ISLAND PADDLING

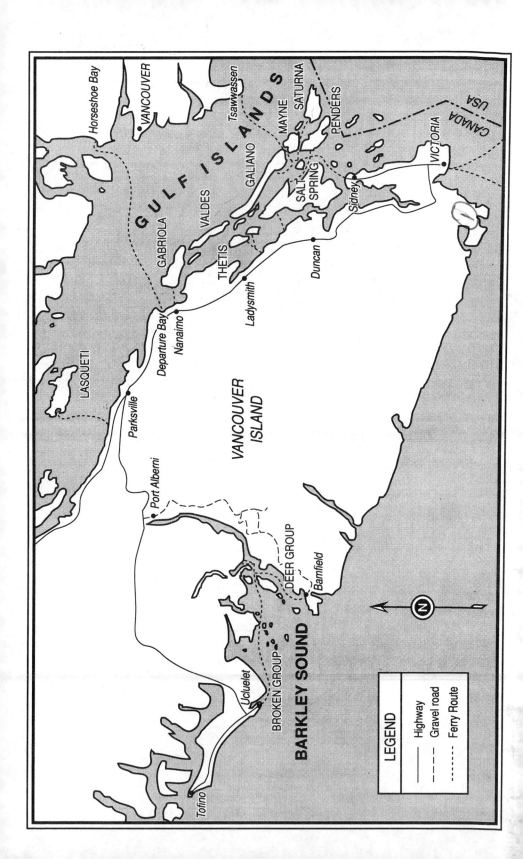

ISLAND PADDLING

A Paddler's Guide to the Gulf Islands and Barkley Sound

MARY ANN SNOWDEN

ORCA BOOK PUBLISHERS

Canadian Cataloguing in Publication Data
Snowden, Mary Ann, 1953-
Island paddling

Includes bibliographical references and index.
ISBN 1-55143-065-7
1. Canoes and canoeing–British Columbia–Gulf Islands–Guidebooks.
2. Canoes and canoeing–British Columbia–Barkley Sound–Guidebooks.
3. Kayaking–British Columbia–Gulf Islands–Guidebooks.   4. Kayaking–. I. Title.
GV776.15.B7S66 1997   797.1'22'0971128   C96-910827-3

Library of Congress Catalog Card Number: 97-65296

Cover design by Christine Toller
Front cover photograph by Gary Green
Back cover photographs by Maurice Robinson
Printed and bound in Canada

Orca Book Publishers   Orca Book Publishers
PO Box 5626, Station B   PO Box 468
Victoria, BC V8R 6S4   Custer, WA 98240-0468
Canada   USA

99 98 97   5 4 3 2 1

For John and Marjorie,
who always welcomed their daughter home.

And to Judy, Kathy and John without whom
I could not have travelled the steepest part of our journey.

ACKNOWLEDGEMENTS

I am not a singlehander. There are many without whom this book wouldn't have happened. But three stand out. First, Audrey Fraggalosch, who not only planted the seed, but also offered encouragement all the way. Second, Harry Neufeld, who was there from the start, and when Namibia called, made sure that all that was necessary for the project was left in my hands. Third, Joanne Nelson, who patiently created the handcrafted maps.

For photographs, thanks to Ken Meadows, Maurice Robinson, Greg Lang, Michael Blades and Ann Kilburtus. And to Bruce Holland and Tracy Cornish (whose name I will not spell incorrectly again), thanks for your extra effort and your large body of photographic works.

To some very patient readers — marine biologist Pam Stacey; fellow paddler David Spittlehouse; Ornithology Curator Wayne Campbell; and Coast Guard Officer Mark Pakenham — thanks for helping to get it right. And for reading over information pertaining to Pacific Rim National Park, my gratitude goes to park staff, in particular, Bill McIntyre, Heather Plewes, Barry Campbell and Catherine Taron.

A special credit goes to Bob Austad at BC Parks who not only provided information but also inadvertently sold me on BC Marine Parks and its unarguable vision to preserve fragile marine environments.

For contributions to the bits and pieces of information — thanks to the staff at Heritage Conservation, to Rob Butler of the Canadian Wildlife Service, and to all the native band managers who willingly provided information with regard to reserve lands.

Others made contributions that were essential. Thanks to Mark Hobson for friendship and support and Julie Draper for producing the line drawings. To Kathy Francis, Linda Priestly, George and Marla Oliver, Tracy Cornish, Tony Wass and my sister Kathy — thanks for sharing some of those nautical miles.

To those whom I met during my travels (your faces are many but your names are few), my sincerest thanks for all your kindness.

Final thanks goes to Brian Henry and Linda Priestly for their individual and infectious love of this coast and their unrelenting support of all my endeavours while I worked at Ocean River Sports; and to Ian McKenzie — for his love of the sea and his sustaining support throughout this project. And last but not least, thanks to Susan Adamson at Orca Books, without whom during revisions I'd not have been as honest, humble and on time.

Mary Ann Snowden, 1997

TABLE OF CONTENTS

INTRODUCTION TO THE GULF ISLANDS

Huddled around the southeast shores of Vancouver Island are a dozen large islands and hundreds of smaller islets collectively called the Gulf Islands. For years the waterways between these islands have attracted countless boaters. Spectacular scenery, low rainfall and the many protected waterways are among the features that add to the appeal of these cruising waters. These same attributes offer ideal paddling conditions for the sea-kayaker and canoeist.

Natural Features

The Gulf Islands and eastern Juan de Fuca waters are sheltered from the extreme weather associated with Vancouver Island's west coast. Winds, especially during the summer months, are often calm, and the climate is relatively dry. Open water distances are short; it is rare that a paddler will travel more than 3 mi before discovering another shore. Strong currents are perhaps the greatest hazard, yet most are predictable and in most instances avoidable.

Mile after mile of shoreline is not only stunningly beautiful but rich in variety. Eroded sandstone cliffs, precipitous bluffs, sand-fringed lagoons and countless tiny islets all add to the paddling experience here. Onshore are historically interesting features: shell middens dating back five thousand years, a turn-of-the-century saltery and the crumbling remains of a leper colony.

The wildlife is as rich and as varied as the landscape. Within the paddler's touching distance are the colourful creatures that occupy the intertidal: flowery plumose anemones, ochre stars, spiny red urchins, limpets and chitons, green anemones and both the California and blue mussels.

Attracted to an abundant food supply are several marine mammals, among them the mink and raccoon that rummage through the kelp for

Coastal areas provide a diversity of natural habitats — dry open forest, tidal lagoon, estuary, rain forest, rocky and sandy shore — each attracting many different migratory and resident birds. Year-round paddlers can expect to see any number of species. (*Bruce Holland*)

crab. Offshore, the harbour seals curiously eye intruders while the river otters frolic with boundless energy. California and Steller sea lions return to these waters each winter and are most often seen by the off-season paddlers either basking on rocky islets or bobbing in the current. The most breathtaking sight is the breaking of the waters by a pod of orca. Although sightings are infrequent, viewing these magnificent whales only metres away is truly an awe-inspiring experience.

Thousands of migratory birds grace the skies and waters around the islands, significantly adding to the appeal of winter paddling. Not all birds are seasonal visitors — throughout the year paddlers can expect to see any number of species that are permanent residents. Most impressive is the bald eagle, the white-headed master. There are an estimated two hundred pairs nesting in the Gulf Islands area. The jet black pelagic and double-crested cormorants, often found close to their cliff-ledge nesting sites, are a common sight. Meanwhile, spindly-legged great blue herons wade through the eel-grass shallows, watching for fish to come within striking distance. Flocks of glaucous-winged gulls scream overhead. Onshore, black oystercatchers chisel away at the mussels exposed at low tide, while the belted kingfisher searches for fish from an elevated perch.

In contrast to the lush rain forest occurring along most of the Pacific coast, dry woodlands are found throughout the Gulf Islands. The area receives a mere 80 cm (32 in) of rain a year. (Prickly pears, found on many of the southern islands, grow in testimony to this dryness.) Douglas fir still dominate the landscape, although many have been logged because of their high commercial value. Frequently associated with the towering firs is the arbutus, Canada's only broadleafed evergreen. Recognizable by its coppery bark and gnarled trunk, this tree prefers sunny locations, especially on bluffs overlooking the sea. Along with the arbutus is the Garry oak. This is BC's only native oak, and although the tree has been depleted by encroaching urbanization, paddlers will still see this gnarled and twisted species growing throughout the islands.

It would be unforgivable to not mention the wildflowers blossoming throughout these dry woodlands in spring. Peak blooming occurs in April and May when the meadows are ablaze with yellow monkeyflowers, blue camas, pink sea-blush, chocolate and white lilies, blue-eyed Mary and the lemon-coloured bloom of the Oregon grape.

Marine Weather

Summer Dry Belt

As the result of a rain shadow cast by Vancouver Island mountain ranges and the Olympic Mountains in Washington State, the Gulf Islands enjoy a relatively dry climate, especially during the summer months. Total annual rainfall rarely exceeds 80 cm (32 in) with Galiano, reportedly the driest of all the islands, receiving less than 57 cm (23 in). Less than 25 percent of the precipitation falls between April and October, and periods of drought extending over four to six weeks are common each summer.

Temperatures are ideal for paddling between May and September. Mean temperatures on the water are over 10°C (50°F) and temperatures in July and August average between 15° and 17°C (approx. 62°F). Because of the cooling effect of sea breezes, maximum temperatures on the water seldom exceed 23°C (73°F).

Winds

Winds in the Strait of Georgia and Juan de Fuca Strait conform to a fairly regular pattern, whereas in the Gulf Islands, they tend to be unpredictable.

In simple terms, two weather regimes establish themselves over this region. One dominates in the summer and the other during the winter. As the summer regime eases in during the spring, the entire Gulf Islands area is subject to strong winds. These winds decrease in frequency, and by summer they are typically calm to light. Winds come up even during fair weather. Lows and fronts can advance in the form of strong southerlies. These winds bring unsettled, rainy weather.

In the Strait of Georgia, northwesterlies not only affect waters within the strait but spill into some of the channels between the Gulf Islands. (Plumper Sound between Saturna and the Penders is often affected by these winds.) In the Juan de Fuca Strait, winds associated with a Pacific high funnel down the strait (blowing up to 20 knots in the afternoon), affecting the waters in eastern Juan de Fuca as well as the Gulf Islands area.

Sea breezes resulting from the differential heating of the land and the water complicate the picture further. They are produced by the greater heating of the land during the day and blow onshore. Usually peaking by mid afternoon, if they are strong enough, they may cause choppy seas.

In the fall, no single wind pattern can be counted on for long. During the winter months, although winds tend to blow from the southeast, they are much more variable, much stronger and blow more frequently. However, even at that time of year, sunny skies and calm weather are possible.

In general, watch for winds from the south during the summer as they tend to bring wet and unstable weather. Be prepared for brisk onshore breezes during the late afternoon. And listen to the continuous weather broadcasts that provide local weather reports and marine weather forecasts for the entire Gulf Islands area.

The wind conditions that are described throughout this book apply to the summer months, unless otherwise specified.

Marine Weather Broadcasts

Environment Canada and the Canadian Coastguard provide continuous marine weather broadcasts for the Gulf Islands. To obtain this information, call (604) 270-7411 (Vancouver) or (250) 656-7515 (Victoria).

On the water it is best to carry a radio that is capable of receiving transmitted broadcasts. Small VHF will pick up at least one of four stations on frequencies (MHz): WX1:162:55, WX2:162.40, WX3:162.475 and 21B:161.65. The smaller, less expensive weather radios will pick up two or three of these same stations.

During the broadcast a general synopsis of systems that will most likely affect coastal waters is provided. In addition, local weather conditions provided by the various reporting stations throughout the Gulf Islands and eastern Juan de Fuca (East Point, Active Pass, Nanaimo, Discovery Point, Trial Islands and Race Rocks) are given. Determine which of these stations is closest to where you plan to paddle. Forecasts are issued four times daily.

An explanation of some of the terms used during these continuous broadcasts follows.

- Wind speeds are given in knots. (Light means wind speeds of 0-11 knots, moderate is 12-19 knots, strong is 20-33 knots.)
- Both wind and swell directions refer to the direction from which they come.
- Marine wind warnings are issued whenever the winds are expected to rise. The warning frequently heard in this area during the summer is "small craft warning." It is not based on

the size of the craft, but on the strength of the wind, and it means 20-33 knot winds are expected.

- The combined wind, wave and swell heights are given in metres.

Sea Conditions

Tides

The Gulf Islands experience four tides over an approximate twenty-five-hour period: a "high" high and a "low" high, a "low" low and a "high" low. The tides fluctuate at their greatest range, 4 m (13 ft), with a new or full moon. These "spring" tides occur approximately twice a month throughout the year. During the moon's first and last quarters the range is generally a little more than half of the "spring" range — referred to as the "neap" tides. (The words "spring" and "neap" are derived from Saxon words meaning "active" and "inactive.") (Washburne)

Tidal predictions for the Gulf Islands appear in Vol. 5 of the *Tide and Current Tables*, published annually by the Canadian Hydrographic Service. When using the *Tide and Current Tables* from April through October, add an hour to compensate for Pacific Daylight Time.

In the Gulf Islands, tides affect paddlers in one of two ways. First, the tides determine water levels onshore. During the summer the lower low tide generally occurs in the morning and the higher high water occurs at night. This means that kayaks and canoes need to be pulled high enough so that they do not float away in the middle of the night. It also means that boats and gear will be carried a longer distance back to the water than they were carried the evening before. The second way that tides affect paddlers is that they also affect current speeds. The strength of currents is roughly proportionate to the difference between high and low water.

Currents

Flooding and ebbing tides in the Gulf Islands create flows that usually run up to 1 and 2 knots. However, they can reach 10 knots in the narrow passes between some islands. When tidal streams reach these speeds, passage by paddle craft is made difficult not only by the fast-moving water but also by the whirlpools, eddies, overfalls and standing waves that are encountered. These hazards present the greatest danger to paddlers; subsequently, narrow passes must be entered during "slack water" times when there is little or no current.

Slack water times (or times of minimum flow) can be predicted using either the *Tide and Current Tables, Vol. 5*, or the *Current Atlas*.

The *Tide and Current Tables* provides maximum flow and slack water times at specific places called Reference Stations. Reference Stations

An overhanging rock is one of the hundreds of sandstone features that adds interest to shoreline paddling in the Gulf Islands. (*Ben Miltner*)

within the islands include Race Passage, Active Pass, Porlier Pass, Gabriola Passage and Dodd Narrows. Based on these major references are the Secondary Stations that show corrected times and flow speeds for local areas. (Paddlers who are not familiar with calculating current speeds at Secondary Stations should refer to "Table One" in the Appendix.)

The *Current Atlas* is comprised of charts that provide pictorial representation of current flows in the Gulf Islands on an hourly basis. It is easy to use and it gives an overall picture of currents, allowing paddlers to determine the best overall route plan.

For the Gulf Islands, use the Canadian Hydrographic Service's *Current Atlas: Juan de Fuca Strait to Strait of Georgia*. Determine which of the charts to refer to by using the *Tide and Current Tables* and making some calculations, or purchase *Washburne's Tables*, published annually by Weatherly Press and available in Canada at most kayak speciality shops. This simple-to-use reference guide takes you directly to the right chart in the atlas "for any hour of any day without need for the tide table, calculations or daylight savings time calculations" (Washburne).

Knowing the direction and speed of currents is useful not only for predicting when to avoid certain areas but also because currents can be used to your advantage. Tides in the Gulf Islands tend to flood to the north and ebb to the south. With knowledge of this general pattern, the paddler would benefit by paddling south in the morning (with an ebb tide) and north in the afternoon (with a flood). Consult the *Current Atlas* while planning your trip as it details the exceptions to this general pattern.

Sea states are not only affected by strong currents. Other less predictable factors can lead to the presence of rip tides and steep standing waves.

Here are a few examples.

- The highest and steepest waves in this area occur when strong currents oppose wind-generated waves. For instance, when northward flooding waters leave Porlier Pass and encounter a northwest wind, steep waves result.
- When the downstream side of an island is surrounded by shallows, tide rips are common.
- When currents converge, turbulent waters result. (A good example of this is off East Point where currents from Tumbo Channel collide with those from Boundary Pass. The seas are made more tumultuous by the adjacent shallows.)
- Off headlands, increased wind, currents and rebounding waves create chaotic seas.

It is well beyond the range of this particular book to detail all conditions that create such difficult waters. Neither are the skills necessary for paddling through hazardous waters outlined in this text. Other books do a far better job of covering both of these topics. David Burch has a section on the problem of "not-so-predictable" currents in his book *Fundamentals of Kayak Navigation*, and John Dowd, in a revised edition of *Sea Kayaking*, provides information on skills and techniques for dealing with turbulent water.

Sea Temperatures

Water temperatures in the Gulf Islands fall to about 7°C (44°F) in winter and seldom exceed 13°C (55°F) in the summer. Most paddlers will never experience the threat of such chilling waters, but this is a hazard that must be considered, first by eliminating the likelihood of a capsize and second by knowing what to do in the event of one.

Refer to the "Safety Considerations" that are outlined later in this chapter.

Fog

Fog is a hazard over the eastern part of Juan de Fuca, forming most frequently in the summer and fall.

Although visibility in the Gulf Islands is rarely affected by fog, it is affected by low-lying cloud and drizzle. Statements regarding visibility are made during marine weather broadcasts if it is expected to be reduced to less than 6 nautical miles.

Paddling duo wash their dishes in the bay at Discovery Island Marine Park. Several marine parks scattered throughout the Gulf Islands offer kayakers extensive camping opportunities. *(Ann Kilbertus)*

Marine Traffic

Some areas within the Gulf Islands are busier than others with boat traffic. For instance, both motorized and sailing craft tend to converge on the narrow passes between the islands at slack water. Sea-going barges and tugs towing log booms are particularly threatening; wait for both tug and boom to pass through. Busier still are the congested areas centred around large marinas. The Sidney area is particularly busy with the traffic that enters and exits Tsehum Harbour and Canoe Bay. Most small boaters (sail and power boaters) exhibit a polite awareness of paddlers, but I have heard of paddle and power craft encounters that have been unpleasant and, in one instance, quite frightening. If in doubt as to whether your presence has been noticed, attempt some sort of communication with oncoming craft. In most cases, a wave of the hand or paddle is sufficient.

Larger vessels — seiners, huge ships and ferries — demand a paddler's respect simply because of their size and lack of manoeuvrability. Large freighters follow the major shipping routes out in the middle of Juan de Fuca and Boundary Pass, so unless a paddler is crossing these open bodies of water, these vessels are of little concern. Ferries, on the other hand, run frequently between Tsawwassen and Swartz Bay and between the Gulf Islands and pose the greatest threat in a number of ways. First of all, the large ferries run up to 18 knots. That is five times faster than we can paddle! If you must cross their path, determine quickly whether you are on a collision course. To do this, hold a steady course (by referring to your compass or a distant landmark), then note the position of the ferry relative to your bow. If the angle relative to your bow and the ferry increases as you converge, this indicates that you will pass beyond the intersection point. If the angle remains the same, you are on a collision course. If there is any doubt as to whether you can make the crossing safely, wait until the ferry has passed. Remember, a kayak or canoe is far more manoeuvrable than a ferry and can achieve a full stop easily. In these instances, your safety is entirely your responsibility. (For further information on navigation through traffic, refer to *Fundamentals of Kayak Navigation* by David Burch.)

Ferries also create swell. On their own these ferry-generated waves are of little concern. It is when they wash onshore or over shallows that trouble could occur. In calm water, an unexpected break could catch the unsuspecting paddler off guard and possibly cause a capsize. Onshore, boats left at the water line are swamped by these large ferry waves that dump on the beach.

One final caution – pay particular attention around ferry docks. Watch that ferries are not about to exit or enter the slip, and stay clear of prop wash. In a hurried attempt to meet a return sailing, I cut across the slip dock entrance just as the ferry approached. I was reprimanded by attendants concerned not only with the potential collision but also with an awareness that their wash could easily wrap my fibreglass kayak around a piling.

Public Lands

Private Property and Crown Foreshore

Most of the shoreline above the high tide line in the Gulf Islands is private property. However, in Canada there is no such thing as a private beach. All foreshore between high and low water is Crown land and is legally accessible to the public. In theory, this means paddlers can go ashore anywhere except where foreshore leases have been granted for private wharves, log booming and marina or port facilities. Most of us, however, are not comfortable with sitting in front of someone's private residence, let alone setting up camp a few metres from their front yard. Fortunately, throughout the islands there are many public accessible locations far more enticing. Beaches that are away from private residences, marine parks and recreation reserves have greater appeal for overnight stopovers, particularly when tide levels are not excessively high.

Coastal Marine Parks

Several marine parks, administered by BC Parks, are found throughout the Canadian Gulf Islands. The larger parks, including Montague Harbour, Beaumont Marine, Pirate's Cove and Sidney Spit, have developed facilities largely catering to recreation boaters and, in the case of Montague Harbour, also to drive-in campers. Other parks such as Winter

Cove, Princess Margaret, Cabbage Island, D'Arcy and newly established Dionisio and Wallace Island are smaller and developed on a limited basis only.

Due to increased use, BC Parks is understandably implementing changes to further protect resources. These changes include the creation of designated campsites, the installation of sanitary facilities and the enforcement of a "No Fires" policy. This includes below-the-high-tide-line beach fires.

There are no garbage disposal facilities within marine parks, except at Montague Harbour. Whatever you pack in, you pack out. Camping fees? Yes, but very reasonable rates apply. In 1997 the per camping party fee averaged $6 a night. Self-registration vaults, located in designated camp areas, depend upon an honour system for collection. In recognition of BC Parks' incredible effort to respond to the tremendous growth in marine park use, paying this meagre fee is the very least we can do.

Historically paddlers overlooked parks in preference for more isolated locales. Interestingly, with the creation of designated campsites, BC Parks is giving back the wilderness we sought by providing us daytime exploration of sheltered coves and inviting headlands – that are not occupied by yet another camping party.

Pacific Marine Heritage Legacy

The Pacific Marine Heritage Legacy, a five-year program designed to expand an integrated network of Pacific coast marine parks, was launched in 1995. The goal, involving both provincial and federal governments, is the acquisition of new lands that collectively will form a new national park system within the Gulf Islands. With the potential addition of water-accessible destinations, the prospects for kayakers are positive indeed. Immediately upon announcing the legacy, several land acquisitions were also announced. The property of greatest interest to paddlers, thus far, is a 95-ha (232 ac) piece on Prevost Island's James Bay. Until such time as the other properties are acquired and the boundaries for the national park are determined, Prevost will be managed on an interim basis by BC Parks. Park facilities will not be developed, as yet. However, paddlers are welcome to visit these now-public lands. Let common sense be your guide so that your impact is minimal, and please respect the rights of private landowners on adjoining properties.

Public Recreation Reserves and Crown Land

There are several islets reserved for public recreation and, although not advertised in any way, they are available for day use and camping. (A half-dozen of these islets are described in the routes in this book.) These environments need to be treated with the utmost respect as the islets are isolated and maintain a natural beauty. Those visitors who do not exercise low-impact camping would not only destroy these little isles but perhaps our privilege to use them. Do not build fires, and when cooking, make sure that all flammable debris is cleared well away from the stove. Pack out everything and leave these unique areas as they were found.

The one piece of Crown land (other than beaches) accessible to paddlers that is used for camping is Blackberry Point on Valdes Island.

No-So-Public Lands

Clearly, the above lands are available for use by everyone, yet there are some lands that fall into a grey area. So that paddlers know what to expect if they choose to land in these areas, they are listed here.

Ecological Reserves

There are presently 120 ecological reserves in BC, preserved because of the unique flora, fauna or marine life found in the area. They are largely established on Crown land, although in some cases private property has been purchased by non-profit organizations and leased back to the Ecological Reserves Program. For example, Brackman Island just north of Swartz Bay was recently purchased by Nature Conservation of Canada and leased to the province as a reserve area.

Seven ecological reserves (Canoe Islets, Rose Islets, Race Rocks, Oak Bay Islands, Brackman Island, Trial Islands and Ten Mile Point) are easily accessed by shallow-draft boats in the Gulf Islands area. Whereas casual non-consumptive, non-motorized use is permitted on most reserves in the province, these areas are particularly delicate (many protect nesting sea birds). They are not intended for public recreational use, and although not strictly prohibited, landing is discouraged.

For information regarding special permission to land, call the Ministry of Parks in Victoria at (250) 387-5002 and ask specifically for the Ecological Reserves Program.

Native Reserve Lands

Many of the reserves in the Gulf Islands are uninhabited, and most of them present features that are attractive to paddlers — easy beach access in sheltered locations accompanied by beautiful woodlands and plenty of level areas for setting up camp. Often we are tempted to go ashore and stay awhile. However, all reserve property (above high tide) is private — owned by the various bands living on Vancouver Island.

In researching for the book, I asked each band what their policy was with regard to paddlers landing on reserves. Their individual requests follow.

Gulf Island Reserves

Valdes Island — The three reserves on Valdes are part of lands administered by the Lyackson Band in Ladysmith. Paddlers once obtained permission to stay overnight by speaking to band members living on the island's Shingle Point. However this small group of inhabitants has recently moved to Vancouver Island. Permission to camp must now be obtained by calling the band office in Ladysmith at (250) 246-5019.

Tent Island – At one time the Penelakut Band (on Kuper Island) leased this island to the province, which in turn used it as a marine park. However, lease agreements terminated long ago. Paddlers are now asked to obtain permission to camp here by phoning the band office on Kuper Island at (250) 246-2321, or by writing the Penelakut Band, Box 3601, Chemainus, BC, V0R 1K0.

Saturna Island – The one reserve on Saturna is adjacent to Narvaez Bay and is under the jurisdiction of the Tsawout Band that is based in Saanichton, north of Victoria. The band requests that you call prior to camping at Fiddler's Cove as it is frequently used by band members for hunting. Although permission to go ashore is most often granted, paddlers will be alerted to safety concerns during hunting. Phone the band office at (250) 652-9101 and ask to speak to the band manager or address enquiries to Band Manager, Tsawout Band, Box 121, Saanichton, BC, V0S 1M0.

Victoria, Sooke and Metchosin Reserves

Chatham and Discovery Islands – Chatham and Discovery reserves are under the jurisdiction of the Victoria-based Songhees Band. Up until recently the band permitted daytime visitors. However, two fires, one in 1993, the other in 1996, led to the public closure of reserve lands on both Chatham and Discovery. The native people monitor the area and will ask those found trespassing to leave. At the time of this book's revision there was no indication that this policy would change. For updated information, call the band office in Victoria at (250) 386-1043 or address enquiries to 1500A Admirals Road, Victoria, BC, V9A 2R1.

Becher Bay Reserve Lands – The Becher Bay Band asks that paddlers restrict their stops to beaches. If you plan to go ashore, please obtain permission from the band council first. Further enquiries can be made by calling the band office at (250) 478-3535 or writing to the Becher Bay Band, 3843 East Sooke Road, Box #4, RR #1, Sooke, BC, V0S 1N0.

Department of National Defence (DND) Lands

Whether or not Crown foreshore is accessible to the public on DND lands appears to depend on how the federally owned land is being used. In an emergency, landing on the beaches fronting DND property is legitimate; however, when military reserves such as those around Rocky Point are used as a munitions depot, security tightens, and small boaters are discouraged from landing anywhere in the vicinity for their own safety. The firing ranges at Albert Head are used for training. Once again, for their own safety, boaters are discouraged from landing. There are no DND lands at all in the Gulf Islands. The few that are within the area covered by this book are located in the Sooke/Metchosin area.

Camping

Getting Away From It All

Paddlers express concern that their need for solitude will not be met in Gulf Islands waterways that appear to be so heavily used by pleasure boaters. In some ways their concern is valid, especially on summer weekends and around parks that cater to the needs of the yachting crowd. Yet by selecting camp areas without mooring buoys, wharves and protected anchorages, particularly in the lesser-developed marine parks or recreation reserves, paddlers can avoid crowded locations. With shallow-draft boats they can also access areas that pleasure boats cannot. For instance, at Pirate's Cove Marine Park, a very popular moorage site is avoided by heading to an adjacent bay that is too exposed for sailors.

Camp in park areas inaccessible to larger craft, or head to camp locations that are unpopular with the cruising set. Chances are that your group will be the only company you keep.

Water

Always carry your own water supply rather than depend on water in an area where summer rains are so infrequent that ground water deficits often occur. Supplies can be topped up at marine parks that have pumps and at marinas. Three litres (approx. 3 qt) per person per day will get you through with some to spare if you are held over by bad weather. Sea water is fine for washing dishes, especially if followed by a fresh-water rinse.

Fires and Stoves

There are many wilderness regions on the Pacific coast where fire danger is minimal, but in an area that receives a mere 75 cm (30 in) of rain a year and experiences weeks of summertime drought, fire is a number one threat. During periods of extreme drought (usually July through September) the Forest Service prohibits all fires in the Gulf Islands. A call to the Forest District Office in Duncan at (250) 746-2700 will determine whether or not a ban is in effect.

Under normal conditions, fires are permitted on beaches below the high tide mark. There are, however, some common sense regulations associated with their burning. Clear debris like mosses and grass within a 1 m (3 ft) of the fire and make sure that stumps, logs and overhanging trees are at least 3 m (10 ft) away.

Because driftwood is scarce in the islands, particularly around public campsites, depend on a small backpacking stove for cooking. Fires leave an offensive scar, and they are not always needed for warmth. For these two reasons I tend to limit using them to the spring and fall.

Shellfish Harvesting and Fishing

Very few paddlers are tempted to collect shellfish during the summer due to the threat of paralytic shellfish poisoning (PSP). For those unfamiliar with PSP, this is a hazard of which you should be aware.

Clams, oysters and mussels can contain a poison that is harmful to humans. These shellfish are filter feeders, which means that they strain the sea water through their gills, extracting the minute organisms for food. From the spring through the fall, a tiny diatom, Gonyaulax, appears in concentrations much larger than normal. It collects in the muscle tissue of various filter feeders, and although it does not harm the bivalve, if the toxins are taken in sufficient quantities, they can make humans very sick and in rare cases can be fatal.

It is impossible for the average person to distinguish between poisonous and safe molluscs. In Canada the federal fisheries department monitors the threat of PSP. Since it is impossible to routinely check every bay and inlet, a general ban is imposed on the collection of shellfish from May through October in many areas surrounding Vancouver Island, including the Gulf Islands and Barkley Sound.

Rather than collect shellfish, try your luck at fishing. Although the best sports fishing occurs in the winter, springs and cohos can be caught in the calmer months, along with smaller chinook and bottomfish (Obee, 1986). In Canada all "fin fish" fishing requires a licence, available at most tackle shops and marinas.

Minimum Impact

I presume that the term "minimum impact" is familiar to most. Rather than elaborate on "how-to," I will reinforce the merits of "leave no trace camping" in this particular area.

Throughout the Pacific Northwest, paddle sports are increasing in popularity, particularly sea-kayaking. With our new sea-borne mobility and our desire for solitude, we are using areas that had few visitors in the past. As individuals or as a single group we have little effect on our environment, but as our numbers increase, we begin to exert a fair influence. Many of the camp areas described in this guide are outside the jurisdiction of parks (recreation reserves). These areas in particular require special care and attention so that our collective impact is minimal. In taking such care we look after our own interests for the future, assuring that these areas will continue as undeveloped and unrestricted sites.

Trip Planning

Paddlers and Ferries

Paddlers following any of the routes described in this guide will undoubtedly board one of more than two dozen ferries that travel between the lower mainland, Vancouver Island and the Gulf Islands.

Ships depart regularly from Tsawwassen, linking paddlers from the mainland to Vancouver Island. No reservations are required for sailings that leave hourly, but expect heavy traffic during the summer and waits anywhere from one to three hours.

Some may choose to depart from the mainland ferry terminal that is north of Vancouver at Horseshoe Bay, thereby accessing Vancouver Island from Nanaimo's Departure Bay terminal. Paddlers living in Vancouver and heading to routes described for the north Gulf Islands and Barkley Sound will likely choose this option. In most other instances, this is the longer route.

Some ferries run directly to the Gulf Islands, departing several times daily from both Swartz Bay and Tsawwassen terminals. Vehicle reservations are required for travel between the mainland and the Gulf Islands but are not required from Vancouver Island to the Gulf Islands. For schedules and reservations, call Vancouver at (604) 669-1211 or Victoria at (250) 386-3431, or write to the BC Ferry Corporation, 1112 Fort St., Victoria, BC, V8V 4V2.

For the Gulf Islands ferry schedule or reservation information, call Vancouver at (604) 669-1211 or Victoria at (250) 386-3431. If calling long distance for either schedule information or reservations call toll free, 1-888-223-3779 from 7 am to 10 pm (P.S.T.) For general twenty-four-hour information, call (250) 381-5335. If you wish to write, send to BC Ferry Corporation, 1112 Fort St., Victoria, BC, V8V 4V2, or visit their home page at Web: http:/bcferries.bc.ca./ferries.

It is cheaper to board without a vehicle, carrying kayaks and gear and paying foot-passenger rates plus a minimal fee for kayaks or canoes. This is not always going to be an option as some launch locations require vehicle access, but if you have a choice, walking on is the least expensive way for paddlers to travel by ferry. There is another hidden advantage to walking on —assured boarding. Three-hour vehicle lineups that occur on busy holiday weekends are best avoided, by anyone's standard.

Sailings are frequent enough to allow many of the routes described in this guide to be paddled as a day's excursion. For instance, paddlers could leave in the morning, park their car at the terminal and walk onto a ferry. By launching adjacent to the terminal and returning in the evening, again as a walk-on, you avoid additional expense.

Ferry operators are generally cooperative toward paddlers with kayaks and all their gear in tow. However, frequent trips between a waiting

Fleet awaiting a launch near Galiano Island's unused Montague Harbour ferry terminal. Adjacent to most Gulf Islands ferry terminals are wharves and beaches suitable for landing. (*Ben Miltner*)

ferry and the terminal's parking area by those attempting to get organized may receive a different sort of response. Make sure boats and gear are consolidated well before the scheduled departure time.

Launching

Suitable launch sites are found adjacent to most terminals in the Gulf Islands. Some are easier to access than others, none require paying a fee and all are described in detail under the launch sections in this book. Most distances between the ferry dock and these water accesses are short, with the longest distance frustratingly experienced by paddlers disembarking from the ferry at Swartz Bay. Boat wheels eliminate some of the inconvenience of this particular .5 km (.3 mi) distance.

Occasionally marinas provide the most convenient launch locations. Most charge a minimal fee (from $3 to $5) for the use of their ramp and associated parking facilities. In my experience, the operators have been most courteous and in some cases have suggested alternative procedures so as to avoid the congestion of vehicles, trailers and boats that surround the ramp. For these extras and for the convenience provided, I gladly pay the minimal fee.

All along the coast of BC there are public wharves, easily recognized by their bright red railings. The floats attached to the wharves are used for moorage by many boaters, yet for paddlers who are willing to lower themselves into their boat from up to 1 m (3 ft) above, they are a convenient launch.

Throughout the islands, and in urban areas on Vancouver Island, there are designated public beach accesses that provide short distance access to shoreline. Many of these are convenient launch locations, and most have nearby parking space.

Navigation Charts

The Canadian Hydrographic Service once published a set of four charts (No. 3310) for the Gulf Islands area. Unfortunately the set is no longer in print. It was replaced in 1995 with chart No. 3313, a cruising atlas that is ideal for the yachtsperson, but its spiral-bound, twenty-four-page format is not so convenient for the paddler. Although it contains interesting supplemental information on weather, distress signals, distance tables, landmarks, etc., most kayakers will end up "tearing out the pages" in order to make the bound format serviceable. In 1997, it retails for about $90.

Individual charts for the Gulf Islands are still available. They are: No. 3340, "Race Rocks to D'Arcy"; No. 3441, "Haro Strait, Boundary Pass and Satellite Channel"; No. 3442, "North Pender to Thetis Island"; No. 3343, "Thetis Island to Nanaimo"; and No. 3641, "Albert Head to Otter Point." All these charts are the same scale — 1:40,000 — and, in 1997, retail for about $20.

Daily Distances

Water distances throughout this book are given in nautical miles (mi). (The length of a nautical mile corresponds to latitudinal minutes and is therefore not subject to metrification.) The speed at which we cover distances is expressed in knots, and 1 knot equals 1 nautical mi per hour. Most kayakers cruise around 3 knots, meaning we are capable of paddling up to 3 nautical mi in one hour.

However, cruising speed and the speed that we actually travel differ for several reasons. First, distances are often calculated following a direct line, yet with a coastline as convoluted as ours, we simply do not paddle a ruler-straight path. (I will confess right now that the distances provided in this guide do not take into consideration every single indentation along each of the coastlines described.) Second, we tend to make plenty of stops to explore and stretch those cramped muscles. Finally, paddling speed depends upon how fast the water itself is moving. An opposing current with a speed of as little as 1 knot affects a small boater's progress. Taking all these variables into account, most of us travel around 2 knots and comfortably cover 10 nautical mi over an average day. Sheer determination and favourable currents would increase this average. However, given normal paddling conditions, figure on this 10 mi as a daily average.

Safety Considerations

The paddler's first line of defence in dealing with a potentially risky situation is to not get into the situation in the first place. Too often time schedules dictate when we go paddling rather than the conditions out there. Know what to expect by listening to weather forecasts — before you go. Determine where there are potentially hazardous waters, and work out a schedule to avoid paddling through at times of high risk. Select routes appropriate to your paddling abilities.

Accidents still occur, even when paddlers are experienced and prepared. Have a plan worked out on how to deal with any number of emergencies — well in advance of their occurrence. And always carry emergency safety equipment.

A few safety reminders follow.

- If you do capsize it is critical to get out of the water in as short a time as possible. Practise both solo and group rescue techniques before your trip. (Refer to *The Coastal Kayaker* by Randy Washburne and *Sea Kayaking* by John Dowd for descriptions of the various sea rescue techniques.)

- If for some reason you cannot get out of the water, you must be able to alert others that you need help. Consider carrying a VHF (two-way radio), and always carry three pyrotechnic distress signals (flares) and a good whistle.

- Wear clothing layers that provide the best in-water insulation. Cuffs that can be closed tight decrease the amount of cold water circulation that will occur around your body.

- The Canadian Coast Guard advises boaters to wear a personal flotation device (PFD) that has enough positive buoyancy to keep the wearer's head well above the water in case they are immersed. Most capsize victims initially experience something referred to as "cold water shock" during which the heart rate increases up to two times its normal rate and breathing increases five times its normal rate. If this person is not wearing a PFD with adequate buoyancy, the effect of their body's reaction to immersion, along with panic and the presence of waves, can lead to their inhaling water and, possibly, to their drowning. (Check the buoyancy provided by your PFD. Put yourself into a vertical position in a pool. Make sure that there is at least 12 cm [5 in] between your lower lip and the level of the water.)

- Hypothermia (body heat loss that can cause death) could result with prolonged exposure to cold. Getting out of the water and back onshore are critical in dealing with this condition, but once ashore, obtaining dry clothing and allowing the body core to return to normal temperatures are essential. Paddlers should familiarize themselves with the symptoms and treatment of hypothermia. (John Dowd, in his book *Sea Kayaking*, covers the subject in detail.)

Off-Season Paddling

Paddle any of the Gulf Islands routes in the winter, and you are in for a rare treat. Most marine traffic comes to a standstill. It is much quieter. There are more sea birds, the sea lions have returned and the steel-grey waters can be mirror-still.

The brazen among us enjoy the overnight solitude in having an entire marine park to ourselves. Others escape to one of the many "Bed and Breakfasts" in the Gulf Islands and plan daytime excursions. Those of us fortunate to be living close to the islands head off for a day's paddle, returning to the comforts of home by evening.

But there are conditions present in winter that must be considered — prior to heading out.

- It is much colder. Be prepared for lower temperatures and the greater likelihood of rain. Remember your hands and head; pogies or gloves (that will keep you warm even when wet) are considered essential, along with a sou'wester for the rain and a toque for the cold.

- The weather is far less predictable and much less forgiving than in the summer. The winds are generally stronger. The rain can be relentless. Pay particular attention to weather forecasts at this time of year, yet be prepared for rapid shifts in both wind direction and intensity.

- Seas reflect the weather conditions. Be prepared for rougher, more unpredictable seas.

- Daylight hours are shorter. Exercise an awareness of the passage of time so as to not get caught unprepared by darkness.

- Take full responsibility for your safety. There is far less marine traffic at this time of year, and so the likelihood of having to deal with an emergency without immediate assistance is far greater. Well in advance, have a plan of action worked out with the entire group for dealing with any number of emergencies.

Trip Selection

It is difficult for inexperienced paddlers to know what trips are suited to their ability level. Harder still is the task that faces this author as she attempts to make this selection process a little easier.

Any sort of trip rating for ocean travel is made difficult by the nature of the seas themselves. Waters that are glass smooth one day are whipped into a maelstrom of waves the next. Saltwater routes paddled several times without incident may suddenly present conditions that are well beyond the most experienced paddler's ability to cope. However, some form of rating is required.

At the beginning of each of the thirty-seven trips described in this guide is a section called "Considerations." Here, the potential hazards that paddlers might expect to encounter on that particular trip are described. Where applicable, these hazards include the following: exposure to winds, where to expect strong currents, where to expect turbulent water, the likelihood of offshore and onshore breakers, the occurrence of fog, the frequency of beach landings and the potential marine traffic hazards. Having described these considerations, routes that are obviously not suited for the novice are described with straightforward statements like, "This is not recommended for the inexperienced." I am assuming that inexperienced, or novice, paddlers have had some paddling experience, perhaps during an introductory sea-kayak course, and that they have done some paddling in lakes or along sheltered stretches of coastline.

I presume that experienced paddlers can predict when conditions are going to be dangerous, know when and how to avoid them and have the skills necessary to cope with rough water. The hazards that are described are "potential" hazards. They will not occur at all times, and in fact they could occur rather infrequently. However, paddlers must base their decision to paddle a particular route on their ability to cope with the worst-case scenarios. Upon reading the considerations, experienced paddlers should be able to determine whether or not the route is suited to their ability.

Remember that no matter what your ability level, you must always make weather considerations the final deciding factor in your route selection process. Inclement weather drastically changes the suitability of all paddling areas. Make it a habit to listen to marine weather forecasts before heading out on any route.

Kayak Tour Companies

There are several tour companies now operating within the Canadian Gulf Islands. In fact, at least one company is now based on each of the larger islands. Most of these owner-operated businesses offer complementary ferry pick-up and drop-off services as well as kayak rentals, convenient for those who wish to walk on to the ferry. Others provide accommodation. Paddling with knowledgeable guides who are trained in first aid and experienced in safety and navigation is for many preferable to self-guided exploration. Be sure of the credibility of the group that interests you. Ask questions regarding guiding certification, length of time it has been in business, previous customer service appraisals, safety considerations, etc.

For current information regarding kayak tour companies in the Gulf

Pelagic birds, such as the cormorants depicted here, are particularly sensitive to our presence during nesting season. Avoid paddling too close to nesting sites from May to August. (*Bruce Holland*)

Islands, call BC Tourism's toll free number, 1-800-663-6000. For a list of kayak specialty shops and rental businesses, see the Appendices at the back of this guide.

Paddling Etiquette

Paddlers, Pinnipeds and Pelagic Birds

Few paddlers intentionally disrupt wildlife, but we do affect them nonetheless — simply because we get in so close to their natural habitat.

Harbour seals and sea lions (generally referred to as pinnipeds) are often encountered. Most vulnerable are harbour seals with their young, especially when paddlers, alarmed to find what appears to be an abandoned pup, try to rescue the orphan. More than likely the mother and pup have been separated for a short period of time while the mother has gone off in search of food. Wait before assuming the pup cannot possibly make it without your assistance.

Dozens of powered craft can pass by a group of seals hauled out on the rocks, and these magnificent mammals barely lift a flipper. Yet as soon as we pass by, they scurry into the water as fast as they are able. Rather than encourage this frantic scramble, if you see a haul-out spot covered with seals, swing well out. By not sending them scurrying for the water, we can more easily observe the seals. (Paddlers with binoculars have a distinct advantage here.)

Sea lions are seemingly not intimidated by us; in fact, in most cases it is quite the opposite. Paddlers attempting to get too close have raised the ire of these large beasts, who then take to the water, swimming to and fro and commanding the intruders' respect simply because of their enormous size. Keep a respectable distance away from sea lions, and they will likely remain stationary on the low-tide rocks.

Birds are particularly sensitive to our presence during the nesting season. The success or failure of a breeding season could depend on our respect for nesting territory. Avoid paddling too close to nesting sites from May through August, and please do not land on any of the island colonies at this time of year.

Onshore Etiquette

I felt it was necessary to include this final section to emphasize the importance of a positive relationship between Gulf Islands' residents and paddlers. It is onshore that we encounter the locals, and this is where we need to exercise the most consideration.

Show respect for the privacy of shoreline residents by staying below the high tide line and, prior to exploring inland, requesting their permission to do so. Their largest concerns centre around fire and litter. By introducing ourselves, explaining our intent and putting them at ease by displaying a common-sense respect for the area, we ensure that future paddlers will be welcome visitors.

When possible, buy locally. Often paddlers are so completely self-sufficient that little is required from local proprietors. We simply pay the launch fee (most often the launch is free), and we are off. Consider buying last-minute provisions at local shops, and en route, restock by purchasing from stores associated with marina complexes. Many of these small facilities depend almost entirely on summertime patronage.

AREA 1 — SOOKE, METCHOSIN

Charts:	– No. 3641, Albert Head to Otter Point, (1:25,000)
	– No. 3442, Race Rocks to D'Arcy Island (1:40,000)
Tides:	– Reference Port: Sooke
	– Secondary Ports: Sooke Basin and Becher Bay
	– Reference Port: Victoria
	– Secondary Port: William Head
Currents:	– Reference Station: Race Passage
Duration:	– Day trips

Launches

All routes are accessed using launches in the Sooke/Metchosin area, west of Victoria.

For Metchosin

The Metchosin launches are accessed from Victoria by following the Old Island Highway (Highway 1A) and then Sooke Road (Highway 14). Turn left at the Metchosin turnoff onto Metchosin Road.

To access the Albert Head launch, follow Metchosin Road to Farhill Road. Turn left. Make another left onto Park Drive and then right on Delgada. Delgada terminates at Albert Head Lagoon Park where the beach launch is only a few metres away and vehicles can be left in an adjacent lot.

To access the Tower Point launch, follow Metchosin Road to Duke Road. Duke Road forms a loop, so proceed to the second junction of Duke Road with Metchosin Road (about 1 km [.6 mi] past the first junction). Turn left and follow Duke Road to Olympic View Drive. At the bottom of Olympic View Drive is a steep staircase that leads to the beach launch. Parking is limited here, but for short-distance access to Witty's Lagoon, this is the best launch.

Access Weir's Beach launch by continuing along Metchosin Road and following signs for William Head. Turn left at Sandgate Road. Weir's

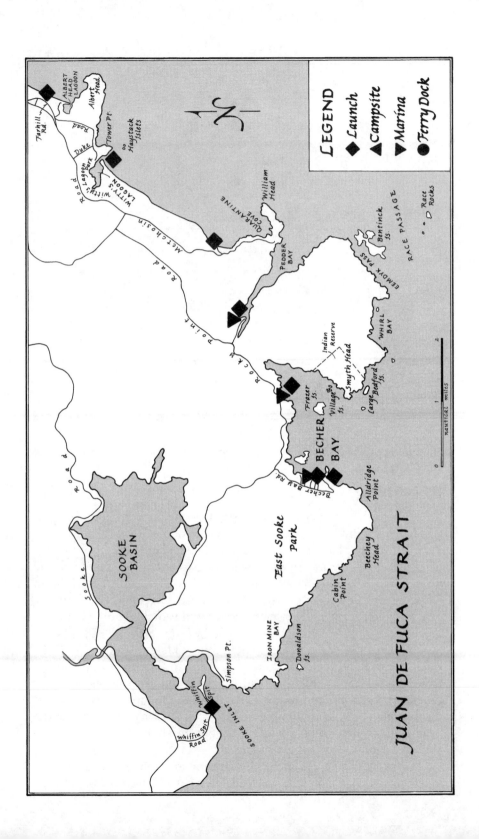

JUAN DE FUCA STRAIT

LEGEND
◆ Launch
▲ Campsite
▼ Marina
● Ferry Dock

N

nautical miles
0   1   2

SOOKE BASIN

East Sooke Park

Sooke Road

Whiffin Spit
Whiffin Spit Road
SOOKE INLET
Simpson Pt.
IRON MINE BAY
▽ Donaldson Is.
Cabin Point
Beechey Head
Alldridge Point
Becher Bay Rd.
BECHER BAY
Frazer Is.
Village Bo Is.
Smyth Head
Indian Reserve
Large Bedford Is.
Bedford Is.
WHIRL BAY
EEMDYK PASS
RACE PASSAGE
Race Rocks
Bentinck Is.
PEDDER BAY
QUARANTINE COVE
William Head
Metchosin Road
Rocky Point Road
WITTY'S LAGOON
Duke Road
Lagoon Park
Tower Pt.
Haystack Islets
Albert Head
ALBERT HEAD LAGOON
Albert Head
Tarhill Rd.

Easily viewed from the water, this "sea monster" petroglyph was long ago bruised into the rock at Alldridge Point. (*Royal British Columbia Museum*)

Beach is found at the terminus of Sandgate, and parking is available nearby.

To get to the Pedder Bay launch, follow Metchosin Road to Happy Valley Road. Turn right, and within .5 km (.3 mi), turn left onto Rocky Point Road. Follow it to the junction at East Sooke Road. An immediate left here will provide access to the Pedder Bay Marina. The marina charges $5 to launch.

Allow forty-five minutes to drive from Victoria to the Metchosin launches.

For Sooke

To access these launches, follow the same route as for Pedder Bay, but continue further along East Sooke Road, looking to the left for the Cheanuh Marina, the first of three launches on Becher Bay. The Cheanuh Marina is owned and operated by the Becher Bay Indian Band, and they usually charge $2 for a kayak launch. (One of the operators explained this varies according to the mood of the attendant.) Plenty of parking space is available here.

Access the second Becher Bay launch by continuing along East Sooke Road to Becher Bay Road. Turn left and follow Becher Bay Road to Pacific Lions Marina. Here, the operators charge $5 to use their ramp and parking area, and although the marina is closed from October to April, the proprietors will open the gate to kayakers year round. Go to the main house for permission to launch during the off-season.

The final Becher Bay launch is accessed by continuing along Becher Bay Road to East Sooke Park. There is a parking lot at the entrance to the park and a hike of approximately 300 m (984 ft) to get to the beach launch. The well-marked trail cuts through the old Aylard Farm and terminates at a stairway that leads down to a sandy beach launch.

Allow approximately one hour to drive from Victoria to the Becher Bay launch sites.

The Whiffen Spit launch is accessed by following the Old Island Highway (Highway 1A) to Sooke Road (Highway 14). Follow Sooke Road to just past the Sooke town centre, then turn left onto Whiffen Spit Road. Lift boats and gear over drift logs on the south-facing shore to reach the launch from the large parking area at the end of Whiffen Spit Road.

It takes about an hour to get to the Whiffen Spit launch from Victoria.

Trip 1 — Becher Bay to Whiffen Spit

Distance: – 6 mi

Highlights

Here is an incredible opportunity to experience exposed coast without having to travel to the distant west coast. Explore windswept bluffs and craggy foreshore and get in for a close-up look at a unique spectrum of marine life especially adapted to survive the rigorous sea conditions. View the only petroglyph in BC to receive heritage status, visible from the water near Alldridge Point.

Considerations

During the summer, the prevailing westerlies that blow down Juan de Fuca Strait often build strength during the day and reach maximum speeds by late afternoon. Winds are generally much stronger here than in the Gulf Islands, so listen to wind forecasts prior to paddling, paying particular attention to conditions reported from the station at Race Rocks.

Even in calm weather, Pacific swell rolls down the strait. On their own these rollers pose little threat; it is when they break onshore or over shallows that they become threatening. Be on a continuous lookout for offshore breakers.

Fog banks that roll down from the open Pacific can affect visibility in this area, especially in the late summer and early fall. Listen to fog predictions for Juan de Fuca Strait prior to paddling, and always carry a compass.

Since winds are common, and because landings along this exposed stretch of coast are infrequent, this route is recommended for experienced paddlers only.

Paddle the route as a round trip or in one direction, launching from one of three Becher Bay launch sites or Whiffen Spit.

Juan de Fuca Petroglyphs

There are seven known petroglyphs along Juan de Fuca Strait, all made in the same manner using a process called bruising. The hardness of the rock in Juan de Fuca required the bruising technique and produced impressions that are hard to see. On the other hand, the Gulf Islands petroglyphs were carved into the softer sandstones, leaving a much deeper impression.

The two Juan de Fuca petroglyphs that are the easiest to see, especially for paddlers as they can be viewed from the water, are at Alldridge Point. The others on Large Bedford, Beechey Head Islet and Otter Point are much more difficult to locate.

When were these petroglyphs made? This is a difficult question to answer for several reasons. First, petroglyphs contain no organic matter and so cannot be radiocarbon dated. Second, there is often no cultural deposit such as a midden site associated with petroglyphs which could be used to estimate when they were made. Finally, the design of the Alldridge Point petroglyphs, although simple, does not necessarily prove that they are older or more primitive than others. The stone in which the figures were executed was such a difficult medium that this alone could explain the simplistic forms.

What is their meaning? Local T'Soke Indian legend has it that the largest of the Alldridge Point petroglyphs represents a mythical sea monster. According to the legend this creature kept attacking the native salmon fishermen and almost wiped out the entire village. The people tried everything they could think of to get rid of the beast, but nothing worked until finally a shaman was summoned. He and the creature engaged in battle, and the shaman won by turning the creature into stone. (Hill and Hill)

The second Alldridge Point petroglyph appears to represent a fish and, although fainter, is visible on a rock face west of the sea monster. Since some petroglyphs were used to indicate a particularly good fishing ground, perhaps this one marks the exceptional fishing grounds off the point.

In 1927 the Alldridge Point petroglyphs became an official Provincial Heritage site. It is one of the few designated sites of native origin, and under heritage laws it is protected against any type of defacement. Rubbings cannot be taken of the petroglyphs. They must be drawn or photographed.

The Route

A major part of this route follows East Sooke Park, a large area covering 1,400 ha (3,500 ac), stretching from Aylard Farm around Beechey Head to Iron Mine Bay and north to Anderson Cove. There are over 60 km

(37 mi) of trails in the park with one trail running parallel to the coast. Paddlers using the park launch will hike through an old orchard that was part of the early 1900s' operations at Aylard Farm.

From the Becher Bay launch sites, head toward Alldridge Point and two petroglyphs "bruised" into a rock face on the inside of the exposed drying reefs located off the point. The "sea monster" is the best known of the Juan de Fuca petroglyphs and is easily seen from the water.

Currents are strong around Beechey Head, with eddylines and whorls common during maximum floods and ebbs. Paddle the backeddies close to shore to avoid major turbulence, and exercise caution when wind-generated waves are made steeper upon meeting an opposing ebb tide.

If conditions permit, paddle the windswept coast between Beechey Head and Simpson Point closely, as these shores support a unique spectrum of marine life. Look for blood stars, flower-shaped anemones, purple sea stars, black chitons and the clusters of gooseneck barnacles and California mussels that are most often associated with exposed headlands.

An exceptional cove northwest of Beechey Head is one of the few that provide a protected beach landing. The area is known locally as Cabin Point, although it is not labelled as such on the chart. An unnamed islet best marks the locale of this stopover. Access the beach by paddling along the east side of it. Several fish-shaped petroglyphs described in *Indian Petroglyphs of the Pacific Northwest* (Hill and Hill) are located on the south side of the islet facing the southeast but are very hard to see. (They are about 8 m [26 ft] above high tide.) If discouraged by what is a difficult search, hike across the headland to the shelter on Cabin Point. This is the "Trap Shack," home to the men who once operated fish traps off Beechey Head. In the early part of this century, pile-driven weir traps were placed along the annual migration route of the salmon, providing the most efficient means of catching the fish to date. The fish trap found along these shores was the last of BC's fish traps to shut down. It operated into the 1950s (Lillard).

Iron Mine Bay north of Donaldson Island also has a gravel beach suitable for landing. The horseshoe-shaped cove is sheltered from prevailing westerlies, and tide-pooling is splendid on the rocky promontories surrounding the beach.

The 1-mi long crossing from Simpson Point to Whiffen Spit is exposed to winds and heavy seas. Watch for turbulence if winds oppose ebb tides flowing out of Sooke Harbour.

Whiffen Spit extends about 1 km (.6 mi) into Sooke Inlet. The elongated gravel bar forms a natural barrier that protects Sooke Harbour and serves well as a put-in or take-out area for kayakers paddling this route.

Trip 2 — Weir's Beach to Becher Bay

Distance: – 7 mi

Highlights

Fascinating history and spectacular scenery are found all along this route. For several decades a quarantine station stood on these shores, and isolated Bentinck Island was home to a handful of lepers, confined to live their final years on a deserted isle. Eemdyk Pass is intriguing, choked with tiny islets, rock reefs and sandy shoals – all supporting an impressive array of marine life. There's some challenging petroglyph exploration to do on Bedford Island, and the alluring beaches nestled in between rock bluffs on Becher Bay are hard to resist.

Considerations

The stretch from Rocky Point to Becher Bay is exposed to prevailing westerlies. Because these winds come up in the afternoon, consider an early morning start to avoid paddling against them. Listen to wind predictions prior to launching for Juan de Fuca Strait, paying particular attention to reports from the station at Race Rocks.

Strong currents in Race Passage affect the tidal flows in the entire area, especially in Eemdyk Pass. Avoid the worst of the currents by hugging the shoreline along Rocky Point, or take advantage of tidal streams and schedule paddling so that your direction and flows are the same.

Fog does occur here, especially in the late summer and early fall.

Given the fair likelihood of winds blowing in this area, and considering that scheduling is required (to avoid stronger currents), this route is not recommended for inexperienced paddlers.

Launch from either Weir's Beach or the Cheanuh Marina.

The Route

Paddle south from Weir's Beach toward Quarantine Cove – so named because from 1894 to 1958 a quarantine station stood on this bay, inspecting all foreign ships bound for Canadian ports. Internment and fumigation buildings housed and cleaned immigrants suspected of carrying disease. During World War I, eighty thousand Chinese passed through the station. Operations peaked in 1927 when over a thousand ships were inspected (Wolferstan). Remnants of the station wharves are all that remain today.

Paddlers are requested to remain outside the several white and orange buoys surrounding the medium security prison at William Head. One of the prison guards is an avid paddler. Be assured, therefore, that your presence will be noted.

Black Oystercatchers

These black, crow-sized birds are easily identified by their long scarlet bill, bright yellow eyes and pink legs. Paddlers are most likely to find them along exposed rock outcrops where they camouflage so well against the dark rocks that we often pass by, unaware of their presence until their shrill incessant call gives them away.

The oystercatcher frequents the rocky surf zone, because it is here that clinging shellfish are so plentiful. The bird's name is a bit of a misnomer as it rarely, if ever, eats oysters. They prefer to chip limpets and barnacles off the rocks, but by far this bird's favourite food is mussels.

Banquet time is during the ebb tide, because at this point in the tidal cycle, the shells of the mussel open as the animal sifts the receding waters for plankton. Into the partially opened shell goes the long red bill of the oystercatcher, and with a definitive snip the abductor muscle, which holds the mussel shells together, is cut before it shuts. After working the half-shells apart, the oystercatcher gulps the meat inside.

Lori Wilson, an avid paddler and frequent contributor to *Sea Kayaker* magazine, describes the oystercatcher as particularly sensitive, especially during nesting season, May to July. She tells of an incident when two oystercatchers became most distressed as humans approached. They temporarily abandoned the nest, and it was then left open to predation from less-timid birds such as gulls and crows. Once it was explained to the intruders that they were distressing the nesting pair, they turned and headed in the opposite direction. The episode shows how the success or failure of a breeding season is often determined by our respect for nesting territory.

All shoreline from the head of Pedder Bay to just east of Large Bedford Island belongs to the Rocky Point Military Reserve. The area is used for both munitions storage and testing, and although much controversy surrounded its establishment in the 1950s, farms were expropriated and the reserve was established. Military presence has certainly protected this huge area from development, but landing anywhere along this beautiful stretch of coast is very much discouraged. Public safety is the main concern. Kayakers lured ashore by an inviting cove can expect to be reprimanded if inadvertently discovered by an officer.

Eemdyk Pass, also referred to as "Choked Passage" because of the countless shoals and islets found throughout, is a kayaker's haven. Here, dozens of harbour seals haul out on drying reefs. At low tide, black oystercatchers probe rocky outcrops, and raccoons explore the kelp-covered shores. Otter and mink fish in the shallows.

It is best to paddle the pass close to slack or when tidal flows and route directions are the same. When paddling against the current, take

Black oystercatchers camouflage well against the dark rocks. Paddlers often hear these birds before they see them. (*Mark Hobson*)

advantage of back eddies and the slower-moving water that is found close to shore. Westerly winds that funnel through this pass could affect paddling progress.

Bentinck Island, once known as the "Island of the Living Dead," has an interesting history. In 1924 the leper colony on D'Arcy Island closed down, and so Bentinck Island, isolated enough to receive immigrants infected with the disease, became the new station. With the introduction of sulpha drugs, leprosy became curable, and in 1956 the last quarantined leper died on this island. For two years after that, you could rent Bentinck Island at $40 a month, but there were no takers. So in 1958 the area was turned over to the Department of National Defence (Wolferstan).

Although the coves that indent Bentinck look inviting, there are also large numbers of warning signs here that read "Blasting — Keep Out." Arms testing does take place in the area, so it is best to observe this shoreline from your "demilitarized craft."

The notable structure out on Christopher Point is an experimental wind generator. Once it spins, an almost deafening hum is emitted (although paddlers are unlikely to hear it as winds that set the generator in motion are strong). This modern-day windmill marks the north entrance to Whirl Bay, an exposed stretch of shoreline that is steep and rocky. The cove behind Shelter Islet provides the only emergency landing, and the surf zone out on Church Point supports large numbers of gooseneck barnacles and California mussels. From here to Large Bedford, long narrow channels pierce the rock cliffs. Tiny shell beaches provide the only break from the craggy bluffs.

Land on the tombolo that links Large Bedford Island to the main shoreline. (Bedford Island and areas adjacent are on reserve land, and although the natives don't mind paddlers landing on beaches, permission must be obtained from the Becher Bay Band before heading inland or camping ashore. Refer to the "Introduction to the Gulf Islands" for details.) Climb to the top of Bedford Island for views over Juan de Fuca Strait and across to the Olympics. In the spring, the entire island is covered with white lilies, pink sea-blush and yellow monkey-flowers.

Two petroglyphs representing human faces are located on a sheer rock face on Large Bedford Island. The carvings supposedly face the southeast and cannot be seen from the sea. I have been unsuccessful in my own search for these carved figures, nor have friends, bribed with the promise of reward, come up with their location.

The area surrounding Smyth Head boasts several small coves, white-shell beaches and tiny islets. One particularly inviting cove that faces north offers shelter from the prevailing winds.

Becher Bay was the scene of an incredible massacre in the early 1800s. Only three of three hundred natives survived a raid by invading Nitinat and Clallam Bands. The survivors, a mother, her son and a niece, sought revenge, and so the three waited until most of the attackers had returned to their homelands and only a small guard party remained on Whiffen Spit. Having walked through the night from Becher Bay to Sooke Basin, the mother approached the guarded spit from landward. Meanwhile, her son crossed the water on a raft and approached from the opposite end of the spit. At the sound of a prearranged owl hoot, they made their way toward each other, slaughtering all sleeping Clallams. Never again did the invaders enter this territory.

Today the Becher Bay Indians living at the head of the bay own and operate the Cheanuh Marina. Traditionally, cheanuh means "salmon." The name is appropriate today since the marina caters to large numbers of sport fishermen.

Trip 3 — Race Rocks

Distances: – Weir's Beach to Race Rocks (8 mi return trip)
 – Pedder Bay to Race Rocks (7 mi return trip)

Highlights

Race Rocks has a variety of marine life unrivalled anywhere within the Gulf Islands. Strong currents bring a continuous supply of plankton to the tiny islets, subsequently drawing large numbers of marine animals to the entire area. Most impressive are the California and Steller sea lions, especially when viewed from a paddler's vantage. Harbour seals also make the islands their home year round, along with hundreds of pelagic birds. Paddlers may be fortunate to view a pod of orca.

Considerations

Race Passage is safe at slack water only; otherwise expect very strong currents, eddies and turbulent water. Since tidal streams reach up to 9 knots in the immediate vicinity of the rocks and up to 6 knots in Race

The light tower on Great Race, surrounded by basking Steller and California sea lions, is visited by a paddler who has taken advantage of slack tide's calmer waters. (*Bruce Holland*)

Passage, paddling here demands scheduling. Slack water is brief — currents pick up speed soon after the turn.

The entire area is exposed to prevailing westerlies; therefore it is advisable to listen to marine weather forecasts, paying particular attention to wind predictions for Juan de Fuca Strait. Fog could also occur.

Given these hazardous conditions, this route is not recommended for the inexperienced. Only those skilled in paddling through fast-moving water and turbulent seas should attempt this route.

Launch from either Weir's Beach or Pedder Bay Marina.

The Route

(For a description of the paddle south of Weir's Beach refer to "Trip 2.")

Launch from Pedder Bay Marina and pass the beautifully situated Lester Pearson College. The college's doors were opened to students world-wide in 1974. During the winter they run an ambitious sea rescue program.

The entire coastline along Rocky Point is part of a military reserve, and landings are discouraged.

Currents are minimal until just south of Rocky Point, when increased flows start to affect paddling. The further south and the closer to Race Passage, the stronger the currents and the greater their effect.

If accurate slack-water scheduling and skill permit a safe paddle to Race Rocks, don't miss this exceptional area. The combination of shallows, drying reefs and continuous current creates a highly productive area for marine life. Most obvious are the California and Steller sea lions either basking on the rocks or bobbing in the current. Hundreds of them return to Race Rocks from distant breeding grounds each winter. Nesting sea birds include pelagic cormorants, glaucous-winged gulls, pigeon guillemots and black oystercatchers. Over one thousand sea birds call this rocky group of islands home each summer. River otters have also taken up residence here, but most spectacular are the pods of orca that occasionally pass through the area. Less obvious but equally as abundant are mussels, anemones, sponges and even a pink coral.

To protect this extremely rich intertidal community, the government designated Race Rocks as an ecological reserve in 1980. The only islet not included in the reserve is Great Race — home to one of the first lighthouses on the BC coast. The striking tower is made from metre-thick granite blocks that were precut, then shipped from Scotland, coming around the Horn as ballast. They were reassembled in 1860 to form the present light station. Over the past 130 years lightkeepers have rescued many boats, but still over thirty-five vessels have met disaster in the vicinity of the rocks. One opportunistic keeper augmented his meagre 1800s' wage with the gold coins he brought up from one of the wrecks (Wolferstan).

In 1997 the Race Rocks light joined the many BC coast light stations that are now automated. Nearby Pearson College expressed concern that the unmanned light station put the maintainance of the adjacent ecological reserve in question. Much to the college's credit, it followed up by wading through the bureaucratic layers of both federal and provincial governments and managed to take over the management of the former station. Pearson now operates an education centre on Great Race and provides an on-site custodian to secure the preservation of this unique marine environment. With permission of the caretaker (just paddle up and ask), visiting paddlers may land on the island.

Trip 4 — Albert Head to Witty's Lagoon

Distances: – Albert Head to Witty's Lagoon entrance (2.5 mi)
 – Lagoon entrance to the Falls (.5 mi)

Highlights

The notable absence of housing is most refreshing, especially given this area's close proximity to a large centre. Views across Juan de Fuca Strait to the snow-capped Olympics enhance the entire route. Paddle through the quiet waters at Witty's Lagoon to the waterfall.

Considerations

Only when winds blow from the south is this area exposed. Currents

Sitting Lady Falls offered a
spectacular backdrop on this winter
paddle in Witty's Lagoon.
(*Bruce Holland*)

are minimal (except at the entrance to Witty's Lagoon on an ebb).

It may not be possible to enter the lagoon by kayak during low tide because the waters at the entrance become too shallow to permit passage.

Novice paddlers will appreciate this route.

Launch from either Albert Head Lagoon or the beach access adjacent to Tower Point.

The Route

Albert Head Lagoon offers refuge to a variety of pelagic birds, but the most impressive among them are the mute swans. This is an introduced species — not to be mistaken for the native Trumpeter Swan. Originally imported from Europe, they long ago escaped captivity and successfully bred in the wild.

Launch from the beach adjacent to the lagoon, and paddle toward Albert Head, an above-the-foreshore area that is owned by the Department of National Defence. The gunhousings, evident as you round the headland, were constructed in World War II. The enclosed artillery was apparently capable of lobbing shells across Juan de Fuca Strait. Today, the barracks are used during the summer for military training sessions. The nearby lighthouse was built after a huge ship, the *Empress of Canada*, went aground here in 1929 (Wolferstan).

Seal escort is almost guaranteed during circumnavigation of the Haystock Islets. In the surrounding shallows, an abundance of kelp and rocky ledges provide an ideal environment for these curious creatures. Onshore, river otter trails weave through the bramble. From a distance the thick undergrowth crowning the Haystocks gives the appearance of old-style haystacks. So strong is the resemblance that it leads to speculation that the islets were originally named "Haystack," but, in the process of chart creation, perhaps an "a" was mistaken for an "o."

Tower Point, part of Witty's Lagoon Park, has beaches on the west side that provide landings. Interestingly, this entire point presents some of the best North American examples of a geologic formation called pillow basalt. These rounded "blobs" of rock are created when lava flows from sea-floor rifts. Sea water contacting the molten rock cools it almost instantly into rounded shells. The material inside each pillow cools at a slower rate. Tower Point is a composite of pillow formations that formed some forty-five million years ago. The "pillows" are easily observed by paddlers all along the shore.

Enter Witty's Lagoon from the north end of the spit, a route that is easiest to negotiate when incoming flood tides overpower outflows from the lagoon. Passage to the lagoon may not be possible during very low tides. (There is a delayed reaction to tides within the lagoon. High tide occurs outside the lagoon sooner than it does inside.)

Stagnant waters, expansive mud beaches and a pungent fragrance are part of the highly productive marine environment at Witty's. Microscopic creatures especially adapted to low salt levels flourish in these seemingly deserted shores, providing abundant food for large crustaceans and in turn creating an invaluable feeding area for hundreds of shore birds. Numerous bird species, including mallards, buffleheads, herons, Canada geese, sandpipers, yellowlegs and kingfishers, are found here. A pair of ospreys and bald eagles nest in the area as well.

The pilings found along the lagoon's north shore were put in place at the turn of the century when the fresh water required by families living out on Tower Point had to be brought in from a few kilometres away. Wood pipes lashed with wire and supported by pilings were part of the gravity-feed system that was installed. The rudimentary structure was apparently difficult to maintain, and freezing winter temperatures and summer droughts took their toll. The pilings are all that remain.

Paddle to the head of the lagoon to Sitting Lady Falls — most spectacular from winter to early summer. The falls are the result of a geologic process called "rebounding." As the weight of the ice was removed following the last glacial period, the land rebounded to former elevations. In the rebounding process, Metchosin Creek was left higher than it stood before the ice advanced. The falls are attempting to erode an even gradient back to the sea.

The park land surrounding the lagoon is worth exploring. Trails follow the lagoon, lead up to the falls and pass through Douglas fir forests. A nature house, about 30 m (100 ft) east of the falls, is open during the summer.

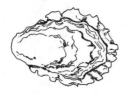

Area II — Oak Bay

Charts:	– No. 3310, Sheet 1, Victoria Harbour to Active Pass (1:40,000) **** No. 3310 out of print as of 1995 ****
	– No. 3313, Cruising Atlas for Gulf Islands
	– No. 3440, Race Rocks to D'Arcy Island (1:40,000)
	– No. 3423, Trial Islands to Cadboro Bay (1:12,000)
Tides:	– Reference Port: Victoria
	– Secondary Port: Oak Bay
Currents:	– Reference Station: Race Passage
	– Secondary Station: Baynes Channel
Duration:	– Day trip or overnight
Camp Locations:	– Discovery Island Marine Park

Launches

Approaches to the following launches are described for paddlers who are heading into Victoria from the Swartz Bay ferry terminal. Paddlers from Victoria can pick up on the route outlined here from wherever it is most convenient for them to do so.

For Chatham and Discovery Islands

To access the Oak Bay launch site, drive from the Swartz Bay ferry terminal along Highway 17 to the centre of Victoria. (Highway 17 eventually becomes Blanshard Street.) Turn left on Fort Street, and follow it to its "Y"-shaped intersection with Oak Bay Avenue. Follow Oak Bay Avenue to Newport Avenue. Turn right and follow Newport Avenue for a couple of blocks, then turn left on Windsor Road. In one block make another right, this time onto Beach Drive. Public access to the waters of Oak Bay is located within a block of this last turn. Because the launch is on the opposite side of the road, you may choose to turn your vehicle around to gain the shortest-distance access to this concrete ramp.

The second launch at Cattle Point is accessed by continuing northward along Beach Drive to the sign indicating "Cattle Point Scenic Loop."

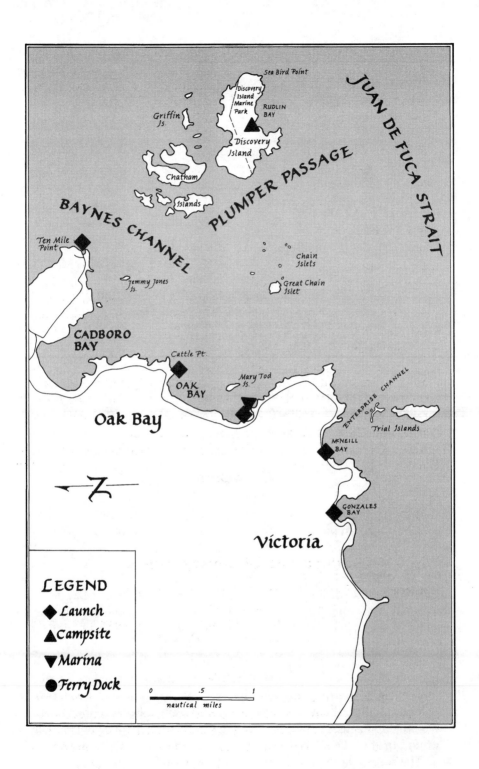

Sea Bird Point

Discovery
Island
Marine
Park

RUDLIN
BAY

Griffin
Is.

Discovery
Island

JUAN DE FUCA STRAIT

PLUMPER PASSAGE

Chatham

Islands

BAYNES CHANNEL

Ten Mile
Point

Jemmy Jones
Is.

Chain
Islets

Great Chain
Islet

CADBORO
BAY

Cattle Pt.

OAK
BAY

Mary Tod
Is.

ENTERPRISE CHANNEL

Trial Islands

Oak Bay

McNEILL
BAY

GONZALES
BAY

Victoria

LEGEND

◆ Launch

▲ Campsite

▼ Marina

● Ferry Dock

0   .5   1
nautical miles

To access one of two boat ramps, follow the loop. There is ample parking here as well.

The third launch is at Ten Mile Point's Smuggler's Cove, also known as Maynard Bay. Continue northward again, along Beach Drive, until it runs into Cadboro Bay Road. Follow Cadboro Bay Road past Cadboro Bay Village to Sea View Road. Turn right onto Sea View Road. It very quickly runs into Tudor Avenue. Follow Tudor Avenue to McAnally, then turn right again. Look for a beach in the elbow of a sharp left on this road. This is Smuggler's Cove. Leave vehicles at the side of McAnally Road, and launch from the adjacent shore.

For Trial Islands

To access the McNeill Bay launch, follow the same route as outlined for the Chatham and Discovery launches, but instead of turning on Fort Street, continue along Blanshard Street to Fairfield Road. Turn left onto Fairfield, and drive along its entire length until it becomes Beach Drive. Follow Beach Drive, and within a short distance, the sea will come into view. This is McNeill Bay. Park along Beach Drive and launch from anywhere along the pebble beach.

To access the second launch on Gonzales Bay, enter Victoria via Blanshard Street (outlined previously), but follow it until it eventually terminates at Douglas Street. Follow Douglas southward to Dallas Road, then turn left. Follow Dallas Road along the seashore to the point where it runs into Crescent Road. Here there is a small park with a lot for vehicles. Park your car and walk down the concrete path to launch from Gonzales Bay's sandy beach.

Trip 5 — Chatham and Discovery Islands

Distances:
- Ten Mile Point to large Chatham Island (1 mi)
- Around the Chathams (2 mi)
- Oak Bay Marina to Discovery Island via the Chain Islets (2.5 mi)
- Circumnavigation of Discovery Island (3 mi)

Highlights

Victoria paddlers love this entire area. Within minutes of launching, they are treated to harbour seals, a sea bird colony and countless islets. Eventually they land on shores that are uninhabited where hectares of fir and arbutus woodlands provide fascinating exploring. An open field in a little-developed marine park is a favourite overnight camp spot.

Considerations

Up until 1996 paddlers had permission to go ashore on the Chatham Islands. This recently changed. The band overseeing this private reserve now enforces a "No Trespassing" policy. (See "Native Reserve Lands" in the "Introduction to the Gulf Islands.") Paddlers must now consider exploration of the Chathams from the water only.

The currents in Plumper Passage and Baynes Channel demand careful consideration as they reach anywhere from 3 to 6 knots. They also demand a crossing during minimum flows or, better yet, at slack. Determine slack water by referring to Baynes Channel, a Secondary Reference for Race Passage.

Expect tide rips during peak flows and, when wind and opposing currents meet, steep standing waves. (Notice the prevalence of "rip" symbols on the chart.)

Although the area boasts predominantly calm days during the summer, strong southeasters could affect these routes; therefore listen to wind forecasts prior to heading out.

Because of the frequency of strong currents, the routes are not recommended for inexperienced paddlers. (During many of Victoria's introductory kayak courses, first-time paddlers are taken out to Discovery Island. In these instances, they are accompanied by paddlers who are very experienced and who know when it is safe to cross.)

The Discovery Island Route

From the launch adjacent to the Oak Bay Marina, paddle past row upon row of jetties and hundreds of sailing craft that moor in this protected bay. By hugging the western shores of Mary Tod Island, avoid confronting the marine traffic that enters the bay from the narrow south entrance.

All along the 2 mi from Mary Tod to Discovery Island are low-tide rocks, tiny islets, offshore shallows and narrow passageways that cause increased tidal flows and, in many instances, tide rips. Although you can avoid most of the turbulence by crossing close to slack, be on the constant lookout for eddylines and the current flows that influence kayaking speed and direction.

The entire Chain Islets' archipelago will delight paddlers. Dozens of harbour seals, whose bobbing heads are often mistaken for the bulb of the giant bull kelp, are a constant presence here. Hundreds of glaucous-winged gulls make Great Chain their guano-splattered domain. Pelagic cormorants also take up residence, along with the black oystercatchers that prefer the low-tide rocks. Due to the sensitive nature of nesting birds, the entire island group is protected as an ecological reserve. Landing at any time of the year is discouraged.

Discovery Island gets its name from the ship commanded by one of Vancouver Island's original explorers, Captain Vancouver. Chatham was

Sleeping volcanic cone, Mount Baker, is often visible during circumnavigation of Discovery and Chatham Islands. (*Maurice Robinson*)

named after the *Discovery*'s consort. Neither of the ships came close to these islands because the expedition followed the continental shore, but the islands were named in their honour during a survey that took place almost sixty-five years later in 1846.

Begin a circumnavigation of Discovery Island by heading to any one of the large sheltered bays on the southwest shore that are within the Discovery Island Marine Park boundary. They serve well as a rest stop following the 2.5-mi crossing from Oak Bay. Carry on with either a clockwise or counterclockwise paddle around Discovery. It is described here in a clockwise sequence.

Paddle the shallow channel between Chatham and Discovery Islands. Expect moving water at peak floods and ebbs — recognizing that flows are fairly gentle and not nearly as complicated as those in Baynes Channel. The entire northern half of Discovery Island is native reserve land. The Songhees Band no longer permits exploring ashore. Paddle mid channel taking in the magnificent little isles that lead to Griffin and Alpha Islets, or on clear days an unobstructed view of Mount Baker.

Griffin and Alpha Islets together form one of several ecological reserves found in this area. More than sixty species of wildflowers grow here. Showy stands of camas, golden paintbrush, pink sea blush and chocolate lilies are prominent in spring, but as the reserve has been established for the protection of this unique flora, observe from the water.

Watch for increased flows in the approach to Seabird Point, take advantage of the close-to-shore backeddies and avoid occasional offshore rips by hugging the coastline. The name of this point isn't taken from water birds but rather from a paddle steamer that caught fire here in 1858. Before she was completely consumed by the blaze, she apparently ran aground to save those on board. The lighthouse was built in

1886. In the summer of 1996 this light station, manned for over one hundred years, became automated.

As the south shore of Discovery is open to prevailing south winds, it is necessary that paddlers check wind forecasts. However, even when seas are calm, there are hazards present that require mentioning. First, submerged rocks, particularly across the entrance to Rudlin Bay, along with adjacent shallows, do cause breakers. Second, the currents in this area are unpredictable. Large backeddies cause flows that run in a direction opposite to what is expected. Finally, there are occasional rips off Commodore Point. These hazards, although worthy of note, are not always present. In fact, most days throughout the summer, paddling along the shores of Rudlin Bay is easy, safe and provides excellent access to Discovery Island Marine Park.

In 1997 BC Marine Parks will begin implementing changes in the formerly undeveloped Discovery Island Marine Park. Paddlers will discover within .5 km (.3 mi) of rounding Seabird Point a marine portal sign perched above a pebble beach that is ideal for landing. On the bench above this shore is an open field that provides ample designated camping space. A pit toilet, picnic tables and an information shelter will be part of the development here. The fee for an overnight stay is $6 per camping party. Initially, an honour payment system will be instituted with the construction of a self-registration vault.

This has to be one of the most stunning of the Gulf Islands marine parks. The sweeping views over Juan de Fuca Strait across to the Olympic Mountains alone make a visit to this spot more than worthwhile. Onshore there is a trail system stretching from the Coast Guard light station to Commodore Point and across to the westernmost shores of the park. Wander through open meadowland or follow pathways shaded by a canopy of arbutus or Garry oak. Sheep have never grazed Discovery. Subsequently, the island has large numbers of plants not found on previously farmed islands like Portland or Prevost. The floral presence is particularly noticeable in spring when the woodlands abound with the colour of blossoming wildflowers.

In the upper meadow explore the locale of the old home site of Captain Ernest Beaumont. For almost fifty years he and his wife lived on this island. Their beautiful home, long ago torn down, overlooked Rudlin Bay. Upon his death in 1967, the Captain left these 60 ha (151 ac) to the province. (He is also responsible for donating the 32 ha (80 ac) on South Pender that make up Beaumont Marine Park.) Once-elaborate gardens, complete with stone-lined ponds and fruit trees, although very overgrown, are still in evidence.

Carry on your from-the-water circumnavigation of Discovery by heading to the island's southwestern shores. Two or three sheltered coves found along this stretch may summon you ashore. Up until the early part of this century, the natives set up seasonal camps in this area.

Seasonal camp, set up by natives on the west side of Discovery Island (note Chatham Island in the background), dates back to the turn of the century. Now uninhabited Gulf Islands reserve lands are owned and overseen by native bands living on Vancouver Island. (*Royal British Columbia Museum*)

From here paddlers may choose to either explore the waters surrounding the Chathams or return to Oak Bay via the Chain Islets.

The Chatham Route

Both Chathams are reserve lands, owned by the Victoria-based Songhees Band. Up until 1996 the natives granted public access to the islands. This changed due to increased concern brought about by careless visitors. Two fires, one in 1993, the other in 1996, lead to public closure. The Songhees Band patrols the area during peak seasons and will ask those who land to move on.

However, I include a description of the Chathams in this revised edition as the waterways that surround the islets are worth exploring. Let tidal flows be your guide as to a clockwise or counterclockwise route. The passes between the two Chathams and between Chatham and Discovery present stronger currents at peak floods and ebbs and, although generally manageable, an extra effort may be required by paddlers who find themselves in opposition to the flow. Crossing eddylines may also be necessary. The route will be described as a clockwise circumnavigation of the larger of the two Chatham Islands. From Discovery head toward the radio towers visible on Chatham's southwest shore.

On the eroded banks of large Chatham (just past the two radio towers) are two grave crosses dated 1917 and 1920. One of the two natives buried here died at the age of twenty-three. According to the marker he was a chief.

Paddle the south side of the island past a tropical-looking sandy shore. Carry on to the eastern shore and a number of sheltered bays that look out to Haro Strait and the American San Juans. At low tide don't miss paddling close to this shoreline in order to take in a colourful and prolific intertidal zone. A meandering, mud-lined lagoon that cuts almost all the way through the island is accessed from this eastern shore. If water levels permit access (high tide only) this unique maritime environment is worth looking into. Large numbers of sea birds, including the heron, kingfisher and bald eagle, are commonly found. In the late afternoon and early evening, huge flocks of crows fly into the area. They are heading to roosting sites found on both Chatham and Discovery Islands.

Return to the lagoon entrance and round the island's northernmost tip. Increased flows and some turbulence are frequently found off the point. Head to the sheltered water in a cove on the northwest side of the island, a delightful nook that has historically been very popular with the Victoria yachting crowd. Carry on to the picturesque channel between the two Chathams. Here, grassy knolls and copper-barked arbutus line the shores of pebbled coves and quiet sheltered bays. Most enticing is a concealed lagoon, only accessible at high tides. Look for its narrow entranceway about halfway along the north shore of small Chatham. Inside this tiny enclave an overwhelming quiet prevails. Carry on with a return to the pass between Chatham and Discovery Islands and a relinking with the Discovery route.

Ten Mile Point Chatham/Discovery Routes

Paddlers may access the Chatham and Discovery Islands from Ten Mile Point's Smuggler's Cove launch. (See "Launches" section.) The tiny islets at the entrance to Smuggler's Cove (also called Maynard Bay) have been declared an ecological reserve. Inhabiting the rock slopes are acorn barnacles, flat plate limpets and, in the cracks and crevices, tiny black periwinkle snails. Harder to see but also present are gumboot chitons, sea urchins, red sea cucumbers and purple ochre stars.

Immediately upon leaving the shelter of this marine-rich cove, paddlers are out in Baynes Channel, a stretch of water that is notorious for tide rips and standing waves. Schedule the crossing close to slack, or expect to be swept along by rushing, turbulent water. If you make a slack-water crossing, anticipate reaching Strongtide Island in about half an hour.

To the inside of Strongtide Island are tiny islets that are ideal for exploring. The narrow passageways form a kayaker's haven. At times of increased flow, the currents are ideal for practising moving-water skills in slow-moving, protected waters.

Head to the channel between the two Chathams and link up with the routes described in the previous Chatham and Discovery Islands sections.

Trip 6 — Trial Islands

Distances: - Gonzales Bay to Trial Islands (1 mi)
- McNeill Bay to Trial Islands (.5 mi)
- Circumnavigation of the Islands (1 mi)

Highlights

Here is a route perfectly suited to an afternoon or evening paddle. Head to the islands for a gourmet picnic on the beach, and return to the launch by sundown. In the spring, take in the rare flowers that blossom on these treeless isles.

Considerations

Depending on the tides, currents of up to 3 knots can be expected between the Trial Islands and McNeill Bay and up to 6 knots off the outer shores of the islands. Eddies and fast-moving water are common. Of greater concern are the steep standing waves that are frequently encountered off the islands' southwest corner. Schedule paddling in the area, and avoid most of the hazardous waters by paddling close to slack.

Because of the scheduling required, and because of the likelihood of "difficult to handle" waters, this route is not recommended for inexperienced paddlers.

Strong currents are often found in Enterprise Channel, so a launch from Gonzales Bay is recommended. The route is described from this preferred launch site.

The Route

Gonzales Bay was originally named Foul Bay, but because of negative connotations, the residents petitioned for a name change. (A major roadway in the area bears the name Foul Bay.) The sand beach at the head of this bay serves as an excellent launch site.

Tucked behind Harling Point and visible from the water is a Chinese cemetery. Before World War II, all Chinese immigrants were returned to their homeland to be buried, but because shipments occurred only once every seven years, bodies were kept waiting in a crypt in Victoria. When the Chinese government started refusing the remains, 849 Chinese were buried at this particular site (Wolferstan).

The flows get stronger during peak floods and ebbs as you get closer to McNeill Bay. Unless you are paddling at slack, avoid this faster-moving water by navigating directly toward the inside of the smaller of the two Trial Islands. Several pebble beaches that line the perimeter of this tiny isle are suitable for landing.

Trial Islands host several rare and endangered plant species. Plant species that have disappeared because of urban development still thrive on these isolated isles. Among the rare species represented are Macoun's meadow-foam, a plant that is extremely sensitive to environmental changes; the golden Indian paintbrush; the chick lupine, reported only in the Puget Sound area and found locally at Trial and Victoria's Holland Point; and the rosy-owl clover. Several other plant species that are almost as scarce grow in the area. Carolina foxtail, Henderson's checkermallow, bear's foot sanicle and the seaside lotus are but a few of these rarely seen plants (Ceska).

In the early 1990s these islands were rightly granted ecological reserve status. In order to protect the unique flora, restrict your stops to beaches and, in the spring, observe the blossoming wildflowers from the shoreline.

Continue a circumnavigation of large Trial Island by passing through the narrow channel between the two islands. Strong winds, a 6-knot current and steep seas led to the 1906 installation of this light station. Manned since that time, this light is slated to become automated by the end of the century. The original lighthouse structure has long since been replaced, but the first lantern room and original lens are on display in Victoria's Bastion Square.

Notice the rip symbols on the chart that indicate the likelihood of turbulence along Trial's outer shores. Other than at times that are close to slack, overfalls, eddies and fast-moving water (at times reaching 6 knots) are common all along this stretch. Conditions are made worse when winds oppose the current, and huge standing waves result. The worst of the maelstrom is found off the island's southwest corner.

Avoid the risks of paddling through such hazardous seas by scheduling a visit to this area. When conditions are right, get in close to the outer shoreline, one of the few stretches of coast in the Gulf Islands that supports a large number of gooseneck barnacles and California mussels.

Victoria's CFAX radio leases a section of Crown land on the island and has erected the towers that are an obvious presence on the west side. To the inside of the towers is a delightful beach appropriate for landing where you can stretch out onshore prior to returning to the Gonzales launch.

Area III — Sidney

Charts:	- No. 3310, Sheet 1, Victoria Harbour to Active Pass (1:40,000) **** No. 3310 out of print as of 1995 **** - No. 3313, Cruising Atlas for Gulf Islands - No. 3441, Haro Strait, Boundary Pass and Satellite Channel (1:40,000)
Tides:	- Reference Port: Fulford Harbour - Secondary Ports: Saanichton Bay, Sidney and Swartz Bay
Currents:	- Reference Station: Race Passage - Secondary Stations: Haro Strait (Hamley Point), Sidney Channel and Swanson Channel
Duration:	- 1 to 3 days
Camp Locations:	- D'Arcy Island Marine Park - Isle de Lis Marine Park on Rum Island - Reay Island - Sidney Spit Marine Park - Princess Margaret Marine Park on Portland Island

Launches

All launches are located in the Sidney area, north of Victoria.

Paddlers from the mainland dock at Swartz Bay, then drive southward on Highway 17. Paddlers from Victoria head northward on Highway 17 to access these launches. Allow fifteen minutes to reach the launches from Swartz Bay, about half an hour from Victoria.

The Island View Beach launch is accessed by turning off Highway 17 onto Island View Road and following it to its seaward terminus. Leave vehicles in the adjacent lot, and launch from the ramp adjacent to Island View Beach Park.

Launch from the government wharf on Saanichton Bay by turning off Highway 17 onto Mount Newton Cross Road. Within a block make a left onto Lochside Drive, then a right on James Island Road. Leave vehicles in the nearby lot, and launch from the government wharf float

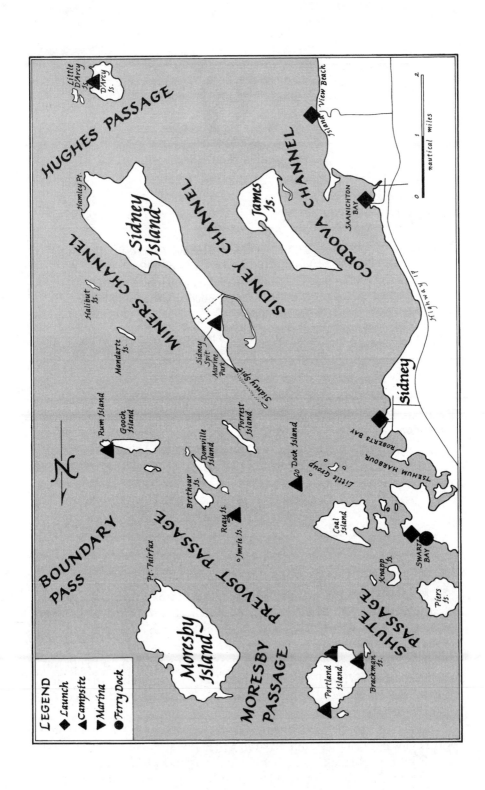

LEGEND
◆ Launch
▲ Campsite
▼ Marina
● Ferry Dock

HUGHES PASSAGE

Little D'Arcy Is.
D'Arcy Is.

Island View Beach

CORDOVA CHANNEL

SAANICHTON BAY

Hamley Pt.

Sidney Island

MINERS CHANNEL

SIDNEY CHANNEL

James Is.

Halibut Is.

Mandarte Is.

Sidney Spit Marine Park

Sidney Spit

Rum Island

Gooch Island

Forrest Island

Brethour Is.

Domville Island

Dock Island

Little Group

Ray Is.

Imrie Is.

Pt. Fairfax

BOUNDARY PASS

PREVOST PASSAGE

Coal Island

Knapp Is.

Sidney

ROBERTS BAY

TSEHUM HARBOUR

SWARTZ BAY

Highway 17

Moresby Island

MORESBY PASSAGE

SHUTE PASSAGE

Piers Is.

Portland Island

Brackman Is.

N

nautical miles
0   2

located at the end of the road.

Drive to the intersection of Highway 17 and Beacon Avenue to access the Sidney launch. Follow Beacon Avenue to Third Avenue, turn left, then right off Third Avenue onto Rothsay Road. Rothsay terminates at a public beach access, and parking is available at the side of the road.

The launch from the government wharf adjacent to the Swartz Bay ferry terminal allows paddlers from the mainland to leave vehicles at Tsawwassen and walk kayaks onto the ferry. Upon arriving at the terminal ask ferry personnel to direct you to the gated exit on the eastern perimeter of the terminal. Bear to the left following the roadway. The government wharf launch at the bottom of Barnacle Road quickly comes into view. Launch from the beach to the left of the wharf. The walking distance from the ferry to the launch is about .5 km (.3 mi).

Paddlers from Victoria access this same launch by following Highway 17 to the Swartz Bay ferry terminal. Take the "CPR Cargo and Canoe Cove" exit just before the terminal entrance. Go straight through at the lights and follow Dolphin Road around to Barnacle Road. A government wharf is located at the terminus of Barnacle Road. Launch from the beach adjacent to the wharf. Be aware that all adjacent parking space is often taken during the summer months.

Trip 7 — South Sidney: James, D'Arcy and Mandarte Islands

Distances:
 - Island View Beach to D'Arcy Island (direct, 3.5 mi)
 - Island View Beach to D'Arcy Island via James and Sidney Islands (5 mi)
 - D'Arcy Island to Mandarte Island (4 mi)
 - Mandarte Island to Island View Beach (7 mi)

Highlights

Paddlers who can get beyond the white-sand beaches on James Island will discover this route has many highlights. Curiously eyeing passers-by are the harbour seals that frequent these waters. D'Arcy Island is now a park but for years was a desolate place where lepers spent their final years. On Mandarte Island, hundreds of nesting birds share every conceivable ledge with the ramshackle bird blinds.

Considerations

This route is exposed to prevailing south winds, especially in the 3.5-mi stretch between the launch and D'Arcy Island.

Three-knot currents in both Cordova and Sidney Channels are occasionally met by opposing winds, thereby creating steep waves. Schedule paddling to avoid the strongest flows by referring to current references for Sidney Channel (on Race Passage) in the *Tide and Current Table* or by using the *Current Atlas,* both published by the Canadian Hydrographic Service.

Given the 3.5-mi crossing and the exposure to winds along this open stretch, this route is not recommended for novice paddlers.

Launch from either Island View Beach or from the government wharf in Saanichton Bay.

The Route

The beach at Island View changes with the season. In winter, high-energy waves lift and carry sand particles out into deeper water, exposing the cobbles and stones along a steeply graded "winter berm." This steepened beach can make launching awkward for paddlers. In summer, gentler wave action leaves more sediments on the beach, reducing its gradient, covering most of the rocks and creating a better launch location.

The tusk of an Imperial mammoth was uncovered here half a century ago. Several specimens buried on James Island and in gravel pits on the Saanich Peninsula have been dated from 17,000 to 20,000 years old.

The crossing from Island View Beach to James Island is about 1 mi.

Paddlers choosing the alternative launch site on Saanichton Bay will use the government wharf — reportedly the smallest public float on the BC coast. The float was originally used by Canadian Explosives Ltd. (now CIL) workers commuting the 1.5 mi to their workplace on James Island.

James Island is the only island in the Gulf Islands area that is completely surrounded by sand. The white beaches have attracted boaters for years, but up until recently landing was strictly forbidden by CIL. It purchased the island in 1913 and up until the 1970s used it as a location for its explosives plant. In the mid 1980s a clean-up program undertaken by CIL and the provincial government removed evidence of the years of industrial use. The island is now in the hands of a development company. Plans include an exclusive village site, golf course, stables, tennis courts and — of greatest interest to paddlers — a public marine park. (Apparently 5 percent of the island must be designated recreational.)

Pull up onto one of James's sandy shores. Considering that on a summer day the lure of sun and sand is sometimes overwhelming, this may be as far as you get! The small lagoon on the west side of James is particularly inviting with its shallow, calm waters.

The crossing from the south end of James Island over to Sidney Island is just over 1 mi and is exposed to winds blowing up Haro Strait. As currents in the channel can reach up to 3 knots, consult the *Current Atlas* or the *Tide and Current Tables* for maximum flow predictions.

This now-disintegrating building was part of a leper colony that operated on D'Arcy at the turn of the century. Little else remains of a thirty-year occupation by Chinese immigrants destined to spend their final years on a lonely Canadian island. (*Tracy Cornish*)

All of Sidney Island, except for the marine park on the north end, is privately owned. The 690-ha (1700-ac) isle was recently bought by a Vancouver-based group who now use the area for tree farming and recreation.

The distance from Sidney Island to D'Arcy is 1 mi, and although currents in Hughes Passage tend to be minimal, they can increase to 2 knots during peak floods and ebbs. Harbour seals frequently haul out on exposed ledges near Sallas Rocks. This group of islets bears the name once given to Sidney Island.

D'Arcy Island Marine Park is rarely used by pleasure boaters as they seem to prefer sheltered anchorages around Sidney Spit. Paddlers will relish these seemingly deserted shores.

Make a stopover in a bay just north of the light on the west side of the island, and land near the visible remains of a concrete wall. This now-disintegrating building was historically part of a leper colony that operated on D'Arcy from 1890 to 1924. Little else remains of a thirty-year occupation by Chinese immigrants condemned to spend their final years on a lonely island in Canada.

Rich intertidal life abounds in the bay south of the light. Look into the low-tide shallows for colourful displays of purple stars, red sea urchins and an usual seaweed, the iridescent algae. The iridescence is produced by an outer cuticle on the algae's fronds. The cuticle is comprised of laminated layers of cells, spaced in such a way that certain wavelengths of the spectrum are absorbed while others are reflected, thereby causing the iridescence (Werthiem).

A Leper Colony

Leprosy was fairly widespread in the Orient at the turn of this century, and so occasionally Chinese immigrants entering Canada were infected with the dreaded disease. Because of the strict policies that demanded complete quarantine of such cases, the Canadian government set up two "lazarettos," one in New Brunswick, the other on the isolated shores of D'Arcy Island. Up until the completion of a recent archaeological study (1989), little was known of the living conditions of the handful of lepers living in exile on D'Arcy Island. Now we understand that in the early years, the lepers lived in row housing on Little D'Arcy, occupying about six units in total and living almost totally isolated. Food supplies were sent to the island every three months, and until more frequent supplies were provided, it was necessary for the lepers to maintain a garden and keep chickens.

In 1905 C.J. Fagan, the province's Secretary to the Public Health Commission, visited the island. He wrote, "There was no pretension made to give medical treatment, and there is no effort made to relieve pain." He went on to recommend that "an effort be made to send the patients to some place where regular and systematic treatment is given."

The government did not follow his recommendations, but at some point a caretaker arrived and lived in the dwelling on large D'Arcy, and food supplies started to arrive weekly. The dilapidated concrete building that remains today was part of this one-and-a-half storey building containing five rooms and a porch and surrounded by a garden.

The rest is speculation, but there can be little doubt that those confined here had little to comfort them. In total exile, they were living away from all that was previously familiar to them. In 1924 the sole inhabitant was transferred to a new station on Bentinck Island, effectively terminating the thirty-year existence of the D'Arcy Island colony.

Windswept trees clinging to a barren shoreline add to the desolate appearance of D'Arcy's south coast. Head to the more inviting camp location situated within a prominent sand-fringed cove. This formerly undeveloped site now has facilities — including a half-dozen tent pads, picnic tables and pit toilets. It is not BC Parks intention to "clip the wings" of those who prefer a wilderness experience but rather to protect fragile environments from overuse. Respect its effort to lessen the impact of our presence and set up camp in designated areas.

A rough trail, voluntarily maintained by a local Power Squadron, heads inland from this point. It crosses the island to the former leper colony, then circumnavigates the north and east shores of D'Arcy.

You may find yourself looking enviably at the shores on Little D'Arcy where there is less undergrowth and more open areas. But Little D'Arcy is not part of the park. It is privately owned.

The Hughes Passage crossing from D'Arcy to Waymond Point is 1 mi. Park-like shores found on the east side of Sidney Island reward the paddler all the way to Hamley Point. Note that Hamley is a secondary current reference in the *Tide and Current Tables.*

Miners Channel was so named because it was part of the main canoe route used by miners heading to the Cariboo Gold Rush. There is occasional turbulence in the channel's shallower waters, especially when winds meet opposing tides. Halibut Island has little appeal except for a shell beach on its northern shore.

Mandarte is a fascinating island to visit, especially in an open boat. This massive bare rock is home to over fifteen thousand nesting birds, all of which fill the air with their raucous calls and pungent odours. Both pelagic and double-crested cormorants claim nesting sites here, with the double-crested dominating the higher elevations and the pelagic nesting on lower ledges. Pigeon guillemots nest under logs and in rock crevices, while glaucous-winged gulls lay claim to the grassy knolls and meadows. This island is also the only place on the inside passage where tufted puffins nest. Their burrows are difficult to spot, but their brightly coloured head and large bill on a black body are unmistakable. Perhaps of greatest interest are the various bird blinds constructed by aspiring ornithologists in their attempt to complete yet another study of life on the Mandarte colony. Apparently there are more Ph.D.'s in zoology per acre on this island than on any other piece of real estate in the province (Wolferstan).

After Mandarte, two route options are open to paddlers. The first option follows the route just described, only in reverse, omitting D'Arcy Island and returning to the Island View or Saanichton Bay launches. The return distance is 7 mi.

The second option takes paddlers to either Sidney or Rum Islands, effectively linking this route with those described in the section on Central Sidney. The crossing from Mandarte to Rum Island is over 1.5 mi. The distance from Mandarte to Sidney Spit is 2 mi.

Trip 8 — Central Sidney:
Little Group, Reay, Rum and Sidney Islands

Distances: - Sidney launch to Rum Island (5.5 mi)
                - Rum Island to Sidney Spit (3 mi)
                - Sidney Spit to Sidney launch (2.5 mi)

Highlights

Miniature islets with secluded beaches are irresistible, and paddlers are sure to be captivated by those found all along this route. Don't miss the Little Group, Greig and Reay Islets with tiny pocket beaches hidden by drying reefs and rocky bluffs. Paddle on to tiny Isle de Lis, an island gem that has been set aside as a park. Walk along the sandy shores that surround Sidney Spit. Set up camp on the shores of a sheltered lagoon on Sidney Island or on the secluded shores of Isle de Lis or Reay Island.

Considerations

Expect currents of up to 3 knots around the islets within the Little Group and in the pass between these islets and the north end of Forrest. (Ebb flows are stronger than floods in this area.) Determine when to expect the stronger flows by referring to currents for Sidney Channel (on Race Passage) in the *Tide and Current Tables* or by looking at flows represented in the *Current Atlas*.

The area is exposed to winds that could blow from the southern quadrants. Check wind predictions prior to launching.

Because it is likely paddlers will have to cross eddylines and paddle through moving water, and because the route is exposed to prevailing winds, it is not recommended for novice paddlers.

Launch from the beach access just north of Sidney. (Because there is a notable similarity to all the buildings located along this shore, take note of surrounding landmarks so as to avoid confusion upon returning to the launch site.)

The Route

Cross over to Little Shell Island, the first islet in the Little Group. Beyond this point, expect tidal flows of up to 3 knots, especially on the ebb and when crossing from Kerr to Dock Island. Ideally, schedule paddling close to slack, or paddle with current flows.

Land on the pebble beach on the north end of Dock, an island reserved for public recreation use. Hike through scrubby Garry oak to a remarkable steep-banked inlet on the island's south shore. The *Nonsuch*, a replica of the Hudson's Bay Company's sixteenth-century vessel, used this location in 1972 to recreate the method used to haul a sailing ship out before docks were constructed, a procedure called careening. She entered the "dock" bow-first, with one side of her resting against logs that were propped vertically along the steep cliffs. During low tide, the crew scrubbed and painted the bottom of the ship. Graffiti, visible on a nearby rock face, commemorates the event.

While the steady flow of motor craft entering and exiting Tsehum Harbour detracts somewhat from Dock Island's appeal as an overnight stopover, it does have its attractions. In particular, wildflower displays on the tiny isle are magnificent in the spring.

Tidal flows between Dock and Forrest Islands can have a significant effect on paddling. If it isn't possible to paddle this section close to

Although sparse vegetation provides little shelter, this Reay Island camp spot offers spectacular views of Boundary Pass, Mount Baker and nearby islands. (*Greg Lang*)

slack, watch for turbulence and eddylines, especially off the south end of Dock Island.

Don't miss a beautiful pebble beach in the sheltered cove on the northeast side of Forrest Island where it is possible to wander along the top of the nearby knoll and look out over the channel. Limit your exploration to below high tide lines, since the island is privately owned.

Passing Greig Island almost guarantees a glimpse of seals either hauled out on exposed reefs or swimming in the luxuriant kelp beds. Glaucous-winged gulls inhabit the treeless isle.

Land on either of two sheltered coves on tiny Reay Island. Reserved for public recreation use, it is possible to camp above the sandstone ledges on this islet. Level ground at the north end provides space for several tents, and although sparse vegetation offers little shelter from strong winds, the rewards of a visit to this recreational reserve are plentiful. Take in panoramic views of Boundary Pass and Mount Baker. Observe resident harbour seals, or simply relax on the secluded pebble beaches. And please, light no fires on this tinder-dry islet. A single errant spark in the early 1990s caused much damage here.

In the pass between Brethour and Domville Islands, gently sloping sandstone shelves rise to arbutus groves on the rocky ledges above. Both islands are private. Brethour Island's owners have posted a unique sign indicating a concern for trespassers. It reads, "Caution – Bull At Large." Domville Island boasts two beautiful beaches separated by a low gravel bar on its narrow south end.

The obvious presence of summer residences on Gooch and Comet Islands reveals the private status of these spots, yet an expansive shell and gravel beach on Comet will likely attract paddlers who require a short-term stopover. For an appropriate camp location, paddle on to Rum Island, watching for moderate current flows in the shallows east of Comet Island.

Rum Island is truly a Gulf Islands gem. The name "Rum" is derived from its use during the 1920s by rumrunners who needed a stepping stone for transporting prohibited spirits into the United States. (The island is less than a mile from the US border.) More recently, Rum Island was used as a summer residence by Mrs. McCaud Nelson, a lover of wildflowers who asked the province to rename Rum Island when it became public at the time of her death. So in 1978 these 4 ha (11 ac) became park land, and it was renamed Isle de Lis (Island of Lilies). Remarkable wildflower displays, including the chocolate lily, continue to grace this tiny isle in spring.

Land kayaks on an easily accessed gravel isthmus linking Rum and Gooch Islands. Hike up the headland of Rum Island to access the half-dozen designated camp sites. In order to preserve the island's fragile environment, tenting is understandably restricted to the recently constructed wood platforms. Fires are prohibited. A self-registration vault accepts the minimal fee charged per camping party. Picnic tables and sanitary facilities are also part of the development on Rum.

Development and restrictions aside, paddlers who choose to make Isle de Lis a destination will not be disappointed. A cross-island trail terminating at Tom Point leads through the open forests and offers spectacular views of Haro Strait, Boundary Pass and the San Juan Islands. The distant droning heard from any vantage on Rum is from the light station on Turn Point. It warns of strong tide rips off the western point of Stuart Island in the American San Juans.

Watch for the swift currents that swirl through the kelp off Tom Point when paddling around to the south side of Rum and Gooch Islands. Note that the shallows of North Cod Reef can generate turbulence during peak floods and ebbs. This stretch of coastline is also exposed to prevailing south winds.

At this point, paddlers can extend this trip by linking up with "Trip 7," or return to the Sidney launch site via Sidney Spit Marine Park. The crossing from Gooch Island to Sidney Spit is about 2 mi.

Notice the pilings driven into the sand bar at Sidney Spit. Apparently, the north end of the spit is gradually disappearing, so pilings were put in place to prevent further erosion. Wolferstan appropriately describes this "valiant effort by the Parks Branch as worthy of King Canute."

Sidney Spit Marine Park is undoubtedly the most popular of all the Gulf Islands anchorages. The wharf and mooring buoys quickly fill with pleasure boats drawn to the park's 140 ha (350 ac) of tree-lined trails and walk-in campsites. There are also numerous picnic tables, a large kitchen shelter and several pit toilets.

Paddling the waters off Isle de Lis. Isle de Lis, or Island of Lilies, was donated to the province by a former owner who loved wildflowers. The entire island is now a marine park. (*Maurice Robinson*)

Paddlers may choose to pass by this busy north end and head to the quiet lagoon south of the spit where there is a huge meadow with space for several dozen tents. This is one of the marine parks that charges a minimal camping fee. A turn-of-the-century brick mill operated on these lagoon shores and at its peak employed about seventy men. Bricks from Island Brick and Tile Limited were used in the construction of Victoria's Empress Hotel. The various hollows that are found in the surrounding area show where clay was once scraped from the surface. Blackberry lovers will marvel at the heavily loaded bushes that now cover the hilly terrain.

Plan an inland excursion. Past owners introduced a number of exotic birds to the island. Among them were the ring-necked and Reeves pheasants, California quail and wild turkeys that are commonly viewed from the island's pathways. Red squirrels and Oregon chipmunks, neither of which is native to the Gulf Islands, were also introduced. The fallow deer that were introduced to James Island in the early 1900s swam to this island in the 1960s. Their escalating numbers have forced the fencing in of some park areas to protect the native plants.

It is likely that within the sheltered lagoon, visiting paddlers will see at least one, if not several, great blue herons. Home to these birds is close to where they can find food and where there is an appropriate nest site. Sidney Spit is an ideal environment for the great blue heron.

Where Are the Blues?

The great blue heron is never far from its nesting colony (heronry). Forty colonies, most under twenty-five nests, are found in the Strait of Georgia, and of all these, four have over a hundred nests. Only one near Point Roberts has over three hundred nests.

Great blue herons return to their natal nesting site in late February from locations that are most often within a 25-km (40 mi) radius of the colony. Monogamous pairs head to their treetop nest where in April they lay four eggs that hatch in May. During the next three weeks, parents must undertake the monumental task of feeding four insatiable mouths. Some chicks die of starvation while others, weakened by the intense competition for food, are pushed out of the nest. Miraculously, two or three will live long enough to fly away on their own (in about the tenth week). Survival remains precarious. Almost 75 percent of the young will not live beyond the first year because the demands placed upon the young birds are immense. Very quickly, they must develop the lightening-precise skills that are necessary for them to catch the large numbers of fish that ensure their survival. Most are incapable of learning the skills fast enough.

The herons' key feeding areas are the eel grass beds. In fact they are so fundamental that biologists have concluded that herony size is proportionate to the size of the eel grass beds closest to the colony. The eel grass beds found in Sidney Lagoon once supported a now abandoned forty-five-pair colony.

Great blue herons are extremely shy birds, a characteristic that frequently works against them in breeding season. If a colony is sufficiently disturbed — perhaps by humans — the rather nervous parents will leave the entire colony en masse. Although the exact reason for a particular mass desertion is unknown, this phenomenon occurred in 1989 and again in the early 1990s at the Sidney Island heronry.

Because of the herons shyness, it is rare that we get close to them, but paddlers often gain access to territory that most people do not. If you do happen upon a herony, do not disturb the nesting inhabitants.

The distance from Sidney Island to the Sidney launch is 2.5 mi, and although currents in this section of the channel are minimal, paddlers may wish to coordinate this northward paddle with a flood tide. (There is a current reference for Sidney Channel on Race Passage.) One final bit of advice — watch for boat traffic as these waters are busy with pleasure craft.

Trip 9 — North Sidney: Portland and Moresby Islands

Distances:
- Swartz Bay to Princess Bay, Portland Island (2.5 mi)
- Circumnavigation of Portland (2.5 mi)
- Brackman Island to Swartz Bay (2 mi)
- Portland to Moresby Island (1 mi)
- Around Moresby to Fairfax Point (3 mi)
- Fairfax Point to Swartz Bay (4.5 mi)

Highlights

The highlight of this trip has to be Princess Margaret Marine Park on Portland Island. Over 160 ha (400 ac) of undeveloped park land are easily accessed by cross-island trails. Wander through overgrown meadows, apple orchards, blackberry thickets and beautiful dry coastal woodlands. Among the offshore islets, a glimpse of playful river otters and shy harbour seals is virtually guaranteed.

Considerations

Ferries are a major consideration in this area, especially in the summer. Most ferries approach the terminal via Gosse Passage (between Piers and Knapp Islands), so it is easy to avoid crossing their path by not paddling in this area. (Small inter-island ferries also use Colburne Passage between Pym and Coal Islands.) Swell from these ferries will not cause a problem until it breaks onshore or over offshore shallows. Watch out for these cresting, ferry-generated waves.

Only in Moresby Passage do currents reach 3 knots, a passage that is easily avoided unless paddlers are heading to Moresby Island.

Winds in the area are usually light during the summer, with prevailing winds blowing from south quadrants.

The route around Portland Island is recommended for novice paddlers, but the route around Moresby is for experienced paddlers only.

Launch from the government wharf adjacent to the Swartz Bay ferry terminal.

The Route

Portland Island

Huge, ferry-generated surf occasionally dumps in on the launch site, so avoid a bad start by putting into the water after the ferries have docked and the waters are calm. Rather than dodge ferries chugging through Gosse Passage, navigate toward Knapp Island.

Before leaving Colburne Passage, look over to Piers Island. Although the developed shores on this tiny isle are of little interest to paddlers, the island itself has an interesting history. Over six hundred

Doukhobours, convicted of parading in the nude, were imprisoned on the island in 1932. A barbed-wire fence separating the men from the women ran down the centre of the island. By 1934 the nearly eight hundred prisoners were released (Wolferstan).

Paddle along the south shore of Knapp Island, and peer into the clear shallows to see the hundreds of clam shells that litter the ocean floor. The fortunate owners of this island have developed several wharves, a covered moorage dock and a magnificent boat house, complete with a marine ways, on the shores of Trader Bay.

While crossing from Knapp to Hood Island (a tiny islet off the southern end of Portland Island), expect minimal currents. (Rarely do the currents exceed 1.5 knots.) From a distance Hood Island appears connected to Portland, but in fact it isn't. Paddle the narrow passage between the two islands, and enter Princess Bay on the south end of Princess Margaret Marine Park.

Up until 1958 Portland Island was privately owned, but it came into the hands of the province when it was exchanged by owner Gavin Mouat for some timber rights. The entire 180 ha (450 ac) became a park when Princess Margaret returned the island to British Columbians in 1961 after receiving it as a gift on her Royal Visit in 1958. Apparently, some tactful negotiating had to occur before the English Crown returned the island to a province that had more or less decided it wanted its present back. In appreciation, this island park was named "Princess Margaret Marine Park." Now maintained by BC Parks, this is one of the marine parks where paddlers pay a nominal fee for an overnight stay. Parks requests that overnight stays be limited to three areas where there are sanitary facilities — at Princess Bay, Arbutus Point and Shell Beach. Water is available from a mid-island pump. To determine its location, see information shelters at any one of the designated camp sites.

Land at the head of the bay to access the weathered remains of an old orchard. In the fall the blackberry bushes here are loaded with ripened fruit. Walk inland through untended pastures to an open meadow where past owner "One-Arm" Sutton built a barn for his thoroughbreds. The Parks Branch has razed the building, but a few bits of it remain among the tall grasses. In 1989 a large herd of domestic sheep considered to have gone wild was removed by the Parks Branch in the hope that someday the island might support the plants and wildflowers that grew prior to the years of constant grazing. Explore the island further by following any number of trails cleared by youth workers a decade ago and maintained until recently by the constant trampling of cloven hooves. Set up camp in the meadow nearest the old orchard, and look out over the bay's aquamarine waters to the Tortoise Islets, or return to your boat to continue on with an exploration of Portland's magnificent shoreline.

From Princess Bay head northward past the Pellow Islets, travelling

Even when fully loaded, kayaks draw less than 15 cm (6 in) of water, allowing paddlers to gain intimate shoreline access. This paddler gets a close look at the colourful and prolific intertidal life clinging to the sandstone ledges. (*Greg Lang*)

along what I'm convinced is the prettiest stretch of Portland's coastline. Arbutus and Douglas fir, sandstone beaches and grassy headlands line the entire shore. Frequently visiting the offshore islets are several river otter. Only once in all of the times I have paddled there have I not seen these playful creatures.

As tempting as some of the headlands along this stretch may appear please respect requests to camp in designated areas only. It is BC Parks' intention to protect these fragile environments from overuse. It needs our cooperation to do so.

In August of 1991 the *MV Church* was sunk off the Pellow Islets. A number of groups including BC Parks and the provincial Reef Society scuttled the *MV Church* so that it could serve as an artificial reef. The 53-m (174 ft) long coastal freighter was thoroughly cleaned. Holes were cut into the hull to allow diver access. As the ship has settled it has been colonized by anemones, sponges and various marine organisms, thereby establishing a very attractive, and now well used, dive site.

Continue on to Portland's north tip, known locally as Arbutus Point and undoubtedly the island's prettiest camp location. A crushed-shell beach provides access to a spacious level area nestled in under the arbutus canopy. A magnificent 180-degree view that encompasses Saltspring's Fulford Harbour, Pender and Moresby Islands and, off in the distance, Rum Island is the reward of all who camp here. On a clear day, Mount Baker's glacier-covered peak breaks the skyline. This is the sunrise and sundown side of Portland, and views of both are fantastic. There's an unusual sand beach nearby, backed by a narrow strip

Who Was "One-Arm" Sutton?

The name "One-Arm" was given to General Frank Sutton, who lost a limb during a bloody battle at Gallipoli in 1915. As the story goes, Sutton led five men into a shell hole, and when a hand grenade was hurled their way, Sutton tossed it back. He did the same with a second one, but only after he caught it in mid air. On the next try, he was not so lucky. The third missile exploded, shredding his arm. Sutton spent the remainder of the war designing weapons, then returned to his family in Shanghai.

In China he rose quickly to the rank of General — only one of three Europeans to receive the honourable position. Generous salaries and the royalties he received from his patented weaponry made him a wealthy man. And as if life wasn't going well enough, he then won an $150,000 sweepstake, a windfall that allowed him to pursue a lifelong dream — the raising and training of thoroughbred horses.

Upon arriving in Vancouver in 1927, he bought a farm, a plane, some placer claims, Vancouver's Rogers and Mutual Life buildings and Portland Island. But the Depression struck and Sutton slid so far into debt that in desperation he took a job as a barker. By selling his assets he was able to salvage some money and returned to China where he worked as a correspondent for Hearst Publications. Soon, he was off again, this time to Korea. For some reason he was thrown out of the country and arrived in Hong Kong to news that the mortgage on Portland Island had been foreclosed.

He was well on the way to yet another fortune when the Japanese overran Hong Kong, and Sutton was placed in a prison camp. It is here that he died at age sixty. (Based on an excerpt from Chettleburg's book, *An Explorers Guide to the Marine Parks of British Columbia*.)

of midden that encloses a tiny salt marsh. Paths from here connect up with trails that encircle the island. For those requiring water — the island's pump is found within a twenty-minute walk.

Recognizing this point is frequently used BC Parks has understandably established facilities here, including six designated sites, pit toilets and an information shelter. A self-registration vault and our honour assures the collection of a very reasonable, per party, camping fee.

Continue shoreline exploration by entering the waters in Satellite Channel. This is the side of Portland where the large ferries pass by on their run between Tsawwassen and Swartz Bay. For some paddlers, ferry swell means fun as attempts to surf on the rolling waves are made. Others are horrified by the erratic seas that are generated when the swell breaks onshore. Swing well out from major headlands to avoid these turbulent waters, and if you do land, pull boats up high onshore to avoid empty cockpits being filled with water.

Just south of Chad Island is a particularly inviting bay, easily distinguished from others by a high knoll that flanks its northern shore. From here, walk inland through the woodlands to a hand pump that provides fresh water. Those who choose to walk farther will discover that the open fields eventually lead to the previously described Princess Bay.

Kanaka Bluff points back to a time in history when native Sandwich Islanders inhabited these shores. They left their homeland in the 1880s when the United States took over the Hawaiian Islands. Rather than live under a republican system, they chose to come to Canada, a country that was ruled by a monarch. Both "Kanaka" and "Pellow" are the anglicised versions of original Hawaiian names.

South of Kanaka Bluff is the last, although certainly not the least, of Portland's camp areas. Land anywhere on the shell beach to access a level area that is large enough to accommodate several tents. Select a spot where the surrounding arbutus will shelter your campsite. Native peoples once camped here, as is evident by the midden that lines this entire shore.

Up until recently, Brackman Island was private land, and in effect it still is, but it has been purchased by the Nature Conservation of Canada. It in turn has leased it to the province, which protects the tiny 4-ha (11 ac) isle as an ecological reserve. Unlike so many of the Gulf Islands, Brackman has never been inhabited, logged or grazed, so several species of plants unique to such a special environment grow here. Magnificent kelp beds off the south tip of the island are also included in the reserve. Visitors are asked to respect this delicate area, and restrict landings to beaches or, better yet, stretch those cramped leg muscles on the 180 ha (450 ac) on nearby Portland.

On the return to Swartz Bay, once again avoid most of the ferry traffic that passes through Gosse Passage by paddling between Knapp and Pim Islands.

Moresby Island

The quickest way to get to Moresby is by crossing Moresby Passage from the Pellow Islets on the northwest corner of Portland Island. As currents reach up to 3 knots in the pass, schedule crossings to avoid the stronger tidal flows.

Ince and Kottner, authors of the book *Sea Kayaking Canada's West Coast*, feel that Moresby Island is "not special." In many respects I agree with their description. However, there are several features that make a visit to this distant isle worthwhile.

What first drew me to these shores was their intriguing history. In the late 1800s, Captain Horatio Robertson left China and built two three-storey octagonal towers — one for his eight sons, the other for himself, his wife and three daughters — on Moresby Island. A 30-m (100 ft) long

Harbour Seals

Undoubtedly, the harbour seal is the most common marine mammal viewed by paddlers on the Pacific coast. We've all seen them — those curious creatures bearing a remarkable resemblance to cats in wetsuits that inspect our passing with large inquisitive eyes. We've seen them stretched out on exposed sandbars and rock ledges, and we have sent them scurrying for the water as we approach their favourite haul-out.

Seals have not always been so plentiful along this coast. Until recently they were hunted for their pelt and killed for bounty, but since 1970 they have been protected, and recovering populations are approaching historic levels. An estimated 2,100 seals in the Strait of Georgia in 1973 increased to 12,500 by 1987 (Bigg and Olesiuk).

Special adaptations allow these incredible creatures to live almost entirely in the sea. To facilitate dives lasting up to twenty minutes, the heartbeat slows, body temperature drops and blood flow is reduced to all but essential organs. Pupils dilate to permit vision at depths of up to 600 m (1900 ft), and thick layers of blubber allow for swimming in water temperatures that seldom exceed 15°C (59°F). Even the newborn seal is ready for life at sea as pups are born fully furred and able to swim. Paddlers are occasionally alarmed to find seemingly abandoned newborns, but the pups are not orphaned. The mother has merely left her young while she feeds herself. Some 2 - 3 kg (4 - 7 lbs) of fish are consumed daily by an adult seal, yet how much of this amount is salmon remains a controversial issue. Fishermen claim seals significantly deplete commercial salmon stocks, yet research indicates that most of the diet is comprised of smaller fish such as sculpins, rockfish and smelts. (Bigg and Olesiuk)

glass-covered balcony linked one tower to the other. While visiting Victoria, the Captain rode in a rickshaw pulled by his coolies. Apparently he was very strict with his Chinese servants, and his somewhat ruthless behaviour forced two of them to escape Moreby Island on a log raft. Nearly dead, they were picked up after several days at sea near Trial Islands (Wolferstan).

Unfortunately, Robertson's extravagant lifestyle is not in evidence today. Since the early 1900s, Moresby Island has been the site of a prosperous farm operation which is visible in the bay on the island's west side.

Navigate toward the sandy bay inside of Reynard Point to view one of the prettiest farms in all the Gulf Islands. A beautiful meadow, pungent with the smell of clover in the spring, adds to the pastoral setting. Although the presence of a private home discourages landing here, paddle the perimeter of the bay where great blue herons fish in the muddy shallows.

Paddle around Reynard Point to access Moresby's western shore

On land, harbour seals are never more than a scramble away from the water. This one didn't move fast enough to get away from a stealthy shutterbug. *(Ken Meadows)*

where "U"-shaped coves are bound to lure you ashore. Spend a couple of hours stretched out in the sun on one of the secluded bays.

Fairfax Point is an absolute gem. Several pocket beaches that surround this southern tip of Moresby Island offer spectacular views across Boundary Pass. Arbutus trees grace the entire area with their unusual copper-coloured bark, and in the spring a yellow flower brightens the personality of the otherwise spiny prickly pear.

Return to the Swartz Bay launch by crossing Prevost Passage and passing tiny Imrie Islet. Isolated from predators such as the raccoon and otter, this barren isle is used as a nesting site by the glaucous-winged gull. During a recent visit, I was impressed by the flock's harried response to the one predator that can access these shores – the bald eagle. What caught my attention was the hundreds of gulls suddenly taking to the air. Within moments the raptor appeared. It seemed there was little the frenzied parents could do except emit their raucous call and circle about in confusion. Only the northwestern crows harassed the unwelcome visitor.

Upon approaching Coal Island, paddlers could feel the effect of tidal flows, especially on the ebb. Swing well out from Charmer Point as this is where flows will tend to be the strongest. Follow the steep-sided shoreline on the north side of Coal, and watch for strong flows again while crossing from Coal to Goudge Island and from Goudge Island to Swartz Head. Perhaps a greater hazard is the large number of pleasure boaters who use the two passes. Be conspicuous, as these boats often move quickly.

Area IV — Saturna, South Pender and the Belle Chain Islets

Charts:	- No. 3310, Sheet 3, East Point to Porlier Pass (1:40,000) **** No. 3310 out of print as of 1995**** - No. 3313, Cruising Atlas for Gulf Islands - No. 3442, North Pender to Thetis Island, and No. 3441, Haro Strait, Boundary Pass and Satellite Channel (1:40,000)
Tides:	- Reference Port: Fulford Harbour - Secondary Ports: Narvaez Bay, Bedwell Harbour and Samuel Island South Shore - Reference Port: Point Atkinson - Secondary Ports: Tumbo Channel and Samuel Island North Shore
Currents:	- Reference Station: Race Passage - Secondary Station: Boundary Passage - Reference Station: Active Pass - Secondary Stations: Boat Passage and Georgeson Passage
Duration:	- 1 to 3 days
Camp Locations:	- Anniversary Island - Unnamed islets off Samuel Island - Cabbage Island Marine Park - Indian Reserve near Narvaez Bay, Saturna Island (Fiddler's Cove) - Beaumont Marine Park on South Pender

Launches

Two launch locations, one on Mayne, the other on Saturna, provide the best access for the routes in this area. Ferries dock with greater frequency on Mayne — an important consideration in deciding which launch is better if you are bound by a tight schedule.

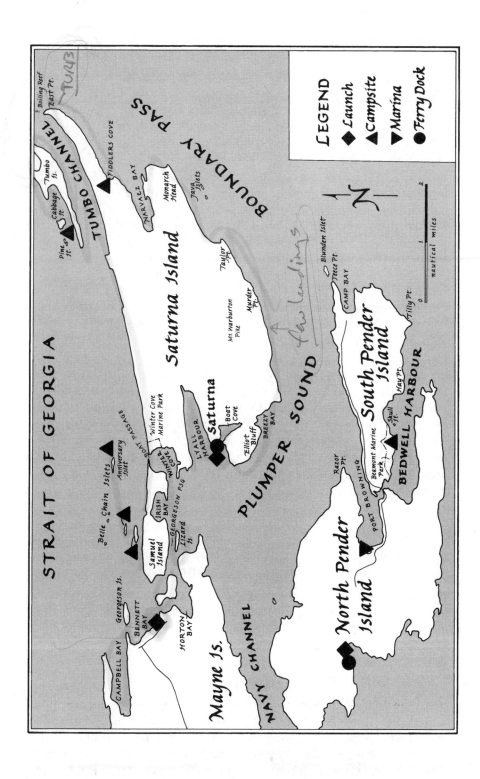

From Mayne Island

To access the Mayne Island launch, board Village Bay-bound ferries. A fifteen-minute drive across the island is necessary to access the launch site. From the ferry terminal, follow Village Bay Road to the Fernhill Road junction where a general store supplies last minute provisions. A left turn leads to Springwater Lodge, Mayne Island's only pub. Here, you may sit out on the balcony overlooking Active Pass, sip a pint and enjoy some pub fare. Return to the intersection of Village Bay Road and Fernhill Road. Follow Fernhill until it becomes Bennett Bay Road. Follow Bennett Bay Road until it turns right and becomes Arbutus Drive, then follow Arbutus Drive. Within a short distance look to the right for Seaview Road, but turn left onto an unnamed lane directly across from it. A beach and an adjacent parking area located at the bottom of this lane provide easy water access.

From Saturna Island

The second launch is from Lyall Harbour's government wharf on Saturna Island. The wharf is adjacent to the ferry terminal, providing paddlers with the option of walking kayaks and gear onto Saturna-bound ferries. Immediately after unloading from the ferry, foot passengers turn left to access the government wharf. Those with vehicles turn right into the parking area in front of the general store, and wait here until remaining ferry traffic passes. (Consider stocking up on last minute provisions here.) Once the ferry has departed, drive down to the government wharf, unload your gear and carry it down the ramp to the floating pier. Leave vehicles in a designated forty-eight-hour parking area about 200 m (650 ft) up from the ferry terminal. On a busy summer weekend, expect to leave your car at the side of East Point Road.

Trip 10 — Saturna Island Circumnavigation

Distances: - Lyall Harbour to Cabbage Island via Winter Cove (6 mi)
           - Cabbage Island to Fiddler's Cove (IR) on south shore of Saturna (5 mi)
           - Fiddler's Cove to Lyall Harbour (7 mi)

Highlights

Saturna Island is the least populated of all the major Gulf Islands. It is largely undeveloped — an appealing attribute as so many of Saturna's shores remain untouched. Paddle the open waters in the Strait of Georgia, and enjoy breathtaking views of Mount Baker. Enter the aquamarine waters around Cabbage Island, and camp in the arbutus woods. Round

East Point where houses are so few and so well hidden that these shores appear uninhabited. Paddle under magnificent sandstone cliffs, enter pocket-shaped Fiddler's Cove and walk along vast stretches of sand, all the while watching for pods of orca out in Boundary Pass — a highlight that truly surpasses them all.

Considerations

Tidal streams in Boat Passage and around East Point demand consideration. Flows in Boat Passage reach up to 7 knots, and at East Point as well as adjacent Boiling Reef, they reach upward of 5 knots. Schedule paddling in both these areas close to slack. Watch for some turbulence off major headlands along the south shore of Saturna.

Southerly winds could affect waters in Boundary Pass, whereas winds from the northwest could affect waters in both the Strait of Georgia and Plumper Passage. Listen to wind predictions prior to paddling, paying particular attention to the East Point Lighthouse reports.

Paddlers who are unfamiliar with calculating when it is safe to paddle through narrow passages must avoid this route. Given the likelihood of turbulent waters around East Point and the lack of suitable landings on the exposed southern shore of Saturna Island, this route is recommended for experienced paddlers only.

The government wharf at Lyall Harbour serves as the best launch for this route. (The three separate trips described for Area IV combine easily to form an extended trip. Launch from either Lyall Harbour on Saturna or from Bennett Bay on Mayne Island if paddling a combination of the three trips.)

The Route

Cross the .5-mi entrance to Lyall Harbour, heading toward the King Islets where shell beaches on the smallest of the two islets are particularly inviting. Minx Reef marks the entrance to Winter Cove, and although the shallows here pose little threat to shallow-draft boats, watch for partially submerged, barnacle-covered rocks.

Located in the tiny cove along the south shore of Winter Cove is St. Christopher's Church. The rebuilt structure, originally a Japanese boathouse, once seated about twenty parishioners. It is no longer used.

The park in the northeast corner of Winter Cove serves well as a stopover while waiting for slack water in Boat Passage. The 89-ha (223 ac) park was originally the site of an aggregates plant; the open pit quarry and furnace produced chipped stones for road building. Upon purchasing the land in 1979, the province established Winter Cove Marine Park. At present there is no overnight camping here, but Parks is attempting to obtain the support of the local community to establish a kayak/walk-in/cycle campground. Call BC Parks at (250) 391-2300 to determine the status of this initiative.

Aquamarine waters and white sands lure kayak sailors ashore on Cabbage Island Marine Park.
(*BC Parks*)

Don't miss hiking the shoreline trail to Winter Point. From the point, look out over Boat Passage, a dramatic portal between Saturna and Samuel Island — only 15-m (50 ft) wide! Water rushes into Winter Cove on the ebb in streams of up to 7 knots and on the flood spills into the strait. Top off fresh water supplies at the hand pump found in the picnic area.

Swift tidal action here creates favourable fishing conditions for the river otter. On one occasion I watched four of these creatures. It seemed that every two minutes they would return to the surface with a small fish — their constant chatter proclaiming the success of their almost playful efforts.

But swift currents create conditions that are not nearly as favourable for the paddler. Enter Boat Passage close to slack only, otherwise expect a vigorous 7-knot ride through the turbulent water.

Once through the pass, either cross over to the Belle Chain Group (see the route description for the Belle Chain Islets) or head along Saturna's eastern shore toward Cabbage Island. Since the 4.5-mi stretch to Cabbage Island is open to northerly winds, check wind conditions for the Strait of Georgia prior to paddling.

There is little in the way of alluring stopovers on this side of Saturna as most beaches are covered with boulders, and the few sandy shores are close to private residences. The approach to Cabbage is studded with tiny islets, a favourite haul-out for seals. Pine Islet, the largest in the islet chain, joins Cabbage at low tide. On one particular morning I observed a black-tail buck and fawn cross the kelp-covered isthmus joining the tiny islet to Cabbage. They had come to browse the undergrowth and, seemingly undaunted by my presence, passed within 5 m (16 ft) of my crouched figure.

Camp locations on Cabbage are not only beautiful but are also easy to access. Land anywhere along the alluring white-sand beach on the island's south side. The entire 4 ha (11 ac) of Cabbage are park land. Forest-sheltered areas close to the sandy shore provide designated camp locations. Pit toilets, a self-registration vault and information shelters are among the BC Parks facilities located here.

Consider swimming in the warm, aquamarine waters of Reef Harbour, or hike out along the northern shores for spectacular views out over the Strait of Georgia and distant mainland peaks. The widespread browning of trees in the middle of the island is not the result of insect attack but rather the effect of salt water. In the winter of 1982, high tides coupled with strong easterlies forced ocean water well above the high tide line, saturating the forest floor with salt.

Nearby Tumbo Island appears most inviting from any number of directions, but the entire island is private land. The often-absent owners hire a caretaker to make sure no one lands on these alluring shores. Admire this island gem from the water.

Appropriately named Boiling Reef off the eastern tip of Saturna gives just cause for concern to paddlers as tide waters swirl around East Point at maximum rates of 5 knots. Turbulent waters extend out from East Point in the form of huge whirls and eddylines all the way across to Tumbo Island. Schedule paddling in the area close to slack, using the *Current Atlas* to get the most accurate representation of tide flows. For those using the *Tide and Current Tables*, slack is determined using the secondary station, Boundary Pass, on the reference, Race Passage. To get to East Point from Tumbo Island, paddle one of three options. The first follows the outer shoreline of Tumbo Island and, unless paddled close to slack, will likely require passing through the most extensive sections of turbulent water. The second follows the inner shores of Tumbo Island, riding the current in Tumbo Channel. (The current in this channel always flows in an easterly direction, a phenomenon that for paddlers heading east works in their favour.) The sandstone cliffs on this side of Tumbo, although not high, are impressive. This second route will, however, require passing through some turbulent water, unless you are going through at slack. The third option avoids much of the East Point turbulence by angling across to Saturna Island before entering Tumbo Channel. Follow Saturna's north shore closely, and round East Point by taking advantage of backeddies.

Most paddlers presume that once they are around East Point, the effect of currents is minimal. Such is not the case. Maximum floods and ebbs create currents of up to 2 knots all the way from East Point to Taylor Point where currents are especially noticeable off major headlands. Take advantage of flows by making sure paddling direction and current direction are the same. On one occasion, I paddled against the current on the 1.5-mi stretch from Monarch Head to Taylor Point. It took forty-five minutes to cover the distance. On another trip, paddling the same distance and riding a flooding current took only twenty minutes. One final note regarding currents in the area —unpredictable backeddies, especially around Narvaez Bay, send currents flowing in the opposite direction from what is expected.

Boundary Pass is a huge body of water separating Canada and the United States. Freighters the size of city blocks use the pass as their gateway to the Strait of Georgia. Unless you are crossing over to the San Juans, their presence has little effect. But the winds that blow up Boundary Pass are a concern for paddlers. Listen to weather predictions, and if strong winds from the south are predicted, assume that they will affect paddling along this southern Saturna shore.

So, you have determined when to paddle around East Point, you know that you are paddling with current flows in Boundary Pass and weather forecasts are predicting calm winds. Is this paddle worth all the scheduling required? You bet! The south shore of Saturna is magnificent. Immediately upon rounding East Point, you will see huge wave-sculpted sandstone cliffs rising 30 m (100 ft) or more to arbutus-covered ledges. Notice the many different ways the few residents here access the water from their homes – 30 m above sea level! Ladders, ropes and railings of various lengths and degrees of maintenance dangle along the cliff face.

Don't miss a stopover in Fiddler's Cove adjacent to Narvaez Bay. (This is reserve land and is therefore private property. Obtain permission to camp by contacting the band manger. See "Indian Reserve Lands" in the "Introduction to the Gulf Islands.") The cove's long sand beach is divided by a tiny islet that joins to the beach at low tide, and the nearby cabin offers temporary shelter from winds. Look for a trail leading away from the beach in the middle of the cove. It winds up the steep bank, traverses the top of nearby bluffs and eventually joins Fiddler's Road, a little-used offshoot of Saturna's East Point Road. Views from the top of the bluffs to the distant San Juans are magnificent, and as these bluffs face south, wildflowers blanket the forest floors early in spring.

Not only does the Tsawout Band permit exploring ashore here, but band members have generously granted the use of Fiddler's Cove for overnight camping. They ask that this privilege not be abused in any way, that fires are not lit and that all that is packed in is also packed out.

Narvaez Bay provides little in the way of alluring stopovers. The mere presence of private residences at the head of the bay and in the sheltered nook on the bay's southern shore discourages land exploration. But the narrow bay adjacent to it boasts an alluring sand beach and open meadow. Unfortunately, the area is part of a tree farm, and signs discourage trespassing above the high tide mark.

The cliffs between Narvaez Bay and Monarch Head are undoubtedly the most magnificent on Saturna's shores. Their 60-m (200 ft) rise significantly dwarfs paddlers below. Falcons and eagles ride the thermals above the highest ledges.

Two coves just inside Monarch Head are accessible only at high tide as at low tide huge boulders block access to the sand beaches above. Those fortunate enough to land can walk through the open arbutus forest to the point. I watched as a pod of six orca passed this point during an unforgettable lunch stop. It is common to view resident orca anywhere within Boundary Pass.

Paddle close to the rocky shoreline between Monarch Head and Bruce Bight, and look into the clear waters for white plumose anemones, red and purple urchins and ochre stars. Here, seals often pull out on exposed rock ledges, raccoons scour the intertidal zone for molluscs and overhead eagles scan the water for prey.

Paddling the pass between Java Islets and Saturna's shore against current flows will noticeably deter progress. Paddle through with the current or close to slack.

Sheltered by Taylor Point is a magnificent sand beach and a meadow owned for years by longtime Saturna residents, the Campbells. At the time of revising (1997), it was rumoured the Campbells had sold. Regardless, the land remains private. Paddlers may access the beach but should respect the privacy of these lands by staying below the high water mark.

Walk around to the outside of Taylor Point, originally owned by George Taylor, who at the turn of the century operated a stone quarry here, as is evidenced by the angular cuts in the rock. Apparently, some of the stone was used in the construction of the Parliament Buildings in Victoria. The dilapidated wharf pilings may well have been part of the same operation. Underwater divers visiting Taylor Point take delight in the numerous bottles and other pieces of junk that were dumped from the wharf long ago.

Most paddlers are by now appreciating a striking absence of homes on Saturna's south shore. But look again. Perched on the high bluff to the right of Taylor Point beach, tucked in the trees in a true aerie-like location, is a Saturna home. It is hard to see and comes into best view from the water.

From Taylor Point to Croker Point, barnacle-covered rock ledges make landings difficult. Yes, a murder did actually occur at Murder Point. An American and his daughter were killed here by natives in the winter of 1863. The story tells of an entire family moving from Waldron Island (US) to Mayne Island in a small boat. When a storm hit, most of the family were transported by a local, while the father and one daughter stayed behind with their possessions. They were attacked by a group of Lamalchi Indians. No one knows exactly why these supposedly innocent victims were murdered; it could be that another completely unconnected incident may have prompted the attack. Eleven natives were implicated, three of whom were convicted of murder and eventually hanged in Victoria.

Dorsal fin of a surfacing orca whale. This fortunate kayaker not only got closer than most, but also had a camera ready. (*Maurice Robinson*)

Orca Whales

In 1964 a sculptor was commissioned by the Vancouver Aquarium to go out and shoot a killer whale and then sculpt a life-size model for the city's new aquarium. A harpoon gun was set up on the southern shores of Saturna Island, and after a two-month vigil and few sightings, a pod of thirteen approached the island shore. The harpoon was fired, injuring a youngster, but the orca did not die. Aquarium staff, having arrived by float plane, decided to move the one-ton whale to Vancouver Harbour where over the next few weeks researchers fought desperately to save the life of the first-ever captive killer whale – Moby Doll. She, who actually turned out to be a he, didn't make it, but Moby's death brought world attention to a little-understood whale species, the orca whale.

Over the next decade the success of this capture led to a lucrative live-captive fishery, with the orca of BC supplying aquariums around the world. Sixty-two were taken between 1965 and 1977 (Bigg, MacAskie and Ellis). The impact the fishery had on local populations caused concern to the informed public and to the many researchers anxious to find out more about the orca.

In response the federal government began to study the occurrence and natural history of these whales in BC. Each one was identified by natural markings found on the dorsal fin and lighter-coloured saddle patches found at the base of the fin. Today, virtually every orca on the BC coast has been identified and numbered.

About 350 of them live in BC waters and are divided into three distinct communities. Two are called "resident," while a third is called "transient." One resident community is found off northern Vancouver Island and the other off southern Vancouver Island. The transient community travels throughout the resident ranges, with all three communities divided into smaller groups called pods. There are between one and fifty individuals in each pod.

The resident community in southern BC waters has three pods, J,K and L, with about eighty-three whales in all. J- and K-pods are the two most likely seen by paddlers visiting the Gulf Islands, whereas L-pod is mostly seen along the southwest coast of Vancouver Island. (It appears as though the "predictable" movements of pods are only predictable for a year or two before they change and start a different routine.) (Baird and Stacey)

Over thirty transient pods have been recorded in these waters as well, but appear infrequently and at irregular times of the year. They do not mingle at all with residents, and their pods are much smaller than the resident pods.

The orca spend a good deal of time foraging, the residents feeding almost entirely on fish while transients prefer marine mammals such as porpoise and seals and, very infrequently, sea lions. In a study continuing over the last four years, whale researchers Baird and Stacey have observed over fifty harbour seal kills in the waters off southern Vancouver Island. Although knowledge of this unusual species has dramatically increased since 1964, studies are far from complete. Many questions still need answering. The public is invited to report strandings or sightings of whales, dolphins and porpoises by calling the toll free number 1-800-665-5939.

Once around the point, paddlers may feel the effect of an ebb tide flowing out of Plumper Sound, although flows seldom exceed 1 knot. Winds from the north and northwest have more of an effect on paddling when winds from the Strait of Georgia spill into Plumper Sound.

At 490 m (1630 ft) Mount Walburton Pike is a striking landmark. An ecological reserve on these slopes protects a virgin stand of Douglas fir. The mountain is named after a unique Oxford graduate, who arrived here in the 1880s and is best remembered for his eccentric and colourful personality. Walburton Pike would often disappear for months on end, wore tailored suits until they fell off his back and went barefoot so often that he could use his toes as if they were fingers. Rated as one of the top big-game hunters in the world, he acquired a reputation as an explorer after making two great journeys into the Canadian north (Wolferstan). Pike bought the farm at the foot of the mountain that eventually bore his name.

The same farm and beach on Breezy Bay have been the site of Saturna's famous Dominion Day Lamb Barbecue. The event that started in 1950 as a school picnic grew so much that, in the 1980s, crowds of two thousand came to join the festivities. In 1989, the fortieth anniversary of the event, the festivities moved to Winter Cove Marine Park.

Elliot Bluff rises 30 m (100 ft) or more above sea level, providing highrise-style accommodation for resident cormorants. Boot Cove is worth exploring if there is time but provides little in the way of beach exploration as most of the shoreline is inhabited. What is most interesting about this cove is a deceptive calm, for although it appears to be sheltered, in fact it is not. Apparently, winds are funnelled by the cove's steep sides, and speeds up to 130 kmh (80 mph) have been recorded. Paddlers can take comfort in knowing that the funnelling occurs during winter months, less so in the spring and autumn and not at all in the summer.

Paddle back to Lyall Harbour to spend a ferry-wait on the balcony of the Lighthouse Pub, overlooking Plumper Sound.

Trip 11 — South Pender

Distances: – Lyall Harbour to Bedwell Harbour (5 mi)
  – Bedwell Harbour to Blunden Islet (3 mi)
  – Blunden Islet to Lyall Harbour (4.5 mi)

Highlights

Recent archaeological excavations on the Pender Canal revealed that native peoples inhabited these shores for at least five thousand years. View these impressive midden sites, then paddle along forested Bedwell Harbour to marine park land. Access an extensive network of little-used trails, then camp under an evergreen canopy. Paddle Pender's outer shores, watching for pods of orca that frequently visit these waters.

Considerations

Currents in Plumper Sound are minimal, and during the summer, winds are often calm to light. However, Plumper Sound is open to winds from northern quadrants. Strong north winds that blow down the Strait of Georgia spill into these waters. The shores of South Pender are exposed to winds from the south. Listen to wind predictions for the general area, paying particular attention to predictions for the strait.

Watch for turbulence off major headlands along the south shore of South Pender, especially around Blunden Islet.

Given the 1.5-mi crossing from Saturna to the Penders and the exposure to winds, this route is not recommended for novice paddlers.

Paddle this route separately or as an extension of the Saturna route by launching from Lyall Harbour on Saturna Island.

Nestled under the bluffs of Mount Norman is 58-ha (143 ac) Beaumont Marine Park. This Pender Island park land was donated to the province by Captain Beaumont, who is also responsible for donating the land that now consitutes nearby Discovery Island Marine Park. (*BC Parks*)

The Route

From Lyall Harbour, head south toward Elliot Bluff, leaving the bluffs at their midpoint and navigating toward Pender's Razor Point. The Plumper Sound crossing is 1.5 mi.

Arbutus-studded Razor Point marks the entrance to Port Browning, at the head of which is a waterside pub serving not only brew, but also pub-style meals.

Some paddlers may elect to miss Port Browning and paddle directly from Razor Point to Mortimer Spit, a narrow band of sand and shells forming one side of Shark Cove. A gently sloped beach is excellent for landing kayaks or canoes. The numerous holes visible in the sand at low tide indicate that there is a large clam population here.

One more stop must be made before entering the Pender Canal. Land on the gravel bar to the right of the bridge. (Pull kayaks well up on shore as pleasure boats frequently use the canal and create a fair bit of swell.) The bank immediately above the beach is comprised of shells deposited over several millennia, creating an impressive shell midden. Recent excavations have produced evidence of native occupation going back five thousand years. A second midden site, equally as significant, is accessed by crossing the road and following the short trail from the right side of the bridge. These lands are owned by the province and protected by heritage conservation laws.

Back to the Pender Canal. At one time, North and South Pender were joined by a narrow spit, and a portage was necessary to avoid rowing all the way around the island. The canal that created the two Penders was

---

5,000 Years on the Pender Canal

Interest in excavating the Pender Canal site was first expressed by archaeologists in the 1960s as severe erosion was destroying the significant midden. But the owners of the property were reticent to agree to excavations. The site was finally purchased by the province, and when various proposals to halt the erosion proved impractical, a decision to excavate was made.

Archaeologists from Simon Fraser University coordinated excavations that occurred over two seasons — the summers of 1984 and 1985. The site, completely cleared of underbrush and gridded in 2-m (6 ft) squares, was painstakingly excavated 10 cm (4 in) at a time. All artifacts were recorded, mapped, numbered and analysed — a huge project when you consider that thousands of archaeological features were discovered. The tiniest bone fragments and bits of flaked stone were all treated as important objects within the assemblage. Slate knives, rock adzes, basalt abraders, bone awls and antler wedges are only a few of the prehistoric tools uncovered. Perhaps most exciting are the burials, some completely intact, others mere scattered remains. A slate box received the most attention. Simply constructed of stone, the cover and four slab walls likely functioned as a storage container.

Although most of the artifacts are dated 2500 to 4000 years old, some are as old as 5,000 years.

---

excavated in 1903. The bridge reuniting North and South Pender was not built until 1955. Flows in the canal reach 3 knots, with currents strongest around the bridge pilings. If you get beyond them, assume passage will be easier through the remainder of the channel. Listen for the rattle call of the kingfisher here. The cutaway banks on the South Pender side of the canal are prime nest-building habitat for these crested birds.

Paddle the north side of Bedwell Harbour to Ainslie Point and a delightful pocket-shaped beach tucked inside the point. Head on to Beaumont Marine Park, an area often passed over by paddlers who prefer more secluded camp locations. During peak summer weekends, the area is very busy, since there are at least eight mooring buoys just offshore of this 32-ha (80 ac) park. But plan an overnight stop in the spring and fall (or even during peak summer months — the campsite on shore is little used as most yachtspeople return to their boats at sundown).

Land on the shell beach that links the small rock peninsula to the mainland. Look closely at the grassy isthmus — it is made up of shell midden. Scattered throughout the adjacent woodlands are a number of walk-in campsites and a pump that pumps water in August! You may feel the choicest tent site is located out on the small yet inviting rocky headland. This is not a park-designated camp location. Leave it for the

The Belted Kingfisher

Paddlers entering the quiet of a salt marsh or narrow passage are often greeted by the kingfisher's distinct rattle-like call. Here is a bird that is usually heard before it is seen.

The belted kingfisher is extremely territorial, defending both nest sites and fishing areas throughout the year. Immediately upon entering its domain, you will hear the rattle-alarm call as the bird flies on ahead — a pattern that is repeated until you reach the limit of the bird's territory, whereupon the kingfisher will swoop back behind you. Watch the next time you encounter the bird as this very predictable behaviour gives a good indication of the size of territory the bird so vigorously defends.

If not flying, these shaggy-headed birds typically perch on an overhanging snag, beaks angled downward, as they watch for prey. At times they hover before plunging headlong into the water, returning to shore where they mince the prey with their dagger-like beak.

Their sturdy bill is used in combination with their feet to dig out a remarkable nesting burrow. A long tunnel extending up to 3 m (10 ft) into a sand bluff or dirt bank has space at the end where the adult lays four to six white eggs. Tunnel entrances 8 – 10 cm (3 – 4 in) in diameter are usually found in steep cutaway banks that are often partially covered with vegetation.

enjoyment of all. The self-registration vault accepts the nominal, per party, camping fee.

Spend some time exercising the lower limbs by walking the shoreline trail toward Ainslie Point. This undulating route eventually leads to recently formed Mount Norman Regional Park, a park that encompasses over 100 ha (247 ac) and includes the 244-m (800 ft) high Mount Norman. As you climb, arbutus-covered bluffs give way to thick Douglas fir and red cedar forests. Logging, which has intermittently occurred over the past several decades, is in evidence about halfway up. Within an hour you will reach the top to take in your just reward — a magnificent view of the San Juans and distant Gulf Islands.

East of Beaumont Marine Park is Bedwell Harbour Resort, a rather posh establishment offering moorage and marina facilities, likely of little interest to paddlers except for a store and waterside pub.

At this point, inexperienced paddlers may choose to retrace the described route back to Saturna, thereby avoiding a paddle around the south end of Pender.

The outer coast of South Pender is exposed to south winds, and currents are noticeable off major headlands, especially off Teece Point and Blunden Islet during peak floods and ebbs. A large number of homes line these shores, and although beaches suitable for landing are frequent, most are adjacent to private residences. A favourite landing spot is just inside and west of Tilly Point where nearby banks appear to be eroding at a great rate.

From Teece Point, return to Saturna, navigating toward the open slopes of Mount Warburton Pike. Wind patterns in this part of the world can be unpredictable. It is common to round Teece Point on a seemingly calm day only to encounter a north wind blowing down Plumper Sound. About two-thirds of the way across the sound and closer to Saturna, southerly winds can have the greater influence. Summer wind strengths are usually manageable, but listen to wind predictions prior to making this 1.5-mi crossing.

Trip 12 — Belle Chain Islets:
South Mayne, Belle Chain Islets and Samuel Island

Distances: –   Bennett Bay to Anniversary Island via the Belle Chain Islets (3 mi)
                      –   Anniversary to Bennett Bay via Georgeson Passage (4 mi)

Highlights

The true highlight of this trip has to be the Belle Chain Islets. Distant coast mountains are an impressive backdrop for this magnificent archipelago. Each year, from fall to spring, California and Steller sea lions haul out on these tiny islets, masterfully commanding respect from all passersby, and year round, harbour seals swim in the surrounding kelp-choked shallows. Camp on one of three island gems, and look across to glacier-capped Mount Baker.

Considerations

Tidal streams reach up to 5 knots in Georgeson Passage and 7 knots in Boat Passage. Flows in both passages demand scheduling so that passing through them occurs close to slack.

During the summer, the winds in the Strait of Georgia that blow from the north demand consideration. Listen to wind predictions for the strait prior to paddling, and pay particular attention to the conditions described from the East Point Light Station.

Because of its exposure to winds in the Strait of Georgia, and because of strong currents in two of its passes, this route is not recommended for novice paddlers.

It can be paddled on its own or as an extension of the Saturna route by launching from either Bennett Bay on Mayne Island or from Lyall Harbour on Saturna Island. The description here assumes launching from Bennett Bay.

The Route

Leave Bennett Bay, and navigate toward the two unnamed islets off the north side of Samuel Island, recognizing that once away from the protection offered by Georgeson Island, the route is exposed to potential northerly winds. Stay clear of the turbulence off Samuel Island's Granger Point, especially when flood waters from Georgeson Passage spill out into the Strait of Georgia. Both Georgeson Island and Georgeson Passage are named after a well-known Gulf Islands family. Two generations of Georgesons manned Saturna's East Point lighthouse for over fifty years.

Neither of the two islets off Samuel's north shore are privately owned, with the largest of the two providing the best camp location. It would be difficult to land in wavy conditions on the sandstone ledges that surround the islet, but in calm weather look for level landings on the easternmost end of the islet. The open forest above provides space for two or three tents. Camp areas on the west end are difficult to access as slippery, kelp-covered rocks make exiting and entering the water a somewhat demanding task. Hike from one end of the islet to the other, passing through open evergreen forests and stepping from one grass-covered knoll to another. Walk through wildflowers in the spring, and look for raccoons year round.

The smaller of the two islets is the furthest out and certainly appears inviting to most passersby. But landings are difficult as the islet is almost entirely surrounded by sloping sandstone, and the undergrowth is as thick as it appears from the water. A determined few may choose to land at the midpoint on the north shore. A tiny clearing, large enough for one tent, does exist in the thick growth of juniper and berry bushes. One major advantage to this camp location is the unobstructed view out to the quarter-mile-distant Belle Chain group.

The highlight of this trip is the Belle Chain Islets. Distant coast mountains create a magnificent backdrop for the rocky archipelago. Exposed ledges are a favourite haul-out for harbour seals. But most impressive are the Steller and California sea lions that return here annually. Early arrivals appear in October and use the islets as a haul-out until the following spring, when they return to distant breeding grounds. Listen for their loud barks from the launch in Bennett Bay to be assured of their presence. For the closest view of these huge pinnipeds, determine current direction, then, from an upstream position, drift alongside the beached lions. Avoid paddling as flailing blades will alert them to your presence. A respectful distance is required —paddle too close and sea lions will plunge into the water and masterfully command your respect. I was fortunate to observe seventeen of these huge pinnipeds, all seemingly unaware of my passing or, perhaps in the very least, unthreatened by my presence.

Anniversary Island, the largest islet in the Belle Chain group, provides an opportunity to camp. Scout out the most level of the rock ledges on the east point, recognizing that even the best of landings will require some manoeuvring over sloping sandstone. A grass knoll immediately above the shore provides camp space for several tents. There are no trees to break approaching winds; therefore this location is best used in calm conditions.

A better camp location is accessed by hiking through an obvious grove of scrub oak and then dropping down to a large grass-covered ledge on the south side of the islet. This delightful enclave is surrounded on three sides by sandstone bluffs. Pitch two or three tents here. Sip a morning coffee, and watch eagles and cormorants attracted to the weather-worn perch of a nearby snag. And listen to the whistle of pigeon guillemots as they fly out from their protective rock crevices. At this point paddlers may choose to extend the route by heading east to Cabbage Island and linking up with "Trip 10." Otherwise, make the .5-mi crossing to the eastern tip of Samuel Island, entering Boat Passage, a dramatic 15-m (50 ft) opening between Samuel and Saturna Islands. The pass demands that paddlers schedule their passing through, since water gushes through the narrow gap at all but slack water. Passage at any time other than slack could be treacherous. Refer to the current reference for Boat Passage in the *Tide and Current Tables*. Further description of both Boat Passage and adjacent Winter Cove are provided in "Trip 10."

The south side of Samuel Island boasts several sandy beaches, most within Irish Bay. I have never landed at Samuel Island as a conscientious caretaker reportedly uses a powerful megaphone to broadcast his discontent to all who land even below high tide levels. The meadow, seen from both Winter Cove and Irish Bay, is the result of the hard labours of one of the original owners of the island, Archie Grey. In the 1930s and 1940s, E.P. Taylor bred and trained racehorses here until he sold the 132-ha (328 ac) island to Charles Lindbergh's daughter for $48,000 (Cummings and Bailey-Cummings). The present owners still keep horses.

Samuel Island has an interesting tide pattern. Tides on the south side of the island are calculated using Fulford Harbour. Tides on the north side are reckoned using Point Atkinson. Range differences between the tide levels often exceed .5 m (1.6 ft), yet the two references are only metres apart.

On to Georgeson Passage, where forested shores flank both sides of a river-like pass. Tidal streams reach up to 4 knots — speeds that a paddler does not wish to be working against. Pass through at slack, or take advantage of a free ride on a gentle flood tide, and watch for eddylines in the shallows off Lizard and Curlew Islands and around the islets off Granger Point.

Plan a side trip into Horton Bay. The waters here, sheltered by Curlew, are often mirror-still. A picturesque farm nestled in the head of the bay enhances the pastoral countryside. Tie up to the government float, and wander up the roadway through lush woodlands.

Return to the launch following the south shore of Bennett Bay.

AREA V — SALTSPRING, PREVOST AND GALIANO ISLANDS

Charts:
- No. 3310, Sheet 3, East Point to Porlier Pass (1:40,000)
  ** No. 3310 out of print as of 1995 **
- No. 3313, Cruising Atlas for Gulf Islands
- No. 3442, North Pender to Thetis Island (1:40,000)

Tides:
- Reference Port: Fulford Harbour
- Secondary Ports: Ganges Harbour and Montague Harbour

Currents:
- Reference Station: Race Passage
- Secondary Stations: Swanson Channel and Trincomali Channel

Duration:
- 1 to 2 days

Camp Locations:
- Montague Harbour Marine Park on Galiano Island
- James Bay on Prevost Island
- Red Islets off Prevost Island

Launches

Long Harbour and the Chain Islands

Both Long Harbour and the Chain Islands routes are accessible to walk-on paddlers from the mainland, as ferries that leave Tsawwassen dock in Long Harbour. Be aware, however, that the launches adjacent to the Long Harbour terminal are not easy to negotiate.

The first launch is accessed from the southeast corner of Long Harbour's terminal. Follow a short pathway to the water's edge, recognizing that at some tides the trail ends rather abruptly, leaving kayaks perched on a rock ledge a couple of metres above the sea. Some tricky manoeuvring may be required to get boats, gear and paddlers down to water level. There is also no protection from ferry wash, so watch for vessels entering and exiting the terminal.

The second, equally difficult, launch is located on the Wellbury Bay

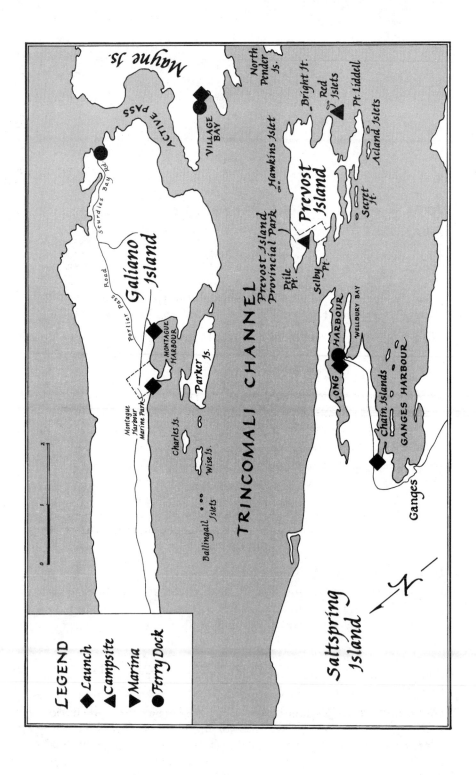

side of the Long Harbour ferry terminal. Look for a short trail leading down from a grassy area adjacent to the ticket booth. Be prepared to negotiate gear over a steep, boulder-strewn descent.

The easiest access to this area is obtained by driving onto a Long Harbour-bound ferry departing from Tsawwassen or a Fulford Harbour-bound ferry departing from Swartz Bay. Either way, head toward Saltspring Island's Ganges Harbour and the nearby Churchill Road launch site. (If you are driving from Ganges Harbour toward Long Harbour look to the right for Churchill Road. It is located within a couple of kilometres of Ganges.) At the end of Churchill Road is a public beach access. Park vehicles and hike the short trail down to Ganges Harbour. The banks along this trail reveal an impressive shell midden.

Prevost Island

The most accessible launch for Prevost Island is Saltspring Island's Churchill Road access. It is described in detail in the previous paragraph. The distance from this launch to Prevost Island's Selby Point is about 3.5 mi.

Also accessible is a launch located at Otter Bay Marina on Pender Island. Otter Bay is within .5 km (.3 mi) of Pender's ferry slip. Paddlers may either walk wheeled kayaks to this launch site or drive to it. Within a couple of hundred metres of leaving the ferry terminal, look to the right for the marina turnoff. The marina deservedly charges a $5 launch fee.

Three other launches for Prevost are adjacent to ferry terminals on Mayne, Pender and Saltspring Islands, making it possible to leave vehicles at Tsawwassen and Swartz Bay terminals and walk on to the ferry. However, be aware that these launches are not easily accessed. Two of the three launches also require crossing ferry-infested Swanson Channel. Ferries run so frequently in the summer it is difficult to time an anxiety-free crossing. A Pender Island kayak tour company wisely makes radio contact with BC Ferries, informing them of crossing parties so that, in the very least, ferries are aware of their presence.

The first launch is adjacent to Saltspring's Long Harbour ferry terminal. A detailed description of this launch is provided in the launch section for Long Harbour and the Chain Islands. The paddling distance from this launch to Prevost Island is 2 mi. Ferries are not a concern on this crossing.

The second launch is accessed immediately to the right of Pender Island's ferry slip. However, negotiating kayaks and gear past a thriving take-out business (that reputably serves the best hamburgers in the Gulf Islands) and over large blocks of concrete makes this launch tricky. Paddling distance to Prevost is about 2 mi. Watch out for ferries.

The third launch is close to Mayne Island's ferry terminal. Immediately upon leaving the ferry, look for a gate in the terminal's fencing and a short trail that leads to a sandy-shore launch. Paddling distance to Prevost is 1.5 mi. Be aware, however, that this crossing is also an extraordinary time-management exercise as paddlers attempt to dodge ferries that frequently enter and exit Active Pass.

Prevost is easily accessed by those paddling in the Sidney area. (Refer to "Trip 9.") From Portland Island, cross to Ruckle Park on the southeast corner of Saltspring, cross Captain Passage to the Channel Islands and then head to Prevost, a total distance of about 5 mi.

Prevost is also accessible to those paddling Galiano routes ("Trip 15"). The distance from Galiano's Montague Harbour to Prevost is about 3 mi. Ferries are not a concern on this Trincomali Channel crossing.

Galiano Island

To access the Galiano Island launch, board ferries bound for the island at either the Swartz Bay or Tsawwassen terminal. From the Sturdies Bay terminal, follow Sturdies Bay Road to Georgeson Bay Road. Turn left and follow Georgeson Bay Road to Montague Harbour Road – a road that terminates at Montague Harbour and the government wharf launch adjacent to a now-unused ferry slip. There is parking available on the road above the dock.

During the summer months, the road to the government wharf may be congested with traffic, making access to this particular launch site difficult. If this is the case, use the public ramp at Montague Harbour Marine Park. There is ample parking adjacent to this launch site.

Trip 13 – Saltspring's Long Harbour and Chain Islands

Distances: – Long Harbour (5 mi round trip)
           – Chain Islands (5 mi round trip)

Highlights

How about a weekend getaway to the Gulf Islands? Stay at one of Saltspring's charming Bed and Breakfasts, and take along kayaks and gear in anticipation of some relaxed, short-distance paddling. Both Long Harbour and the Chain Group beg to be explored during a winter reprieve.

Paddle the mirror-still lagoon at the head of Long Harbour, and explore the nearby estuary, or take shelter in a cove behind the tiny islets that mark the entrance to the harbour. Head over to the Chain Group, a delightful archipelago that is not only beautiful but is also historically fascinating.

Thriving on exposed rocky bluffs throughout the Gulf Islands is the arbutus. Arbutus, or madrone, is the only broadleafed evergreen that grows in Canada. (*Bruce Holland*)

Considerations

Currents are minimal in both Ganges and Long Harbours. Winds are generally calm during the summer. However, both harbours are open to the occasional southeaster. Watch for ferries pulling in and out of the Long Harbour terminal.

At most times, these are excellent routes for novice paddlers.

The Route

Long Harbour

From the Long Harbour ferry terminal, paddle to the head of the inlet where docks, mooring buoys and private homes are plentiful. Beyond this development, the inlet narrows to a passageway leading to a secluded lagoon, where the already quiet waters are hushed further by the thick forest that surrounds these shores. At the end of the lagoon is a small estuary, and at high tide, deeper waters allow passage through to the marshy terminus.

Return to the main harbour, and follow its north shore to Nose Point. This entire stretch of coast is part of a development called "Maracaibo Estates." The homes are few and well hidden, as their natural wood finish blends in well with the forest environment. White-shell beaches are frequent along the route. Clamshell Island, in the middle of the harbour, calls out to be explored. However, steep, rocky banks deter landing. Those disappointed by poor access may take comfort in knowing

---

The Arbutus

The arbutus, or madrone, is Canada's only broadleafed evergreen. Specially adapted oval leaves are glossy on the upper side, allowing water to run off them easily. In the event of freezing temperatures, an icy coating does not develop on the leaves. The tree's most outstanding characteristics are its peeling green bark and its twisted, copper-coloured trunk. In March it blooms with clusters of creamy white flowers. In the fall the blossoms develop into small orange-red berries. The arbutus thrives on exposed rocky bluffs overlooking the sea throughout the Gulf Islands where even under the best conditions it rarely exceeds 12 m (40 ft).

---

the island supports a prolific growth of prickly pear. Out toward Nose Point, thick rain forest gives way to open woodlands, and a small cove, sheltered from wind and view by a cluster of tiny islets, is worth exploring. From the cove, stroll through open arbutus forest to Nose Point.

At this point paddlers may choose to link up with the Chain Islands or Prevost Island routes or simply return to the ferry terminal following Long Harbour's southern shore. There are many more homes on this side of Long Harbour. The most impressive complex serves as an outstation for the Royal Vancouver Yacht Club.

If paddling near the ferry terminal, be aware that because Long Harbour is so narrow, the ferries that arrive twice daily must go beyond the dock and then back up into the slip.

Head to the Chain Islands in the middle of Ganges Harbour for some interesting shoreline exploration.

Recent history is in evidence on First Sister Island. Upon purchasing the island in the 1920s, an immigrant Scotsman decided he should live in a home reminiscent of his homeland, and so this rather colourful individual proceeded to construct a scaled-down version of an authentic Scottish castle. Alas, the unfortunate fellow was also fond of alcoholic beverage, and it eventually did him in. An American subsequently purchased the medieval real estate but soon discovered it was not only much too primitive, but that it was also impossible to heat! He had a large portion of it torn down. However, the remains of the original castle are visible on the island today.

A beautiful white-shell beach on the west end of Third Sister Island shouldn't be missed.

Several mammals inhabit these waters. Expect to see mink and river otter, and perhaps fallow deer. On a particular winter paddle, I sat and watched a deer swim to the most easterly islet of the Deadman Group. The young buck went ashore and proceeded to browse the undergrowth, seemingly undaunted by my presence. These deer frequently swim across saltwater passages in the hopes of reaching better forage.

The Sea Urchin

What is most remarkable about the urchin is a complex chewing mechanism composed of forty bones and sixty muscles. It is called "Aristotle's Lantern" since it reminded the scientist/philosopher Aristotle of a many-sided lantern. Located on its underside, this mouth scrapes and tears plant material from the sea floor, quickly changing an expansive garden of kelp into a pavement of pink cructose algae.

Understandably, the spiny urchin has few predators, so juveniles settle close to the adults where they are protected under the canopy of spines.

Urchins are commercially fished in BC waters to meet the demands of an inexhaustible Japanese market. The roe, extracted from the urchin and placed in shallow trays for export, is consumed raw and must therefore arrive fresh and in prime condition.

In the summer, Ganges Harbour becomes very busy, as it is a major thoroughfare for boat traffic. At the head of the harbour is the community of Ganges, one of the largest in the Gulf Islands, offering a variety of services and facilities. Grocery stores, a health food shop, two bakeries, restaurants, craft stores and a liquor outlet may be of interest to paddlers — all within two blocks of the government wharves.

Trip 14 — Prevost Island

Distances: – Circumnavigation of Prevost Island (7.5 mi)
  – Circumnavigation of Prevost, including the inlets (12 mi)

Highlights

Since 1924 Prevost Island has been farmed by the DeBurgh family, and to this day the tended fields and rough pastures support domestic herds. The resulting pastoral countryside stands out in distinct contrast to the busier Gulf Islands.

In 1996 a stunning piece of property surrounding the island's James Bay became park land. An overnight visit to a delightful isle that has maintained its charm and quiet isolation is now possible.

Considerations

Currents are minimal. The only riffling of waters occurs off Selby Point (during peak tide flows only).

Winds are generally calm, and only when strong winds blow from the southern quadrants do the waves steepen to a significant height.

As crossings exceed 1 mi, novice paddlers should exercise caution.

The greatest hazard is the ferries that frequently run through Swanson Channel. This risk is avoided by crossing to Prevost from Saltspring or Galiano Islands.

The route is described here, assuming a launch from Saltspring Island's Churchill Road access.

The Route

Paddle the northern shore of Ganges Harbour heading toward Scott Point. (See "Trip 13," the Chain Islands section, for a description.) From Scott Point cross over to Nose Point, then begin a .5-mi crossing over to Prevost's Selby Point. Captain Passage narrows here, and as a result, currents can pick up speed. However, it is easy to get around Selby Point, even when paddling against flows.

Up until recently paddlers did not have other than below high tide line access to Prevost shores. However, in 1995, 95 ha (235 ac) of land surrounding James Bay (including O'Reilly Beach and the entire Peile Point peninsula) were purchased by the provincial and federal governments. At the time of this writing, long-term development plans were not in place, but eventually these lands will become part of a newly established national park system within the Canadian Gulf Islands. In the meantime, James Bay park lands are overseen by BC Parks and for the time being will remain undeveloped. (For additional information regarding the future development of a national park in this area, see "Pacific Marine Heritage Legacy" in the "Introduction to the Gulf Islands.")

O'Reilly Beach is the local name given the cove halfway along the western shore of James Bay. A large meadow and orchard add to the pastoral appeal of this sheltered shore. Tent sites are plentiful. Choose to set up camp in level grassland or on an arbutus-sheltered ledge overlooking James Bay.

There is plenty of opportunity for on-foot exploration in this newly formed park. Wander inland through open fields and forest trails. Or simply explore the shoreline around the bay. The more intrepid paddler may choose to hike the 1-km (.6 mi) long distance out to Peile Point.

I have observed paddlers camped out on Peile Point — an attractive setting as it provides views of both sunrise and sunset. The access however appeared difficult. The party's canoe lay from high point to low point in a near-vertical line. I suspect reentry with the morning's low water levels was tricky.

Weekend visitors to Prevost may choose to depart from James Bay Saturday morning to circumnavigate Prevost and return to camp by Saturday evening.

Paddle from Peile to Portlock Point. Although the rocky shoreline and thick forest growing right down to the water don't provide land access along this stretch of coast, the views to the rock bluffs on Galiano and down to Active Pass are magnificent. In the spring herring attract hundreds of migratory birds to this area, including oldsquaws, scooters and Brandt's cormorants.

The Hawkins Islets are a paddler's paradise. Low tides expose nearby reefs where harbour seals bask in the sun. Magnificent displays of the red sea urchin are visible in the shadows off the south islet. In spring, the wildflowers that cover these islets create a vivid palate of colour. Chocolate lilies, pink sea-blush, yellow buttercups, blue camas, white saxifrage and blue-eyed Mary all bloom simultaneously.

As Hawkins Islets have recreation reserve status, paddlers may go ashore. Access is however very limited. I have camped solo on the islet but was perched somewhat precariously on the little available level land. Parties of more than one will likely choose to take in Hawkins from water level only.

The light on Portlock Point heralds an attractive shell beach in Richardson Bay. If you choose to land here be sure to place kayaks high enough to avoid ferry-generated swell from dumping into open cockpits.

Groves of arbutus and Garry oaks, drying reefs off the Bright Islets, ferries passing and views down Swanson Channel all add to the spectacular stretch of coast from Portlock Point to the Bright Islets. The Bright Islets are a recreation reserve but cannot be considered an overnight camp location. Steep rocky shores limit access, and there is no level ground for tents. Admire these intriguing isles from the water.

The beautiful Red Islets are also a recreation reserve and camp space is available here. Land on either of two white-shell beaches on the outer tip of the largest islet. At high water, access is straightforward, but at low water, it is necessary to carry kayaks over exposed rocks. Look for level camp areas in the open forest and on grassy knolls where there is enough space for two or three tents. One particularly beautiful spot is up on a rock bluff that looks out over Swanson Channel. Another camp area is accessed by heading to the shell beach that faces Prevost. Just above the high tide line is limited space to pitch one, perhaps two small tents.

Arbutus cling tenaciously to the tops of the rock bluffs from Point Lidell to Glenthorne Passage. Offshore, the Ackland Islands jut abruptly from sea level to a crown of evergreen. The islands' close proximity to Prevost creates a delightful passage, where seals observe passing paddlers.

Secret Island is no secret. Cabins front onto both Captain and Glenthorne Passages. Glenthorne Passage is no secret either. On a summer day, many boaters seek shelter here and for good reason – it is exceptionally beautiful. To fully appreciate this specific area's charm, plan a visit here in the spring or fall.

Paddle along the shore where the isthmus between Glenthorne and

Annette Inlet reaches its narrowest point. The banks are speckled white with shells that form a large midden. The dock visible at the head of the inlet is the main access to the farm on Prevost. Paddle out through Glenthorne Passage to an unnamed island off the north end of Secret Island. It is uninhabited and has a lovely shell beach.

Annette is the longest inlet indenting Prevost, about 1 mi in length. Several shell middens found along the bank indicate that native people frequently visited these shores. Herons commonly fish the shallows at the head of the inlet.

Don't miss Selby Cove. Steep overhanging cliffs on the western shore are lush with the green of ferns and forest. A meadow at the head of the inlet enhances the pastoral landscape. Park land fronts a section of the eastern shore. Steep slopes, however, make access to the park from this vantage impractical.

Either return to camp in James Bay or to Saltspring's Churchill Road launch.

Trip 15 — Galiano Island — Montague Harbour

Distances: – Montague Harbour to Ballingal Islets (3 mi)
  – Ballingal Islets to Montague Harbour via Galiano shoreline (4 mi)

Highlights

Some paddlers may choose to avoid this area during the busier summer months, but paddled in the off-season, this route is special. Particularly noteworthy are the hundreds of migratory birds that return annually to these waters. Remarkable at any time of year is the unusual tree-nesting site of double-crested cormorants on the Ballingal Islets and the spectacular, naturally sculpted sandstone cliffs on the shores of Galiano Island.

Considerations

For the most part, currents in this area are minimal, seldom exceeding 1.5 knots. (Paddlers may wish to coordinate a northward paddle with a flood tide and a southward paddle with the ebb.) The stronger currents swirling around the tiny islets off the west end of Parker Island are usually manageable and easily avoided.

Winds here are generally calm, but watch for occasional southerlies that blow up Trincomali Channel.

The likelihood of favourable paddling conditions makes this a suitable route for novice paddlers.

Galiano is the only Gulf Island that has a kayak tour and rental company operating right on the island. For further information, turn to the Appendices.

The trip described here assumes launch from the government wharf adjacent to the ferry slip at Montague Harbour.

The Route

Prior to launching, paddlers may wish to pay a visit to the Montague Harbour Marina. The operators run a small store where you can stock up on a few last-minute provisions.

From the launch, head directly to the channel between Parker Island and Gray Peninsula, as many of the features attractive to paddlers are located outside the confines of this sheltered harbour.

Gray Peninsula is part of Montague Harbour Marine Park, and immediately upon rounding the easternmost point of this landmark, you will see a beautiful sand beach, one of several beaches in the park. This may be a little too soon for a rest stop, but for those leaving the harbour, this spot serves well as a stopover.

Two sandy coves are found on either side of the low isthmus on Parker Island, with the north-facing cove now serving as the permanent home to a beached barge. The barge was apparently moored near here in the early 1980s by an enterprising individual who drew a number of friends to this rather plush on-water accommodation. Obviously, things went awry as the decaying hulk is all that remains today.

Paddle along the outer shoreline of the tiny islets west of Parker, paying particular attention to the faster-moving currents between the east point of Wise Island and the offshore islet. Oystercatchers are typically seen on this tiny rock outcrop.

All of the islets in this area are privately owned, and residents on the outer shores of Wise have created some rather interesting dwellings on the rocky bluffs overlooking the water. One of the inhabitants accesses his getaway cabin by kayak.

The Ballingal Islets are undoubtedly the highlight of this trip. Nowhere in the Pacific Northwest can you observe a cormorant nesting site as unusual as the one found on this tiny isle. Since the 1920s, the double-crested cormorants have built their stick-nests in two weather-worn junipers; by 1939 the tree-nesting colony had increased to thirty-three nests, many of which still exist today (Wolferstan). Certainly, double-crested cormorants prefer isolated places for nesting and breeding, but it is indeed rare to find them choosing to nest in a tree. (The many cormorant colonies found in cliff locations throughout the Gulf Islands belong to the pelagic species.) To preserve this remarkable site, these islets have been designated a provincial nature park, and visitors are asked to observe from a distance.

From the Ballingal Islets, head shoreward. The waterfront along the most obvious cliff face is well worth exploring. Large sandstone grottos

Silica and calcite cements that bind minerals in sandstone dissolve in sea water, producing the intricate outcrops adding interest to shoreline paddling. (*Tracy Cornish*)

have been carved out at the base of 60-m (200 ft) high bluffs. Pelagic cormorants live highrise style on the narrow ledges, and at sea level various intertidal creatures are both colourful and plentiful and are best observed at low tide.

The only pebble beach, easily accessed by paddlers along this section of the route, is located east of these impressive cliffs. A public access from shoreward may mean sharing the space with others, but the locals are not only friendly but in my experience also quite informative.

At this stage paddlers may choose to follow Galiano's shores up toward Retreat Cove in order to link up with "Trip 20 – Wallace Island Marine Park" or "Trip 23 – Valdes Island: Valdes, Gabriola, the Flat Tops and Galiano Island." The distance to Retreat Cove is a little over 2 mi. It's an additional 5 mi to North Galiano's Spanish Hills' government wharf.

For those choosing to return to Montague Harbour, follow the shoreline closely as it is made interesting by a number of unusual sandstone shapes carved by wave erosion. Most impressive is a natural carving referred to by locals as Mushroom Rock.

Legend tells of concealed caves along this Galiano shore and secret passages climbing to exits on bluffs above Montague Harbour. Remember the murder that took place at Murder Point on the southern shores of Saturna in the 1860s? (If not, the story is told in "Trip 10.") Apparently, the party guilty of committing the crime hid in these caves until the leader of the assailants was discovered.

Sandstones of the Strait

Even a brief look at a chart of the Gulf Islands region shows a characteristic alignment of the islands, whose shapes are generally elongated from northwest to southeast. The islands are the eroded crests and edges of sedimentary rock layers that were compressed into a series of parallel folds millions of years ago by tectonic forces acting from the southwest.

All the sandstones you see in this region are part of the Nanaimo Group, a sequence of deposits totalling over 16 km (10 mi) in thickness. These layers include conglomerates, coal seams, shales and sandstones that underlie most of Vancouver Island's east coast, in addition to forming most of the Gulf Islands.

The spectacular erosive features seen in these rocks have all been created since glacial ice last disappeared from the Strait of Georgia about 13,000 years ago. The silica and calcite cements that bind the particles of quartz and other minerals in sandstone are easily dissolved by sea water. Wherever waves act on softer zones of these rocks, erosion is accelerated, producing intricate "fretted" or "honeycombed" outcrops. Especially impressive are the major overhanging "galleries" – some of which were used by early Spanish explorers in this area to cache provisions. Post-glacial "rebound" of the region over several thousand years gradually lifted some of the sculptured cliffs above the reach of the waves.

Garry oak, juniper, arbutus and Douglas fir, all drought adaptive, grace the cliffs along this shore. Even the prickly pear cactus grows on these south-facing shores. Interestingly, Galiano is one of the driest of all the Gulf Islands, receiving a mere 80 cm (32 in) of rain a year.

What makes paddling so exceptional from the fall through the spring are the countless birds that over-winter in this area. In fact, most paddlers will likely encounter at least a dozen species during a day's excursion in the "off-season." In the early fall, both arctic and common loons return to these waters, along with huge numbers of surf and common scooters. These are quickly followed by the returning Barrow's and common goldeneye. During the winter, the three mergansers –hooded, common and red-headed – are found here, along with grebes, buffleheads and scaups, while in the spring, the mergansers and loons, now in full breeding plumage, are joined by migratory Brandt's geese. Hummingbirds, drawn to the warmth of south-facing bluffs, return to the cliffs early each spring.

Expect to see several resident eagles, blue herons, kingfishers, pigeon guillemots and oystercatchers –all of them year-round inhabitants.

Montague Harbour Marine Park was the first marine park established in BC (1959) and to this day remains very popular with many pleasure boaters. It has earned a reputation as being the busiest of all the marine parks. (The park has a wharf and several mooring buoys and is also accessible to car campers.) For this reason, many paddlers may wish to pass it over during the summer months. However, in June and September you could well expect no one else to be using the several walk-in locations that are located well away from car-accessible sites. (This marine park charges a camping fee — $12.50 when this guide was revised in 1997.)

As you paddle the shoreline along the north side of the park, note the white-shell beach. This entire stretch of shore was inhabited from almost three thousand years ago to the arrival of white men by natives, who over the countless years of occupation discarded the shells that form the midden. Storms have subsequently eroded the beach, leaving the shell fragments visible today (Wolferstan).

Perhaps the only difficulty paddlers will have in this area is a mental one stimulated by the half-dozen power lines that manage to cross just about every beach and cove on Gray Peninsula and Parker Island. Passing 38 m (125 ft) overhead, they are certainly not a navigational hazard, but the sight of them is rather irksome.

Area VI — Sansum Narrows

Charts:	– No. 3310, Sheet 2, Tsehum Harbour to Ladysmith Harbour (1:40,000) ** **No. 3310 out of print as of 1995** **
	– No. 3313, Cruising Atlas for Gulf Islands
	– No. 3442, North Pender to Thetis Island, and No. 3441, Haro Strait, Boundary Pass and Satellite Channel (1:40,000)
Tides:	– Reference Port: Fulford Harbour
	– Secondary Ports: Maple Bay and Cowichan Bay
Currents:	– Reference Station: Active Pass
	– Secondary Station: Sansum Narrows
Duration:	– Day trips
Camp Locations:	– Beach behind Musgrave Island

Launches

To access the Cowichan Bay launch, follow Highway 1 north from Victoria. South of Duncan, take the Cowichan Bay turnoff, and follow Cowichan Bay Road to Cowichan Bay. There is a public boat ramp and plenty of parking space just north of this seaside community. Allow an hour to drive from Victoria to Cowichan Bay. Access the Maple Bay and Genoa Bay launches by following Highway 1 to Duncan. From the centre of town, follow signs to Maple Bay. Make a left turn onto Beaumont Avenue, and within several hundred metres, look for the Maple Bay Rowing Club. Launch from the public ramp adjacent to the club. A large parking area provides ample space to leave vehicles. Allow an hour to drive to the Maple Bay launch from Victoria.

To access the launch at Genoa Bay, follow the same route as outlined for Maple Bay, only prior to reaching Maple Bay, take the well-marked Genoa Bay turnoff. The winding gravel road terminates at Genoa Bay where paddlers may launch from the ramp at the Genoa Bay Marina. The proprietors do not charge a kayak launching fee, nor do they charge for use of the adjacent lot, but tell them of your intentions. Allow a little over an hour to get to Genoa Bay from Victoria.

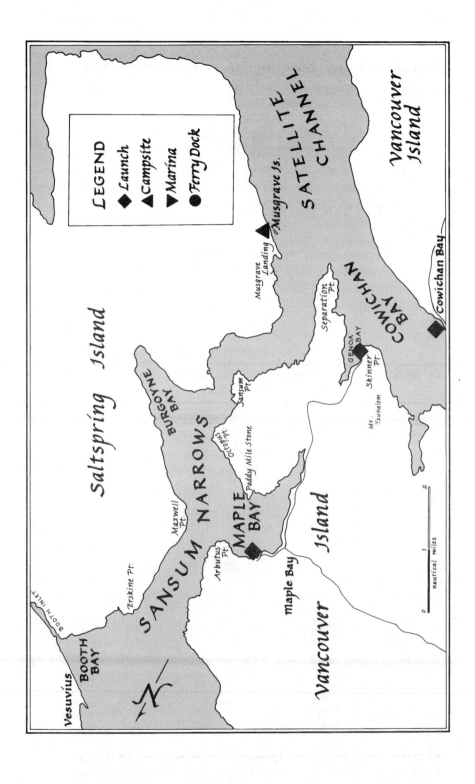

Trip 16 — Cowichan Bay to Musgrave Landing

Distance: 6 mi (round trip)

Highlights

What makes this paddle so delightful is exploring a little-known reserve area on Saltspring Island. Wander through open meadows where sheep contentedly graze, and follow a bubbling creek to a secluded waterfall, then camp in the coolness of a forest-sheltered site behind Musgrave Island.

Considerations

Both Cowichan Bay and Satellite Channels are open to occasional afternoon winds that are at times quite fresh. Currents are strongest between Separation Point and Musgrave Landing. In my experience, the *Current Atlas* provides the most accurate representation of flows in Sansum Narrows, although they can also be predicted by using the *Tide and Current Tables*. (Both are published by the Canadian Hydrographic Service). Steep waves result when currents flowing out of the narrows meet opposing winds from Satellite Channel.

Given open-water crossings that exceed 1 mi and the likelihood of turbulent water, this route is not recommended for novice paddlers.

Launch from Cowichan Bay.

The Route

Paddle the northern shoreline of Cowichan Bay, or head straight across the bay to Separation Point. This 2-mi crossing can be affected by brisk southeasterlies, as can the 1-mi Sansum Narrows crossing. Check weather conditions prior to paddling these open waters.

Having crossed to Saltspring, look for a dilapidated government wharf within the confines of the delightfully secluded Musgrave Landing. This previously isolated area is changing as the southern point has been subdivided, and a mooring dock associated with the development now assumes much space in the cove.

But the one attraction that makes Musgrave Landing a worthwhile destination point is a short walk away. Beach kayaks, and follow an overgrown road from the old wharf to the main gravel road. Then, .5 km (.3 mi) along this upward climb, look to the right for another roadway leading into a greenbelt reserve — an area set aside for public recreation use. (There are no signs indicating this is a greenbelt area.) These 34 ha (87 ac) were once used as a farm; sheep continue to roam the open pastures. Pass through the meadows, following a rough trail that eventually drops down into a creek bed. A short distance upstream, a secluded waterfall cascades into a crystal-clear pool. The surrounding rain forest provides a magnificent backdrop for falls that are most impressive in the spring.

Retrace your route back to the main gravel road, but as you begin the descent back to Musgrave Landing, look to the left for yet another overgrown trail. Follow it down to a pebble beach facing out to an island, unnamed on the chart but known locally as Musgrave Island. Return to this beach with kayaks as there is a delightful campsite in the forest above the shore. Walk along the shore to where the creek spills out from the old farm onto the beach.

Trip 17 — Maple Bay to Genoa Bay

Distance: 8 mi

Highlights

Schedule paddling so as to take advantage of the free ride offered by currents in fiord-like Sansum Narrows. Falcons and eagles soar above precipitous cliffs, and secluded coves offer enchanting rest stops. Don't miss the Genoa Bay Marina. Undoubtedly the most charming marina in all the Gulf Islands, it boasts a cafe that serves great pie!

Considerations

The currents through Sansum Narrows occasionally reach up to 3 knots; therefore, paddle from north to south with an ebb tide and from south to north with a flood. (Paddlers who are unfamiliar with this kind of scheduling may find themselves paddling in opposition to the flows and, although not in danger, will quite likely become frustrated.)

Southerly winds tend to funnel through the narrows, and at times significantly affect progress. When these winds meet an opposing ebb current, steep waves are likely to occur at the south end of the narrows.

If paddling south, launch from Maple Bay. Launch from Genoa Bay if paddling north. A one-way paddle requires leaving a vehicle at either launch, but it only takes ten minutes to drive from Maple Bay to Genoa Bay.

Given currents that reach up to 3 knots and the likelihood of turbulence at the south end of the narrows, this route is not recommended for novice paddlers.

The Route

Paddle the perimeter of Maple Bay to Paddy Mile Stone. From here to Octopus Point the shallows support an eel-grass environment. Look closely as eel grass provides shelter for many animals from microscopic life forms to larger creatures such as crabs, moonsnails and limpets. Diatoms are microscopic organisms that, if present in large enough numbers, constitute the furry olive-brown coating that covers the eel grass leaves. The tangled mat of grass is also teeming with small fish.

Consider a side trip to Burgoyne Bay. Mount Maxwell looms 595 m (1,952 ft) above the bay — an excellent place to watch turkey vultures, bald eagles and human hang gliders. Land at the government wharf at the head of the bay, and stroll along an idyllic country road that winds inland past several of Saltspring's sheep farms.

Sansum Point marks the entrance to a channel that is as close to a coastal fiord as could ever be found in the Gulf Islands. Steep rock bluffs rise up from the narrows to 690-m (2300 ft) Bruce Peak on Saltspring Island and 240-m (800 ft) Stoney Hill on Vancouver Island. Eagles and vultures soar above the cliffs. Down below, aquaculture farms have set up their rearing pens.

Burial Islet, so named as it served as a native burial ground, offers little in the way of alluring stopovers, but it is an excellent shoreline to follow as, at low tide, the intertidal life here is quite remarkable. Especially beautiful are the white plumose anemones. These gorgeous metridiums take on quite a different appearance at low tide when the feathery tentacles, visible at high tide, are retracted. All that remains is a drooping, slimy stalk.

Rocky shoreline from Sansum Point to Separation Point discourages landing. A single gravel beach just north of the point provides the only shore access. Rounding Separation Point may require crossing eddylines, and if winds from Satellite Channel meet an opposing ebb tide, expect steep waves in this area.

Several shell and gravel beaches break up the rocky shore between Separation Point and Genoa Bay. The large bight located halfway along this stretch of coast has a sheltered pebble beach fronting a large grassy meadow. The driftwood lean-tos, fire pits and makeshift benches all testify to its popularity.

Genoa Bay Marina is truly one of the most charming in all the Gulf Islands. The cafe, where a casual and friendly atmosphere is immediately apparent, leans out over the water and looks down on an assortment of seaworthy craft from houseboats to fishing boats. Delicious home-cooked meals are served here from May through October. Don't miss this opportunity for coffee and pie.

Those familiar with the "Brother XII" story will be interested to know that Genoa Bay was once home to the Brother's ship, the *Lady Royal*. Before he made his hurried getaway, Brother XII caused so much damage to the *Lady Royal* that she sank. Eventually, she was brought to the surface and sold to T.A. Coulson, who had her towed to Genoa Bay. Coulson embarked upon a monumental repair job — referred to locally as "Coulson's Folly" (Gould).

One of the largest sawmills in BC operated continuously on these shores from 1895 until 1925, when the owners shut her down because of severe water problems. Fresh water for the mill's boilers had to be brought in by tanker scow from Burgoyne Bay, and too often the scows were late arriving (Gould).

Looking to stretch those cockpit-confined muscles? A short walk up the main Genoa Bay road connects hikers to a footpath that winds its way out to Skinner Point. The trail continues on to Skinner Bluff, then up to the 510-m (1700 ft) peak of Mount Tzuhalem. The route is steep, but the views of surrounding Gulf Islands are magnificent. Allow at least an hour to get to the top.

Trip 18 — Maple Bay to Vesuvius

Distances: - Maple Bay to Vesuvius (5 mi)
- Maple Bay to Vesuvius via the shoreline of Booth Bay and Booth Inlet (7 mi)

Highlights

Launch from a delightful seaside community, and paddle isolated Saltspring shores beneath the towering peaks that contribute to the fiord-like appearance of Sansum Narrows. Cross open waters at the entrance to Booth Bay, or enter a fascinating marine environment found within Booth Inlet. And don't miss Vesuvius — a tiny Saltspring community that boasts a delightful waterside pub complete with a balcony where paddlers can indulge in sumptuous pub fare prior to returning home.

Considerations

Currents in this section of Sansum Narrows seldom exceed 1.5 knots; however, paddlers may wish to coordinate a northward paddle with a flood and a southward paddle with the ebb. (Although the chart indicates flows of 3 knots, the *Current Atlas* provides the most accurate representation of current flows in this part of the narrows, indicating that flows do not exceed 1.5 knots.)

Southerly winds do affect these waters, but during the summer, waves rarely build to a significant height.

This route is not suited for novice paddlers given the 2-mi stretch of open water across the entrance to Booth Bay. (This open stretch is avoided by paddling the shoreline, but that increases the return trip length to 14 mi.)

Launch from Maple Bay.

The Route

The resort community of Maple Bay has several commercial facilities. Of particular interest to paddlers are the general store located just above the government wharf and a waterside pub located a couple of hundred metres north of the launch.

From the launch, follow rocky shoreline to Arbutus Point, then cross the .5-mi wide Sansum Narrows, navigating toward Maxwell Point. From here the northward stretch along isolated shores is particularly beautiful as little development has occurred on this part of Saltspring. Rock bluffs rise from the sea to grass-patched ledges where elevated knolls support Garry oak and arbutus forests. In the spring these dry coastal woodlands abound with the colour of blossoming wildflowers. A gravel beach just south of Erskine Point provides the best place to land.

For the shortest paddling distance to Vesuvius, leave Erskine Point and traverse the waters at the entrance to Booth Bay, an open crossing of 2 mi.

An extended route follows the entire shoreline of Booth Bay, along which is found Arbutus Beach. Here the creek draining Lake Maxwell empties into the sea, and an expansive sand and gravel beach surrounding the outfall provides easy access and an excellent lunch stop. However, as this area is accessible by road, expect to share this spot with Saltspring residents, especially on a sunny summer day.

Continue on to the entrance to Booth Inlet, easily distinguished by the sandbar that flanks its south shore. This inlet is best explored at high tide (at low tide gumboots may be required). During peak floods, the water that rushes through the narrow entrance provides an exhilarating ride. However, the waters inside the inlet are calm. Even the shore birds are silent as they probe the silty banks. Within the confined waters, pungent salty odours fill the air. The paddle concludes at the bridge, as beyond it the water is too shallow for passage. From here, the town of Ganges is only 2 km (1.2 mi), a distance that island residents considered dredging so as to join Booth Bay to Ganges Harbour. Turn back to the head of Booth Bay and the 1-mi paddle to Vesuvius.

Vesuvius is a delightful seaside village with an idyllic location and waterside facilities that certainly make it a worthwhile destination point. Two locations provide landing access, the government wharf and a nearby beach. Space is limited at the single-float government dock, but if there is room, this access is closest to nearby facilities. The beach at the head of Vesuvius Bay has a stairway leading to Langley Street. Follow it to Vesuvius Bay Road, then turn left to access a well-known Gulf Islands stopover — the Vesuvius pub. This very popular watering hole operates above the government wharf and not only provides brew but also serves excellent pub fare in a relaxed West Coast atmosphere. And don't miss a visit to the Vesuvius Bay General Store as this tiny establishment, located a few hundred metres up Vesuvius Bay Road, is one of those remarkable country stores that stocks just about everything.

The *Vesuvius Queen* docks at the adjacent ferry slip. She is one of the smallest of the Gulf Islands ferry fleet, carrying commuters from Saltspring to Crofton. The wash from her wake is not a threat, but paddlers should note that she moves in and out of the slip not only quickly but also frequently.

On the return trip, cross from Erskine Point to Grave Point. The route southward from Grave Point passes uninhabited shores, and the steep cliffs behind rise up to 510-m (1700 ft) Maple Mountain.

Area VII — Central Gulf Islands

Charts:	– No. 3310, Sheet 2, Tsehum Harbour to Ladysmith Harbour and Sheet 3, East Point to Porlier Pass (1:40,000) **** No. 3310 out of print as of 1995 **** – No. 3313, Cruising Atlas for Gulf Islands – No. 3442, North Pender to Thetis Island (1:40,000)
Tides:	– Reference Port: Fulford Harbour – Secondary Ports: Preedy Harbour and Chemainus
Currents:	– Reference Station: Race Passage – Secondary Station: Trincomali Channel
Duration:	– 2 to 3 days
Camp Locations:	– Tent Island (with permission from Kuper Indian Band) – Wallace Island Marine Park – Dionisio Point Provincial Park – Islet south of Reid Island

Launches

For Thetis, Kuper, Tent and Reid Islands

Launch from Chemainus on Vancouver Island, from Preedy Harbour on Thetis Island, from Southey Point on the north end of Saltspring Island or from the north end of Galiano Island.

To access the Chemainus launch, follow Highway 1 from Victoria to north of Duncan. Turn off the highway, following signs to Chemainus and the Thetis-Kuper ferry. The route eventually heads down Oak Street through the "old town" part of Chemainus. Turn left off Oak onto Esplanade, and follow it around to Kin Park. Leave vehicles in the nearby lot, and launch from the ramp adjacent to the park.

To access the Preedy Harbour launch, follow the same route as for the Chemainus launch, but follow Oak Street down to the Thetis-Kuper ferry terminal. Either board the ferry with vehicles, or unload gear and walk on. An area just ahead and to the left of the ferry lineup provides

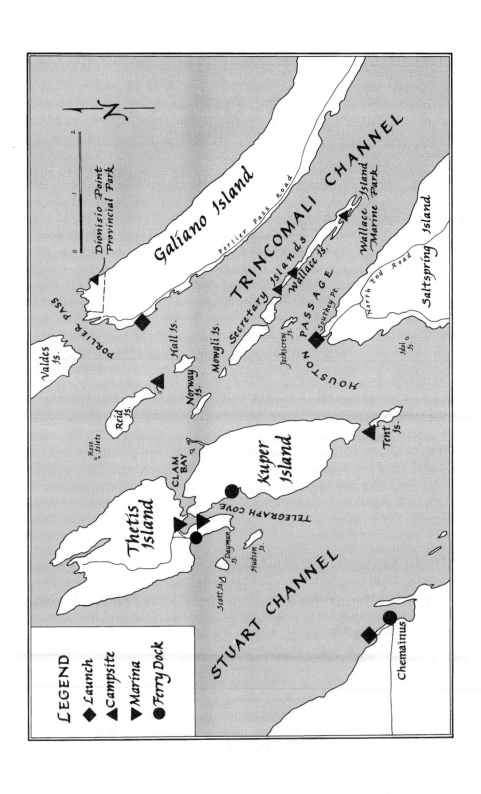

space to unload. Vehicles left in Chemainus can be left in the lot already described near Kin Park.

The launch on Thetis Island's Preedy Harbour is adjacent to the ferry slip. Immediately upon leaving the ferry at Preedy Harbour, look to the left for a short trail leading to a pebble beach. It serves as an excellent launch area. Vehicles can be left parked on the road above the ferry dock.

Access to the launch on the north end of Galiano is described in the launch section for "Area VIII."

For Saltspring Island North

To access launch areas on the north end of Saltspring, paddlers board Saltspring-bound ferries at either the Tsawwassen or Swartz Bay terminal. From either of the two Saltspring terminals, follow signs to Ganges. To get to launch sites at Southey Point from Ganges, follow signs to Vesuvius and then to Southey Point via North End Road. Turn right off North End Road onto Southey Point Road to gain access to a sheltered bay launch at the end of this road. Limited roadside parking is possible. A second launch is accessed by turning off Southey Point Road onto Arbutus Road. A short trail leads to a beach at the end of Arbutus Road. Again, limited roadside parking is available.

To get to Fernwood launch, follow above directions for Southey Point only make a right turn approximately 4 km (2.5 mi) along North End Road (measure from intersection of North End and Vesuvius Bay Roads) onto Fernwood Road. A government wharf where Fernwood Road joins North Beach Road serves as a launch site for Wallace Island. But better yet, head further north along North Beach Road and within a couple of hundred metres there is a steep access to a boat launch. This location provides easy water access and there is parking on North Beach Road.

Trip 19 — Thetis, Kuper, Tent and Reid Islands

Distances: – Chemainus to Kuper Island (3 mi)
               – Thetis Island (Preedy Harbour) to Tent Island (3.5 mi)
               – Tent Island to Reid Island (4.5 mi)
               – Reid Island to Thetis Island (Preedy Harbour) (4 mi)

Highlights

Here is a delightful route that is easily paddled in a weekend by leaving Thetis early Friday evening, camping on Tent Island Friday night, spending Saturday night camped near Reid and returning to Thetis by Sunday afternoon.

Don't miss the pelagic cormorant colonies on cliff faces along Kuper and Tent Islands, beautiful sand-fringed bays on Tent and the remains of a Japanese saltery on Reid Island.

Considerations

During the summer, winds in this area are usually calm, although waters are occasionally affected by southeasters blowing up Trincomali and Stuart Channels.

Paddlers may choose to ride a flood when heading north and an ebb when heading south, but for the most part, currents are minimal. The only turbulence due to tidal flows is found off Southey Point during peak floods and ebbs.

Novice paddlers who have listened to wind forecasts and know that southeasters are not likely to affect these waters will enjoy the favourable paddling conditions in this area. (The 3-mi crossing of Stuart Channel is easily avoided by novice paddlers by taking the ferry to Thetis Island.)

Launch from either Chemainus or Preedy Harbour.

The Route

If you haven't seen the murals painted on many of the buildings in the town of Chemainus, they are a worthwhile side trip. And if last minute provisions are required, there is a general store close to the Thetis-Kuper ferry terminal. The Chemainus bakery, two blocks up from the terminal, has an irresistible selection of baked goods.

Crossing the open waters of Stuart Channel (3 mi) in the summer is straightforward as winds are usually calm (watch for occasional southeasters) and currents in the channel are minimal. Navigate toward Active Point at the approximate centre of Kuper Island. On the horizon Kuper appears flatter than the somewhat hilly Thetis Island.

Paddlers launching from Preedy Harbour will note that, although the foreshore on the south end of Thetis is developed, paddling along these shores is most pleasant. Kuper Island is an Indian reserve, and except for the village at the north end of the island and the ferry terminal on Telegraph Harbour, it remains relatively natural. Paddle south along the rocky cliffs toward Augustus Point where pelagic cormorants nest on the narrow ledges.

Lamalchi Bay is named after a Cowichan tribe who originally lived at the south end of Kuper. A village once stood on the bay. However, due to drastic population reductions in the late 1800s (due to smallpox and tuberculosis), the few remaining Lamalchis amalgamated with the Penelakuts at the north end of Kuper. The only piece of land on Kuper Island not included in the reserve is on Lamalchi Bay. It was not included when the reserve boundaries were set in 1916 because it was the site of a church founded by the North American Society for the Propagation of the Gospel.

Tent Island was a provincial park until yearly lease agreements with the Penelakut Band on Kuper Island ended. It remains a popular overnight camp spot, but now visitors are asked to contact the band office prior to camping ashore. (See "Native Reserve Lands" in the "Introduction to the Gulf Islands " for further information.) Paddlers will quickly discover the area is very popular with boaters who moor in the large bay on the west side of Tent. They may wish to head to a secluded sand beach (just north of the popular moorage) where there is ample space for several tents in the arbutus forest above. (Avoid a view of the smoke from the Crofton pulp mill by choosing a tent location that faces north.) After dark, walk the water's edge, and stir the nearby waters. Do the rippled waters give off tiny pinpricks of light? If so, you are observing a rather unusual phenomenon called bioluminescence.

Paddle the 1.5 mi around Tent Island. Large numbers of moonsnails and their casings are found in the pass between Tent and Kuper, cormorants nest on the cliff edges on the island's southwest end and nearby North Reef is a prime bottom-fishing area. (Look for its well-marked shallows on the chart.)

The crossing to Jackscrew is .5 mi. From here, paddlers may choose to head to Wallace Island (see "Trip 20" description) or continue northward toward the Secretaries.

The Secretaries appear most inviting with their open arbutus and evergreen woodlands. However, North and South Secretary are privately owned. A sand bank joins the two islands at all but high tide. Appropriately, the native name for the area is Shemetsen, meaning "goes dry" (Rozen). When shellfish harvesting is permitted, the exposed mud flat provides the persevering digger with a sumptuous meal of clams.

The perimeters of Mowgli and Norway Islands are rocky, and the few protected beaches are close to private residences. Land on an unnamed bay on the south end of Hall Island – an easily accessed beach stop where a combination of sandy shores and rocky reefs provides interesting exploration. This entire island was at one time owned by Anna Morgan, also named the "Mystery Duchess, Hermit of the Isle of Echoes." She lived in total isolation here from 1907 to 1933 (Wolferstan).

Camp on a tiny unnamed islet on the southern tip of Reid Island. It is a recreation reserve. The only landing is on the rocky south end where exposed flat ledges provide rather awkward kayak access. Some tricky manoeuvring of boats and gear over rock ledges is required, but in my estimation, the effort is worth it. Weathered juniper and arbutus trees grace this entire islet. Flat grassy areas on the south and northwest corners are ideal campsites, accommodating two or three tents and offering panoramic views through Porlier Pass and down Trincomali Channel. Exercise extreme caution if you use a cookstove as this island is often tinder dry. Do not light fires.

Bioluminescence

Sea water is rich with tiny plankton that experience a population explosion during the summer (encouraged by warm water and increased sunlight). One particular species, Noctiluca (meaning "night light"), displays a remarkable ability to be luminescent.

Noctiluca contains an enzyme, luciferase, and an organic compound, luciferin. When disturbed, the enzyme initiates a chemical reaction between luciferin and oxygen, and a pulse of light energy results. The movement of a paddle through the water, or feet through the sand, shifts the plankton, putting it in contact with the required oxygen. None of the energy released occurs as heat, the reference to "cold light." This phenomenon is best observed on a moonless night in the late summer.

Reid Island was purchased in 1852 for $2.52 by Joe Silvey, the first Portuguese immigrant in Canada granted British citizenship. The wooded isle is still privately owned but remains largely undeveloped. Plan to stop at the pebble beach in the sheltered bay facing Thetis. (On the chart, "Piles" mark the north end of the beach.) Hidden behind the thick blackberry bramble at the south end of this bay are the remains of a Japanese saltery, established here in about 1908. Apparently, this operation employed about 150 men. The dry salt herring shipped from here went to Nanaimo, then on to export markets in the Orient. With the establishment of several other salteries on adjacent islands (Valdes and Galiano), Nanaimo became a major herring centre. Operations peaked in 1910 when 27,800 tons of salt herring were exported (Forester and Forester). With the relocation of all Japanese during World War II, salteries were shut down. Government legislation disallowed Japanese returning to their confiscated lands, and subsequently fish processing ended here.

Less than a mile to the north of Reid Island are the Rose Islets, established as an ecological reserve to protect representative marine wildlife. In 1968, 180 pairs of double-crested cormorants nested here. By 1983 the nesting pairs had diminished to 12, and by 1986 only 2 pairs of birds remained. The decline is attributed to human disturbance. Several pairs have returned, but it is most important that they are not startled, especially during nesting season from April through August. Other bird species frequenting the Rose group include black oyster-catchers (3 pairs), harlequin ducks, pigeon guillemots and glaucous-winged gulls (116 pairs).

For a close-up look at a colourful spectrum of intertidal creatures, follow the kelp-covered shores. Look for bat stars and purple stars, rock and kelp crabs, the acorn and thatched barnacle, tube worms and anemones. And look below the water for the red sea urchin and sunflower star.

The crossing from the Rose Islets to Clam Bay is just over 1 mi. Currents are minor. The outstanding white shell-beaches of Penelakut Spit mark the entrance to Clam Bay. (The native community behind is home to Kuper Island's Penelakut tribe.) At one time a traditional village composed of fifteen longhouses stood out on the spit where extended families of up to twenty individuals lived in each house. The Indian word for the village is "Penalexeth," meaning "buried houses on the beach" (Rozen).

The dredged pass between Thetis and Kuper Islands poses little threat to the kayaker. Tidal currents are minimal, flooding east and ebbing west. Some have likened the waterway to an irrigation ditch during low tides. At high tides, soft muddy banks line the shallow passage. The north shore is populated by Thetis Island residents, while native homes dot the Kuper Island side.

Two marinas operate in the sheltered waters of Telegraph Harbour and attract many boaters. Kayakers can stop for groceries, or enjoy the waterfront pub. If you are coordinating your trip with ferry schedules, allow an hour to paddle from the pub to the Preedy Harbour ferry dock. To paddle from Telegraph Harbour to Chemainus, allow approximately two hours.

Trip 20 — Wallace Island Marine Park

Distances: – Southey Point to Wallace Island Park (1 mi)
 – Fernwood Wharf to Wallace Island Park (1 mi)

Highlights

Head out from any of the launch sites described for Saltspring Island North and within an hour arrive at one of the newest of BC's marine parks — Wallace Island. It is little wonder that such colourful historic residents were drawn here. Sheltered coves, offshore islets, a midland trail meandering through juniper, fir and arbutus forests, historical remains and virtually assured glimpses of harbour seals, eagles and otter are only a few of the features that make a visit to this easily accessed island more than worthwhile.

The Route

Up until recently Wallace Island's alluring coves and forest trails were not accessible to paddlers. Fortunately all but 4 ha (11 ac) were purchased by the province in 1990 and Wallace was declared a park.

Visitors to these shores cannot help but ponder the lives of past residents. Jeremiah Chivers, a retired gold miner, died on the island at

Low tide at Chivers Point, Wallace Island Marine Park. (*Mary Ann Snowden*)

High tide at Chivers Point. During the summer, low tide occurs during the morning while higher water occurs at night. This means kayaks need to be pulled up high enough so as not to drift away at night. It also means hiking gear and boats back to low water levels in the morning. (*Tracy Cornish*)

the age of ninety-two. All that remains of his solitary thirty-eight-year influence are the twisted fruit trees lining Conover Cove. The American, David Conover, who credits himself for discovering Marilyn Monroe in his autobiographical *Finding Marilyn*, was full of dreams of an ideal existence when he purchased the island in 1946. Subsequent books, *Once Upon an Island* and *One Man's Island*, describe the victories and setbacks of his twenty-year residency. The cabins that remain in Conover Cove were part of Conover Resort, which once included guest cottages, a recreation hall and various support buildings.

A winter paddle to Wallace transported me to a virtually deserted isle. The 1-mi crossing from Saltspring's Southey Point ended on a secluded beach at Chivers Point. On a summer weekend undoubtedly numerous paddlers would already have settled here, having chosen one of the several tent locations. Up until recently paddlers predictably set up camp on the elevated headlands that define the bay at Chivers Point, understandably drawn to the views of nearby Galiano and Saltspring Islands. However, so that these areas are protected from overuse, BC Parks has wisely set up designated camp locations. Dispersed along the trail, these six forest-sheltered sites offer secluded camping and leave Chivers Point and beaches for the general use of all who visit. Pit toilets are also a part of the recent Parks' development here.

An obvious southward trail will beckon to most visitors. Follow the forest-lined route. In winter expect to see the hoof prints of resident black-tail deer. Within forty minutes this undulating path widens and shortly thereafter spills into an open meadow. Rusting farm implements lay in testimony to previous inhabitants. A water pump, maintained by BC Parks, is located here — however, signs advise boiling this water before drinking it. Carry on and in five minutes the historic buildings associated with Conover Cove come into view. In summer anticipate that many others will be taking advantage of the recreational resources situated around the cove. Good anchorage and a moorage dock understandably attract many boaters. Tent and picnic sites, toilets and visitor services are also available. Solitude-seeking paddlers may choose to pass the cove and follow the right-bearing 1-km (.6 mi) long trail that leads to Panther Point. Eagles, river otter and seals are commonly observed from this quiet promontory.

Wallace Island is not unlike many of the surrounding Gulf Islands in that mild winters are followed by very dry summers. As fire hazards are high, camp fires are not permitted — not even below the high tide line. BC Parks requests paddlers to camp at one of three designated areas — Conover Cove and Chivers and Cabin Points. A minimal user fee applies and is collected on an honour system by depositing in the associated self-registration vault.

Cabin Point is the least visited of the three designated camp locations. It is located about half a nautical mile south of Chivers Point on the east side of the island. Its beauty is as alluring as its isolation. A picturesque rocky outcrop defines the western perimeter of a sand-sheltered bay. Little remains of the cabin that once occupied this site. Parks has taken advantage of the level ground associated with it by setting up several designated campsites. Hike past these tent locations and carry on up the bank to the junction of the trail that travels the length of Wallace.

Not all of Wallace Island is within the park. Please respect the private lands located north of Conover Cove on the western shore.

Upon leaving Wallace, paddlers may return to the Southey Point launch or easily link up with other routes, particularly those described in the North Gulf Islands section. It is a short distance from Wallace across to Galiano's Dionisio Point Provincial Park. For a description of Dionisio, see "Trip 23 – Valdes Island: Valdes, Gabriola, the Flat Tops and Galiano Island."

Area VIII — North Gulf Islands

Charts:
- No. 3310, Sheet 4, Porlier Pass to Departure Bay (1:40,000) ** **No. 3310 out of print as of 1995** **
- No. 3313, Cruising Atlas for Gulf Islands
- No. 3443, Thetis Island to Nanaimo (1:40,000)

Tides:
- Reference Port: Fulford Harbour
- Secondary Port: Degnen Bay
- Reference Port: Point Atkinson
- Secondary Ports: Silva Bay and Valdes Island

Currents:
- Reference Stations: Gabriola Passage, Porlier Pass and Dodd Narrows
- Secondary Station: False Narrows

Duration:
- 2 to 4 days

Camp Locations:
- Whaleboat Island
- Pirate's Cove Marine Park on De Courcy Island
- Unnamed islet in the Flat Tops
- Blackberry Point
- Reserve lands on Valdes Island (with permission from Lyackson Band Office)
- Dionisio Point Provincial Park
- Unnamed islet adjacent to Kendrick Island

Launches

From Vancouver Island

Access Vancouver Island's Yellow Point by following Highway 1 north of Ladysmith. Turn off at Cedar Road, following signs for Cedar, Harmac and Yellow Point. Leave Cedar Road at the Yellow Point turnoff. Follow Yellow Point Road to about .5-km (.3 mi) north of Yellow Point Lodge where you turn onto Westby Road and enter Blue Heron Park. Leave vehicles in the adjacent parking area, and launch from the park's beach. Allow an hour and a half to drive from Victoria to this launch.

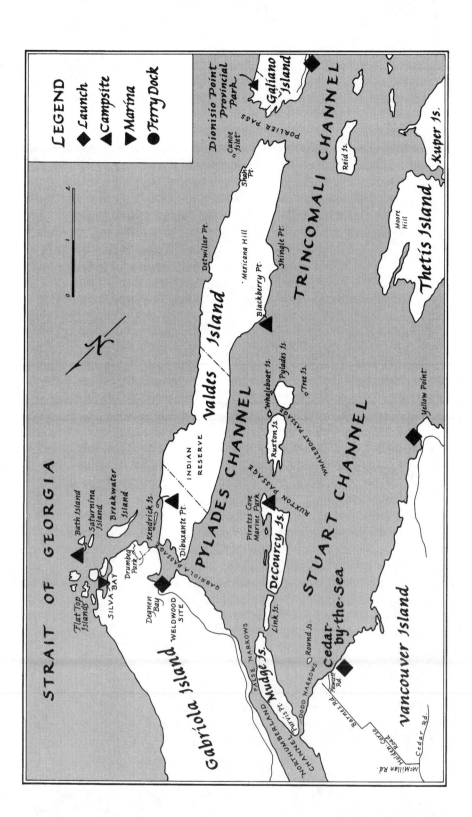

Access Vancouver Island's Cedar-By-The-Sea launch by following Highway 1 to just north of Ladysmith. Turn off at Cedar Road, and follow signs for Cedar, Harmac and Yellowpoint. Follow Cedar Road north to McMillan Road, turn right, then right again onto Holden-Corso Road. Follow Holden-Corso to Barnes Road, and follow Barnes to Fawcett Road. Turn right and drive down Fawcett to its terminus. Launch from the public boat ramp, leaving vehicles parked in the nearby lot. Allow an hour and a half to drive from Victoria to this launch.

From Gabriola Island

To access Gabriola Island's Degnen Bay launch, take Highway 1 north from Victoria to Nanaimo, then follow signs to Nanaimo's Gabriola ferry terminal. (Paddlers from the mainland docking at Nanaimo's Departure Bay terminal, follow signs to the centre of Nanaimo and then to the Gabriola ferry.) The Gabriola ferry docks at Descanso Bay on Gabriola Island. From the terminal, follow South Road to Degnen Bay Road, then turn right and follow Degnen Bay Road to its seaward terminus. Launch from the government wharf or from the adjacent beach, leaving vehicles parked along Degnen Bay Road. Allow an hour and a half to drive from Victoria to Nanaimo, plus twenty minutes to drive from Descanso Bay to the Degnen Bay launch.

From Galiano Island

Launching from Galiano Island is most convenient for paddlers from the mainland, because travelling to Galiano from Tsawwassen requires only one ferry sailing.

To access this launch, board a Galiano-bound ferry at either Tsawwassen or Swartz Bay. Ferries dock at Galiano Island's Sturdies Bay. Leave the ferry terminal, and follow Sturdies Bay Road to Porlier Pass Road, then turn right and follow Porlier Pass Road almost the entire length of Galiano Island. Launch from the government wharf at North Galiano, adjacent to the Spanish Hills Store.

Trip 21 — De Courcy Group:
Link, De Courcy, Ruxton and Pylades Islands

Distances: – Cedar-By-The-Sea to Whaleboat Island via west side of
                    De Courcy Group (6 mi)
                 – Whaleboat Island to Cedar-By-The-Sea via the east side of
                    the De Courcy Group (5.5 mi)

Highlights

If the shores along this route could talk, we would hear of Brother XII and his bizarre religious cult, of buried gold and smuggling, even of brainwashing and strange disappearances. The tales would be made all the more colourful by absurd place names like "The City Of Refuge," "Gospel Cove" and the "Fortress For The Future," all areas ruled by the preposterous Brother and his whip-wielding consort, Madame Zee. Brother XII disappeared from the islands more than fifty years ago, yet these places remain much the same today. There are no ferries here and no commercial facilities. The few summer homes found along these shores exist without electric power and telephone service. A quiet ambience prevails in this little-developed archipelago.

Considerations

This route is the only one in the north Gulf Islands that does not require paddling through one of four major passes within the north Gulf Islands area. Currents are minimal (although paddlers may wish to coordinate paddling north with a flood and south with an ebb), and winds, except for occasional southeasters blowing up Trincomali and evening westerlies, are usually calm. (Paddlers should, however, listen to wind predictions prior to heading out.) The only notable turbulence occurs during maximum ebbs in the waters surrounding Round Island and around tiny islets in Ruxton Passage.

Given the favourable paddling conditions that are usually found in this area, the route is recommended for the inexperienced.

The Route

Launch from Cedar-By-The-Sea, a seaside community that was once the headquarters for the Aquarian Foundation (1927) before Brother XII moved the colony to De Courcy Island.

Embark on a Stuart Channel crossing by heading toward Round Island and then crossing from Round Island to the north end of Link Island (1 mi). As currents in the northern sections of Stuart Channel are influenced by flows in Dodd Narrows, paddlers can expect increased tidal flows in this area. Watch for eddylines and whorls off the south and east sides of Round Island during a strong ebb.

Link and Mudge Islands are actually joined by an extensive shell beach (tombolo). This picturesque tombolo is made up of two U-shaped coves mirroring each other. A shellfish recreation reserve permits the harvesting of the bountiful clams and oysters in the east-facing bay (except in the summer, when the area is most often closed because of PSP).

On a May visit, I was awed by the presence of an industrious group of Vietnamese clam diggers who, over several hours, raked baby clams from the intertidal zone. The harvest was packed into 20-kg (50 lb) sacks and loaded into nearby skiffs, whereupon the combined weight of clams and clam diggers left only a few centimetres of freeboard. I

Getting in for a closer look at eroded sandstone. Convoluted shapes and intricate rock patterns, carved by the sea, are commonly found on cliff faces in the north Gulf Islands. (*Greg Lang*)

was informed later that an opening for clam harvesting was declared that morning. I had just witnessed a day's work for the itinerant crew.

In an emergency the extensive tombolo beach might serve as a camp location as it is below the high tide line. However, locals have observed a number of paddlers camped on the oh-so-tempting meadows immediately above high tide lines. These lands are private and must be respected as such. In a previous edition of this book I erroneously described the unnamed islet on the east side of the tombolo as a suitable camp location. This islet is deeded to Link Island and is private property and not to be used by paddlers. Carry on to Pirate's Cove Marine Park or Blackberry Point for an overnight stay.

Paddle south along the west sides of Link and De Courcy, passing eroded sandstone cliffs. Convoluted rock and honey-combed hollows result as the sea relentlessly carves the sandstone face. These cliffs jut up from the sea so abruptly that it is easy to get in for a close-up look. Photographers especially will delight at the shadows cast in the evening light. The narrow passage between Link and De Courcy is appropriately called "Hole in the Wall." The narrow gap dries at low tide.

Whereas the western shore of Link is devoid of housing, the western shore of De Courcy is not. Several summer homes are tucked into the forest above the sandstone ledges. Those interested in the history of the Brother XII colony will want to look at the homestead about halfway along this shore. The barn and orchard were apparently once part of cult operations. (Respect the privacy of the current owners by observing these buildings from the water.)

Paddlers may choose to turn left at the south end of De Courcy Island and head directly to Pirate's Cove Marine Park (described on a following page). Others may wish to explore Ruxton and Pylades Islands. If so, cross the .5-mi wide Ruxton Passage. Current are minimal except in shallow waters between the drying reefs of the northernmost finger

Brother XII

Of all the offbeat religions that seem to flourish on the Pacific coast, there was none quite so bizarre as the Aquarian Foundation led by the notorious Brother XII. Somehow this preposterous guru (his real name was Edward Wilson) convinced intelligent, wealthy people from all over the world to come and join him in building a "Fortress for the Future" in the northern Gulf Islands.

In 1928 notable individuals flocked to the Aquarian base at Cedar-By-The-Sea: James Lippincott of Lippincott Publishing Company; Maurice Von Platten, a millionaire pipe-organ builder from Chicago; and Will Comfort, a writer from the *Saturday Evening Post*. Mary Connally left the affluent social circles of North Carolina and turned over all her life savings to the Foundation so that it was able to purchase De Courcy Islands. Here, the disciples began the arduous task of creating a self-sufficient colony. Greenhouses, orchards, storehouses and even a sawmill were constructed by the loyal followers.

Early on there was dissension among the Aquarians – especially upon the arrival of Isis. (Isis, formerly Mrs. Baumgartner, was convinced by Wilson that she was the reincarnation of the ancient fertility goddess and that she was destined to join him in holy union to create the new messiah.) Wilson, who had systematically bugged the entire colony, was able to pick up every expression of disloyalty. Dissenters were not only identified but were also quoted word for word. Awed by their leader's supposed supernatural powers, they were hushed.

Then there was the most absurd character of all – Madame Zee. Formerly Mrs. Skottowe, a banker's widow from Saskatchewan, she was introduced to the colony as the Brother's right hand. She promptly began overseeing the already overworked colonists. Mary Connally, the Aquarian who had so generously bought the De Courcys, suffered the most under this whip-wielding tyrant.

The Brother and the rather fiendish Zee headed to England where they purchased the *Lady Royal*, a 22-m (72 ft) trawler. Sailing without auxiliary engines, they returned to the Gulf Islands a year later. Several colonists had become used to a more relaxed existence, and when they expressed their dissatisfaction at the Brother's return, they were subsequently banished. In an attempt to regain money invested in the colony, these expatriates filed suit against their former guru. Incredible tales collected over the previous six years were disclosed in court.

Before the trial was completed, the diabolical pair mysteriously disappeared. A newspaper entry printed in 1934 in Switzerland tells of the Brother's probable end. It noted that Julian Skottowe had died. Brother XII, who presumably took the name of Zee's first husband, was buried in Neuchatel. No trace of Madame Zee was ever found.

on Ruxton. An inviting shell beach at the head of Herring Bay is often blocked from view as during the summer this bay often fills with boats.

Ruxton is subdivided but remains largely undeveloped. Steep sandstone cliffs along the western shore increase in height from north to south. Garry oaks, arbutus and cormorants are found wherever they can grab a foothold. In spring these cliffs are splashed with the orange of Indian paintbrush.

Paddle a short distance around the south shore of Ruxton to view the "Great Whaleboat Passage Steam and Traction Company" —a unique West Coast sauna, complete with cedar shakes and multi-paned windows that offer views of the water. Connected to the beautiful home above is an addition sign-posted the "On Sweet" — undoubtedly the most attractive outhouse in all the Gulf Islands. A half-door permits the occupant full view of Whaleboat Passage.

Tiny Tree Island is most inviting, but even though it is uninhabited, it is private land. Exploring above the high tide line is trespassing, so limit your stops to one of several white-shell beaches. There is a shell midden in the cove facing Pylades Island.

Rocky shoreline, steep topography and a thick forest do not tempt a stopover on Pylades Island. The only landing is on the island's northeast corner where a gravel beach faces Valdes Island.

Observe the tiny unnamed island northeast of Pylades from your kayak only. Attached to Pylades at low tide, this islet is private land. Pylades Island residents are concerned about recreational use and will request anyone landing here to move on.

Three-ha (7 ac) Whaleboat Island is an undeveloped marine park with a shoreline completely lined with sandstone and large boulders that continue up through the scrub and evergreen forest. There are no beaches to land on. Overnighters who are willing to sleep under the stars with only space for a single sleeping pad will discover there is room to camp on the northernmost point. Only as a desperate measure would most paddlers choose to go ashore. This island was called Eagle Island prior to becoming a park in 1981.

There are several summer cottages along the eastern shore of Ruxton Island. Seals typically haul out on the drying reefs between Ruxton and De Courcy Islands.

Pirate's Cove, named "Gospel Cove" by the Aquarians, is now a 30-ha (76 ac) marine park. There are two coves in the park, and by far the most popular with recreation boaters is the "U"-shaped bay facing the northwest. Paddlers will likely prefer landing in the lesser-used south-facing cove. From this beach, trails lead to designated campsites. There is a water pump above the cove. A user fee for overnight stays applies here, and remember this is a pack-in, pack-out park. As with all BC marine parks there are no disposal facilities.

Paddle the shallow pass between the long, narrow islet and the mid-eastern shore of De Courcy Island. This rich intertidal area is abundant with clams and oysters — but of greater note is the large number of sand dollars, more than I've seen anywhere in the Gulf Islands. Beachcombers will delight at this opportunity to collect the empty shells. (Remove only those shells that have lost their spiny covering and are white in colour.)

Continue paddling the cottage-lined eastern shore of De Courcy, and return to Cedar-By-The-Sea by paddling between Link and De Courcy Islands. Otherwise, portage across the gravel bar between Link and Mudge Islands.

Two routes easily extend this trip. Cross Pylades Channel to join up to "Trip 23" (Valdes Island), or return to Cedar-By-The-Sea via False and Dodd Narrows ("Trip 22").

Trip 22 — False Narrows and Dodd Narrows

Distance: – Link Island to Cedar-By-The-Sea via False and Dodd Narrows (4 mi)

Highlights

An impressive "conveyor belt" of water, Dodd Narrows has tidal streams reaching 10 knots. View the perilous, full-flood waters as they disgorge into Northumberland Channel from the bluffs on Mudge Island. In the winter months, paddle the waters fronting the Harmac mill to view the dozens of sea lions that overwinter here. Look for the huge pinnipeds hauled out on the log booms or rafting up in the water.

Considerations

The 10-knot currents in Dodd Narrows and the currents that run about half that speed in False Narrows absolutely demand consideration. Schedule passing through Dodd Narrows at slack only, and pass through False Narrows close to slack.

Expect turbulent water not only in the channels, but also in areas where tidal streams spill into Northumberland and Pylades Channels. (Steep waves are especially common when the flood waters from Dodd Narrows disgorge into Northumberland Channel. Approach this area with caution.)

Except for offshore breezes and occasional southeasters, summer winds in this area are calm.

This route is not recommended for inexperienced paddlers.

The Route

Since currents in False Narrows reach up to 4.5 knots, schedule paddling through so that route direction and current are not at odds. Better still, go through with a slower-moving flood tide (within an approximate hour of slack) and take advantage of the gentler-moving east-to-west flow.

Both Mudge and Gabriola Islands' shores are lined with summer cottages and permanent residences. Few areas look interesting enough to justify landing except for one area known locally as "The Brickyard." Look for a beach cobbled with bricks on Gabriola's shore, where broken pieces of brick, stamped with "Dominion," are the only remnants of a factory that operated here from 1895 to 1952.

The Harmac mill smokestacks that welcome paddlers to Northumberland Channel are optimistically described by Bill Wolferstan as being visible for miles around and therefore providing a convenient indication of wind direction, as well as many brilliant sunsets.

Occasional visitors to Northumberland Channel are the California sea lions. When they overwinter in this area their loud honking barks can be heard for miles. Typically they haul out on log booms adjacent to the mill or simply raft up. Usual rafting posture is with flippers extended out of the water, likely to minimize heat loss (Bigg and Olesiuk). Paddlers choosing to cross over for a close-up view of these large pinnipeds should favour the Gabriola shore and cross to Harmac well away from Dodd Narrows. (Water disgorges from the narrows into Northumberland Channel, and seas pile up forming huge "haystacks," a condition paddlers must avoid.)

Approach Dodd Narrows from the tip of Mudge Island, and while waiting for slack, climb the adjacent rock bluffs for lofty views of a perilous gap once called Nanaimo Rapids. At full flood, this gorge of water runs up to 10 knots. It is totally impassable by sea-kayak an hour before slack. Half an hour later, it begins to look promising. Finally, fifteen minutes prior to slack, the narrows are passable, but even then, enter the passage with some caution. You may discover a tug with several booms in tow heralding this moment as his own to pass through.

Along the 1.5-mi return stretch to Cedar-By-The-Sea, few places permit or inspire landing. Pull out at the Fawcett Road ramp.

Trip 23 — Valdes Island:
Valdes, Gabriola, the Flat Tops and Galiano Islands

Distances:
- Galiano Island along the west side of Valdes Island to Degnen Bay (10.5 mi)
- Degnen Bay, Gabriola Passage and Flat Top Islands (6 mi)
- East side of Valdes Island to Porlier Pass and return to the launch (8.5 mi)

Highlights

Valdes Island is almost completely uninhabited. Paddle the western shore to one of the most beautiful camp areas in all the Gulf Islands, Blackberry Point. Explore the island's interior by following any one of a number of old logging roads. Paddle along sandstone cliffs to take in the convoluted shapes and intricate patterns carved by the sea. Don't miss a stopover at Degnen Bay and Gabriola's petroglyphs. Finally, paddle the exposed shores on the east side of Valdes where the Strait of Georgia and the distant Coast Mountains provide a spectacular backdrop, heralding one of the best marine park set-ups for kayakers, Galiano's Dionisio Point Provincial Park.

Considerations

Two major passes, Porlier Pass at the south end of Valdes and Gabriola Passage at the north end, have tidal streams reaching up to 9 knots. It is therefore necessary that paddlers schedule paddling through them close to slack.

Currents are otherwise minimal, although paddlers may choose to schedule paddling north with a flood and south with an ebb.

Waters on the outside of Valdes Island and around the Flat Top Islands are exposed to prevailing northwest winds in Strait of Georgia. Listen to wind predictions prior to paddling this stretch.

Waters on the inside of Valdes are sheltered from most winds, but open to occasional southerly squalls blowing up Trincomali and Pylades Channels.

Given the speed of the currents in the narrow passes and the exposure to winds along the outside of Valdes, this route is not recommended for inexperienced paddlers.

Launch from Degnen Bay on Gabriola Island or from North Galiano's Spanish Hills Store. The route described here assumes a launch from Galiano and circumnavigation of Valdes in a clockwise direction.

The Route

Launch from the government wharf on the north end of Galiano Island (adjacent to the Spanish Hills Store) and head toward Porlier Pass. As tidal streams reach up to 9 knots in the pass, swing well out from the entrance to avoid being swept into the channel. Navigate toward Cardale Point on the south end of Valdes Island.

Up until the beginning of this century, a large native population inhabited the southern shores of Valdes, living in one of three permanent villages. The largest village, Laysken, spread north and south of Shingle Point and had as many as ten houses and a population of two hundred. A smaller village at Cardale Point had five houses and a total population of one hundred. The smallest site included three or four houses stretching from Cayento Point to Vernaci Point (Rozen). The villages were abandoned when populations became so depleted that the remaining few inhabitants had to join up with related bands.

Paddlers requesting permission to camp on any of the reserve lands on Valdes are asked to contact the Lyackson Band Office in Chemainus. Up until recently, permission could be obtained by speaking directly to natives living on Shingle Point; however, this handful of inhabitants has relocated to Vancouver Island. (See "Native Reserve Lands" in the "Introduction to the Gulf Islands.")

Blackberry Point is Crown land and a stopover haven. Immediately impressive is the extensive sand beach surrounding the point. Equally attractive is the meadow that provides level ground for tenting. (This meadow is used intermittently by a small-scale logging enterprise. When in use the area becomes a barren tract lined with logs. Fortunately within short periods of time it returns to a more pristine state.) Others may prefer the arbutus-sheltered locations. Either way, the available camp space is so extensive that sharing the point with others does not detract from this area's appeal. It also faces west, so evening hours of sunlight are extended and views of sunsets are spectacular. There is plenty of opportunity for hiking along sandy shores and exploring old logging roads as well.

The cliffs that surround Blackberry Point are set farther back than their close-to-shore counterparts on north Valdes, but are equally spectacular as they rise up over 150 m (500 ft). Yes, it is possible to climb to the top of the cliffs, but from a cove about .5-mi north of Blackberry Point. The cove, obviously used as a landing for past logging, marks the beginning of the steep ascent. Land on the pebble beach and start out using the old roadway, then break off in a easterly direction toward Mexicana Hill. Although no single trail leads to the destination, the route becomes obvious — simply head upward toward the cliff tops. Those who question whether or not the vertical climb is worth the effort will put aside doubt as views from 150 m (500 ft) begin to appear. The final vista includes all the islands from Galiano to Gabriola. Pause for a while. Twenty eagles were counted soaring above the cliffs during an early May visit. Look across Pylades Channel to Thetis Island. Ac-

Most of the shoreline on the east side of Valdes is rocky, and there are few suitable landings. Paddlers here have taken advantage of the level sandstone ledge, exposed at low tide. (*Greg Lang*)

cording to native legend, an underground tunnel connects Thetis to Valdes Island. Young men reportedly descended into a cavern on Mexicana Hill and walked 3 mi under the sea to the exit on Thetis Island's Moore Hill in an act that was supposed to be part of a puberty ritual.

Continue along the western shore of Valdes to about midway along the reserve shoreline. Here is an obvious indentation, easily pinpointed using the chart, where, during all but the dry months, a fresh water creek empties into the sea. Beach your kayak and climb the nearby knoll to a large open meadow where intrepid individuals may choose to acknowledge the lure of an old logging road. Meadowlands and views over Pylades Channel make this site an excellent camp location. However, permission to stay overnight must be obtained beforehand from the Lyackson Band Office in Chemainus.

Valdes Island was logged in the 1950s, and as a result, the entire island is crisscrossed by a network of overgrown roadways. Pull out onto rock ledges located at the base of any number of old landings that, although covered with undergrowth, are still visible. Quickly link up with old byways that lead to the interior, passing through the salal, heading up along rock bluffs and entering evergreen and arbutus forests. Roads frequently break into open areas where rusting drums and thick chain are all that remain of past logging.

Sandstone galleries on the north end of Valdes are simply the most magnificent of all the ones found in the Gulf Islands. Steep cliffs rise abruptly to over 60 m (200 ft) and are intricately carved by wave erosion.

The imagination is inspired as the convoluted shapes take on the look of sea serpents, huge beehives and mushroom-shaped clouds. Consider paddling along these cliff faces at low tide for an added treat. The displays of intertidal life at this time are fantastic! In the upper reaches, blue mussels and acorn barnacles firmly attach themselves to the vertical rocks. A middle zone is coloured with congregations of green anemone, cream-coloured thatched barnacles, purple stars, white tube worms and red and brown crab. Below, the white plumose anemone sweep the plankton-rich water for food, and the soft-skinned leather star seek the next victim.

In the late 1920s, Brother XII purchased 160 ha (400 ac) on the north end of Valdes and built his "House of Mystery" near Dibuxante Point. Today, the entire bay south of the point is a booming ground where tugs patiently wait for slack water in Gabriola Passage.

From Dibuxante Point, cross Gabriola Passage to Degnen Bay. Although the worst flows in Gabriola Passage occur further to the east, expect eddylines, fast-moving water and turbulence in this part of the channel, especially in the shallows that surround the light. Avoid difficult-to-handle conditions by crossing close to slack.

Although Degnen Bay has no facilities, this secluded port has a delightful West Coast charm all its own. In the off-season, fishboats tie up at the government wharf. Paddle past the wharf toward the head of the bay to view the "killer whale" petroglyph that is found between the last two piers on the northeast shore. At low tide, land on the gravel beach. The well-known petroglyph is about 5 m (16 ft) below the high tide line, carved into a sloping sandstone ledge. The property behind is owned by Mrs. Cliff, whose daughter wrote the book, *Gabriola: Petroglyph Island* (Bentley and Bentley). Mrs. Cliff is used to visitors and doesn't mind viewers as long as the carving and her privacy are respected. She warns of the rocks on the beach becoming very slippery when they are wet.

There is another petroglyph site on Gabriola that must not be missed. It is called the "Weldwood Site." A hike is required, so pull kayaks up high on the beach near the government wharf (anticipate an hour-long absence from the boats). Follow the gravel road from the wharf to its intersection with South Road. Turn left, and just past the intersection with Thompson Road, look for the United Church. Follow the church's driveway up to the parking area, then look to the right for a forest trail. Within several hundred metres, the path makes a left turn toward a very visible clearing (two stone boulders mark the entrance). This remarkable opening in the forest contains sandstone slabs with more than fifty carved petroglyphs. The largest of the petroglyphs is thought to represent a mythical sea serpent.

Paddlers may decide to spend more time in Degnen Bay while waiting for slack water in Gabriola Passage. The passage is the smallest of

Weldwood Site

Two amateur archaeologists, Ted and Mary Bentley, recorded and produced rubbings of various petroglyphs on Gabriola Island, but in 1976 they discovered the island's most significant site.

Many island residents knew of the site location due to its distinct setting — a natural clearing surrounded by forest — but none dreamed that hidden under the thin layer of grass and moss were so many ancient carvings. One Gabriola pioneer remembers playing on the site as a child while others remember logging operations during World War II. (Scratch marks from steel treads are still visible.)

When the Bentleys made their discovery, the property was owned by Weldwood of Canada. Weldwood offered support in protecting the area when informed of the significant petroglyphs on its land by deeding the land to the Crown. The site is now protected by the province.

By 1980 over fifty petroglyphs were recorded here. Among the figures represented are faces, weird humanoids, bird-like creatures, fish and mythical sea creatures, as well as geometric designs such as a foot, eyes, concentric circles, "S" shapes, curves and lines (Mary Bentley).

What purpose did the site serve to ancient peoples? Since such an aura of mystery and seclusion surrounds this forest opening, some speculate it may have been used as a sacred centre. How old is the site? The age of petroglyphs is not easily determined. One figure shows a depression possibly representing a labret carved beneath a humanoid's mouth. This "T"-shaped bone, worn by females on the lower lip, was a beautifying device used from 500 B.C. to about 500 A.D. Possibly these carvings were executed about this time.

The precise meaning and exact age of these petroglyphs are not known, yet these unanswered questions only add to the mystery and inspire our imaginations.

Paddlers searching for detailed information on these petroglyphs should have a look at *Gabriola: Petroglyph Island*, by Ted and Mary Bentley.

the three major passes leading into the Gulf Islands and has currents reaching up to 8 knots. Between Cordero Point and Jan Josef Point, expect the fastest-moving water. Watch for turbulent water in the shallows off Kendrick Island and surrounding the two adjacent lights.

Be aware that many other vessels converge on the pass near slack. Tugs with full booms will labour through the narrows, as will every imaginable pleasure craft that uses this shortcut between ports in Vancouver and the Gulf Islands. Kayakers will be dwarfed by this entourage and should be sure that other vessels are aware of their presence.

Once through the passage, follow the shoreline of Drumbeg Park.

Although camping is not permitted, the area is worth exploring. Wander through the 20 ha (50 ac) of forest, or walk from the beach to a beautiful meadow that looks out over the water.

Gabriola's Silva Bay is a major marine centre. Powerboats and sailboats move in and out of the port, taking full advantage of fuel, repair, lodging and moorage facilities. All shores that line the bay are crowded with commercial facilities, private floats and a Royal Vancouver Yacht Club outstation. Of greatest interest to paddlers are a couple of grocery stores, a marine pub and a restaurant. If you want seclusion, head to the quieter ambience of the Flat Top Islands.

In the Flat Tops there are sheltered channels and exposed stretches of coast along the outer islands. Homes are sparse, but "private" signs are not. If paddlers don't mind being confined to their kayak or below high tide line on the beaches, this delightful archipelago offers some excellent touring. Don't miss the windswept shores of Carlos Island where a single arbutus grows horizontally, revealing the exposed nature of this tiny islet. In April, blankets of yellow monkey-flowers spread out between the boulders.

You may choose to camp on the larger of two unnamed islets between Saturnina and Bath Islands, but at high tide, steep-sided shores make landings difficult here. (At low tide, landings are easier since the islet is joined to Saturnina by a gravel beach.) Level areas accommodate a couple of small tents, but this treeless isle is exposed. To sum things up, this is a suitable overnight stopover if winds are calm and you are willing to deal with tricky access.

Members of the West Vancouver Yacht Club obviously recognize the sheltered waters behind Kendrick as they have set up an outstation here. Camping is available on the unnamed islet closest to Kendrick (the islet and Kendrick join at low tide), but once again, shores surrounding this islet are steep and rocky and landings, although possible, are usually difficult. In the morning, be prepared to manoeuvre kayaks over slippery rocks to access the water. The best camp spot is on the northwest side of the islet where an elevated location is partially protected from winds by a backdrop of trees and brush.

Upon leaving these sheltered waters, paddlers enter exposed waters within the Strait of Georgia. Most of the shoreline on the east side of Valdes Island is rocky, and there are few suitable landings. Check wind forecasts for the Strait of Georgia prior to paddling this stretch of coast.

One of the few sand beaches is in an unnamed cove about halfway along the reserve area, where you can land on a sandy beach and explore the interior of the island by following numerous old logging roads. There is a freshwater stream nearby, but don't depend on it as a source of water, because during the summer, flows taper off. It is possible to camp here, but once again, permission to use these reserve lands must be obtained prior to landing.

Paddling through Porlier Pass at slack. Within four hours, current flows up to 9 knots will turn these calm waters into a rip-infested sea. (*Rene Zich*)

Exposed rocky coast continues from here to Detwiller Point. Most of the homes on Valdes Island are found between Detwiller and Shah Points. Since there are no ferries to Valdes, these homes are accessible by boat only. A delightful little cove behind Shah Point is worth exploring. An arbutus-lined meadow and magnificent views to distant Coast Mountains add to the appeal of this stopover. Offshore are the Canoe Islets, an ecological reserve and home to over one hundred nesting glaucous-winged gulls. California and Steller sea lions use these bare rocks as a winter haul-out.

Porlier Pass has tidal streams reaching 9 knots, and although the bays offer some protection from the faster-moving water, you will encounter huge tide rips, eddies and standing waves out in the rock-congested pass. Use the *Tide and Current Tables* to determine slack water. Unpredictable eddies and huge rips are also a problem in the 1-mi-long crossing from Valdes to Dionisio Point. Avoid this crossing, except close to slack water.

Dionisio Point Provincial Park is a "must do." These 147 ha (360 ac) overlooking Porlier Pass were only recently granted park status. Driftwood shacks used to line these shores, built by loggers and coal miners who used them while fishing in Porlier Pass. Several of the cabins were almost fifty years old when a second occupation began in the early 1970s by those seeking an alternative West Coast lifestyle. Eventually all buildings were razed in an attempt to open up the area for public use. For the next decade recreational vehicles pulled up, having travelled a rough four-wheel-drive road to gain access. Unfortunately the bay was subsequently subject to overcrowding and some abuse of the natural environment. In the early 1990s Dionisio Point Provincial Park was formed.

Stunningly picturesque is sand-fringed Coon Bay, joined by a narrow isthmus to arbutus-studded Dionisio Point and curving around to Steven's Point. Coon Bay and the adjacent sandstone-ledged bay dry at low tide, providing opportunity to explore the diverse intertidal life associated with these different habitats. Inland, kilometres of interpretive trails run through the understorey of Douglas fir, hemlock and cedar forests. Pathways that parallel the shores of the Strait of Georgia and Porlier Pass spill onto open headlands providing unimpaired views across the strait to the mainland's Coast Mountains and Valdes Island. In positive evidence is BC Parks' attempt to revegetate fragile areas. Steven's and Dionisio Points both show signs of a return to original vegetation now that camping is restricted to designated sites.

The development of Dionisio is, from a kayaker's perspective, BC Marine Parks at its best. The park is accessible to vehicles but the road access is rough, and the few campsites that do exist are placed well away from parking, thereby virtually eliminating recreation vehicle use. (In 1996 no vehicles entered the park as the road access was blocked due to an unsettled dispute involving Galiano Islanders, various levels of government and a controversial subdivision development. The contentious issues were still unresolved early in 1997, at which time the road remained impassable.) Cyclists, day users and walk-in campers are predominantly attracted to this park. More attractive to kayakers however is a section of the park developed specifically for paddlers. It is water accessed only and is located along Galiano's eastern shore. Paddle past Coon Bay, and within 500 metres a BC Marine Parks portal sign comes into view. Land on the gently sloping sandstone ledges, and lift kayaks and gear up a convenient, Parks-constructed stairway. Immediately accessible are 15 designated sites, unobtrusively developed, forest bordered, complete with evergreen-framed water views. Additional facilities include pit toilets, a self-registration vault (a $7 fee applied in 1997) and a Parks information shelter. Most impressive is a simple, yet innovative, kayak rack. Conveniently constructed close to the stairway, it provides empty kayaks above-tide storage. A ten-minute hike along the interpretive trail leads back to Coon Bay where a freshwater pump and a well-organized system for recyclables are situated. Otherwise, this is a pack-in, pack-out set-up. Understandably, a strict "No Fires" regulation is enforced here.

Reluctantly, paddlers will leave Dionisio to return to the Spanish Hills Store launch. Enter Porlier Pass at slack to safely paddle Galiano's northern shoreline. The two lighthouses on Race and Virago Points have guided vessels through the pass for nearly a century. Both are now automated. The dilapidated boardwalk and quaint shingle-sided houses on Lighthouse Bay are on private reserve land. The natives live closer to Acala Point and do grant access to those who ask permission. Paddle the final stretch from Acala Point following the northwest shore of Galiano to return to the government wharf near the Spanish Hills Store.

Natural Features

Barkley Sound offers 800 square km (312 sq. mi) of spectacular paddling – a West Coast indentation that contains countless islands and islets, forming two distinct island clusters – the Deer Group and the Broken Group Islands. Along the outer rim of isles, seas break against the sheer cliffs. Whether mantled in fog or shining brilliant in the sunlight, the drama of crashing waves is breathtaking. The inner islands are more serene in character. Here the coastal rain forests are surrounded by sand-fringed bays, quiet coves and sheltered waterways.

Rivalling the spectacular landscape is an incredible diversity of marine life. Of all the world's temperate seashores, nowhere is there a greater variety of species than those found on the North Pacific coast. Several factors account for this, but most significant are the presence of nutrient-rich bottom water and the warming effect generated by prevailing westerlies. On the Pacific coast, there are over ninety species of starfish and forty-one species of shrimp compared with a respective twenty and three on the Atlantic coast (Wyett).

The abundant marine life is attractive to a variety of mammals that are both resident and seasonal visitors. Several hundred California and Steller sea lions overwinter at specific haul-out locations found within Barkley Sound. Year round, there are the inquisitive-faced harbour seals. Pelagic wanderers, such as the grey whale, regularly feed in the sound, along with the local harbour porpoise. In sheltered coves there are raccoon, mink and river otter, and in the forest, the Columbian black-tail deer.

In surf-swept environments, green anemones, California mussels, gooseneck and thatched barnacles and orange and purple sea stars cling to the rock ledges. Inhabiting the quieter, sheltered waters are Japanese oysters, moonsnails, bat stars and leather stars.

Abundant food and ideal nesting habitat draw hundreds of sea birds to Barkley Sound. In all seasons, belted kingfishers and great blue her-

To be a happy camper, raingear is essential here. Go to Barkley Sound prepared for many forms of west coast wet – rain, low-lying cloud, fog and drizzle. *(Mark Hobson)*

ons search for fish in tide pools and shallow waters, while further off-shore cormorants sometimes dive 40 m (130 ft) to obtain a meal. Onshore, black oystercatchers pry limpets and mussels from the dark rocks. On a deserted isle, pigeon guillemots choose a nesting site, and from weatherworn snags bald eagles search for prey. These are a few of the resident birds found in these waters. In the spring and fall, the variety of birds multiplies considerably as migrants stop en route to distant breeding grounds. The arctic loon, Canada goose and western sandpiper are among the species seen during these seasonal migrations.

Abundant rainfall and mild temperatures are the primary reasons for the lush vegetation that covers these islands. Mature forests grow to towering heights. Sitka spruce, western hemlock and western red cedar are the predominant species. Below, thickets of salal and salmonberry compete for space. A forest floor that is cluttered with deadfall provides nutrients that support the dense fern thickets and carpets of moss. Collectively, this tangled mass of flora and forest forms an almost impenetrable barrier. Travel by land is often difficult. But more than any other feature, it is the intricate network of waterways connecting the islands and islets that draw countless paddlers to this area each summer. Crossings from one island to the next (once you are within the islands) seldom exceed 1 mi, and although occasional rough seas force paddlers ashore, many of the inner waterways are protected from prevailing winds and swell. Here is an environment that couldn't be more suited to travel by canoe and kayak.

Marine Weather

West Coast Wet

The climate on the West Coast is largely governed by the masses of air that move in off the Pacific. They tend to have a moderating effect on coastal temperatures, so that in the winter when the rest of Canada is besieged by freezing cold, here the temperature rarely drops below zero. In the summer, temperatures average around 17°C (about 62°F).

Pacific air also brings moisture — and lots of it! Precipitation at Tofino averages 300 cm (120 in) per year, with 80 percent falling during a six-month wet season extending from October through March. From June through September, the average rainfall is a mere 46 cm (18 in), which means less than 15 percent of the year's average precipitation falls during the peak paddling months. Unfortunately, these statistics far from guarantee blue skies during a summer paddling trip. It can rain at any time, and even with blue skies, fog is a common occurrence. It rolls in with little warning and can stay for days.

Regardless of the time of year, rain gear is considered essential here. A couple of hours in a West Coast downpour is all that is needed to convince those who didn't bring it along that it would have been better if they had. Consider the better quality wet-weather wear, because so often the waterproof jacket that was "such a bargain" splits at the seam, and, in the middle of a deluge, starts to leak. Almost as ineffective are today's waterproof breathables. They tend to lose their ability to resist water in a salty environment. The folks in outdoor speciality shops can tell you about recommended alternatives. A sou'wester and a reasonable pair of over-the-ankle rubber boots are also a necessary part of a "wet coast" ensemble.

Winds

During the summer months, the prevailing westerly winds blow in a predictable manner. They are calm in the early morning, build strength during the day, peak by mid afternoon, then drop again by dusk. Although they tend to remain light (1–11 knots), they can increase to moderate strengths of 12–19 knots.

This pattern is so predictable that paddlers can use an awareness of it to determine when and where to paddle. For instance, the outer islands reduce the impact of winds on the inner waters so that during the summer, sheltered waterways experience less of the effect of prevailing westerlies. Meanwhile, the outer islands and the islands that line Loudoun, Imperial Eagle and Trevor Channels take the winds full force. Therefore, schedule paddling along exposed coastlines in the early morning, before the winds begin to blow. Paddle through protected waters later in the day, knowing that westerlies generally peak by mid afternoon.

Paddling in the fog near Dodd Island in the Broken Group Islands. Compasses and compass skills are prerequisites for a paddling trip to Barkley Sound. (*Bruce Holland*)

Variations on this wind pattern do occur. The southeasters that prevail during the winter months also blow during the summer, tending to bring unsettled weather and rain. They have a particularly powerful effect in Imperial Eagle and Coaster Channels, churning calm waters into steep seas. On many occasions, paddlers heading westward through Coaster Channel are caught just as a southeaster blows in. They are always relieved to arrive safely at Turret Island's campsite.

Fog — It's a Grey Matter
The condition perhaps most despised by anyone paddling the West Coast during the summer months is fog. It usually coincides with long periods of good weather (just as you are getting used to blue skies!), when warm, moist air from the Pacific meets the cooler water along the shore. The resulting condensation may persist for several days. Although the month of August appears to have the highest incidence of fog, the grey banks can roll in at any time from June through October.

If the fog is light, solar heat burns it off during the day. Heavy fog takes longer to dissipate, dispersing only when the wind changes direction, bringing cooler, moister air from another part of the ocean (often an indication of changing weather and approaching storms).

Visibility is drastically reduced when fog banks advance. Compasses and compass skills are prerequisites for any paddling trip to Barkley Sound. (David Burch does an excellent job of describing fog navigation in his book *Fundamentals of Kayak Navigation*.)

Fog conditions are forecast during marine weather broadcasts.

Marine Weather Broadcasts
Always carry a radio capable of picking up the continuous marine

weather broadcasts for this area. VHF radios pick up Canadian Coastguard broadcasts on the following frequencies: WX1: 162.55, WX2: 162.40, WX3: 162.475 and 21B: 161.65. Within Barkley Sound, the smaller, less expensive weather radios most often pick up one station only, an American marine broadcast from Neah Bay in Washington State (WX1: 162.55).

For conditions that apply to Barkley Sound, listen specifically to forecasts for Vancouver Island South and to local weather conditions at Amphitrite Point, located at the western entrance to Barkley Sound, and at Cape Beale, located at the eastern entrance to the sound.

Forecasts attempt to give representative values over the open Pacific. The weather conditions described for these Pacific waters are going to be modified by the geography of the islands within Barkley Sound. This doesn't mean forecast conditions do not affect the sound – obviously if strong westerlies are predicted, these winds do affect the outer islands and the waters in Loudoun, Imperial Eagle, Coaster and Trevor Channels. But during the summer months, the sound's inner waterways are semi-protected from the general conditions that prevail in exposed areas. Use weather forecasts to determine when caution needs to be exercised in a route-selection process, when it is safe to paddle exposed shorelines and when it is best to avoid them.

Fog conditions are predicted during weather broadcasts, followed by a statement regarding visibility (if it is expected to be significantly reduced). Fog predictions for the outer coast do apply to Barkley Sound, especially the outer islands.

Meanings of some of the terms used during these broadcasts are provided in the section on "Marine Weather Broadcasts" in the "Introduction to the Gulf Islands."

Sea Conditions

Tides and Currents

There are two high and two low tides on the West Coast within an approximate twenty-five-hour period. Paddlers who prefer setting up camp on the beach can take comfort in knowing the highest tide levels occur during the winter months. Another plus for summer paddlers – the lowest tides occur from June through September, providing an excellent opportunity to view the rich spectrum of intertidal life.

Tidal predictions for the West Coast appear in Vol. 6 of the *Tide and Current Tables*, published annually by the Canadian Hydrographic Service. Remember to add one hour to the times when Pacific Daylight Time is in effect, April through October. Measurements for tide levels within Barkley Sound are based on Tofino, using Bamfield, Ucluelet and the Stopper Islands as Secondary Ports. In the summer, ranges seldom exceed 3.5 m (12 ft).

Currents are much less significant here than in the narrow passages on the inside of Vancouver Island. Flows rarely exceed 1 knot, and only in a few instances do they reach 2 knots. By far, wind and swell conditions demand the greater consideration.

Swell

The Pacific swells that roll onto the outer edge of Barkley Sound on their own pose few problems. In fact, paddling in and out of the rollers is very much a part of the West Coast experience. It is when these giant waves meet the shore that trouble could occur. These rollers tend to crash over the jagged rocks, then wash back to the sea, colliding with the next wave. The resulting turbulence could cause a capsize. Avoid paddling through these erratic seas by swinging well out from exposed headlands.

Another even less desirable condition occurs when swell pushes in over offshore shallows, forcing the huge waves to crest and break. These are referred to as "offshore breakers." They are found throughout Barkley Sound and break with little warning, even in the calmest conditions. (Their somewhat erratic presence is determined by tide levels.) Because of their rather deceptive nature, they are indeed a hazard, and paddlers need to be on a constant lookout for them.

Swell conditions are complicated further when prevailing westerlies blow. Wind-generated waves and swell waves are of different lengths. Put the two together and you have steep, choppy seas – not a desirable condition by any paddler's standard. Prior to paddling in exposed areas, listen to marine weather broadcasts, paying particular attention to the combined wind and swell heights. Low swell means less than 2 m (6.5 ft), moderate is 2–4 m and heavy is more than 4 m (13 ft).

Sea Temperatures

Ocean temperatures, although warmer in the summer, do not get above 12°C (54°F) – an extremely threatening temperature in the event of a capsize. For more information on the risks involved with a capsize – how to be prepared and how to cope with these cold waters in the event of one – refer to the "Safety Considerations" in the "Introduction to the Gulf Islands."

Public Lands

The Deer Group

The Deer Group, occupying the eastern part of Barkley Sound, is not part of Pacific Rim National Park and is less frequently visited than the Broken Group Islands.

Most of these islands are Crown land. The exceptions are Helby Island, most of the shoreline that lines Robbers Passage and Indian reserves on Diana, Haines, Helby and Tzartus Islands. Thus officially, most lands within the Deer Group are available to the public and can be used for overnight camping. Yet what most paddlers will discover is that dense forest and high tides play the most significant role in determining where to camp. Beaches do not extend above high tide, and clearings in the forest are infrequent; therefore appropriate camp locations are few. There are, however, several sites that are close enough to each other so that it is possible to move from one campsite to another with a day of paddling.

Water is as hard to come by and is as inadequate for drinking as in the Broken Group. Pack in your own supply – about 3 litre (3 qt) per person per day, and if you are supplementing with local water supplies, be sure to boil the liquid for at least ten minutes.

Driftwood is hard to find in areas surrounding campsites, but it isn't hard to find en route. The trickiest part is finding space for it in a fully loaded boat!

Not-So-Public Lands

Native Reserves in Barkley Sound

All reserves are private and in Barkley Sound are owned by the Ohiat and Sheshaht Bands.

Deer Group reserves are located on Diana, Helby and Tzartus Islands. The Ohiats living at Pachena Bay request they be contacted prior to anyone landing on these traditional lands. Recently hired staff monitor land use and safety concerns in these areas. Permission to visit (this does not include overnight stays) will be granted through the purchase of a yearly pass. A minimal fee is charged. Address enquiries to the Ohiat Administration, PO Box 70, Bamfield, BC, V0R 1B0, or phone (250) 728-3414.

Broken Island reserves are located on Effingham, Keith and Nettle Islands and are administered by the Sheshaht Band in Port Alberni. Written permission to explore ashore must be obtained by addressing enquiries to the Band Manager, Sheshaht Band Office, PO Box 1218, Port Alberni, BC, V9Y 7M1, or phone (250) 724-1225.

Camping

The Broken Group Islands and Pacific Rim National Park

In 1971 the Canadian government purchased the Broken Group Islands, thereby ensuring the preservation of a major part of Barkley Sound. As a result, this entire group of islands is now within Pacific Rim National Park.

The national park system is committed to preserving the natural, fragile environments found within park boundaries. In order to lessen the impact from the ever-increasing recreational use, the park confines all camping to designated areas. Wardens patrol the area and will ask those camping outside official sites to move. Chart No. 3670, published by the Canadian Hydrographic Service, provides detailed information as to the location of designated campsites and water supplies. A very reasonable camping fee is collected at each of these designated sites, May through September. In 1997 the fee was $5 per night per person.

Parks Canada has determined approximately how many tent sites there are at each of the designated areas. The tent sites are not numbered at these various locations, nor do park personnel enforce these approximations. These statistics are simply presented here to give an idea of the relative size of each camp area: Hand Island, 16; Clarke Island, 16; Willis Island, 14; Gilbert Island, 9; Turret Island, 15; Dodd Island, 10; Benson Island, 12; Gibraltar Island, 11.

As you can see, all areas are relatively small, leading many paddlers to wild speculation as to which of the designated campsites is the least used — with the hope they might find themselves the only visitor on an uninhabited shore. It is difficult to determine which campsites receive the heaviest use. Certainly Hand Island is popular as most paddlers entering the Broken Group from Toquart Bay land there first. Gibraltar also receives much use as it is closest to the drop-off point for the passenger ships MV Lady Rose and MV Frances Barkley. Willis, Turret and Clarke also get large numbers of visitors, and Gilbert is popular with sport fishermen who want quick access to prime fishing grounds off Cree Island. In summary, expect to share your chosen site with others. Solitude seekers are simply out of luck here. Besides, once you are out on the water exploring there are plenty of secret places where you can be completely on your own. The company of others back at camp, all sharing similar experiences, is often most pleasant. In fact, the comradeship that develops between paddlers who constantly cross paths is quite remarkable.

The unique wilderness that attracts so many paddlers to these islands is maintained by the underdevelopment of the campsites. Pit privies and forest clearings are as developed as they get. Firewood, picnic tables and cooking facilities are not provided. Neither is garbage disposal. You must pack out all your garbage. Because this area receives so many visitors, this pack-in, pack-out philosophy cannot be overemphasized.

National park wardens regularly go out on patrol. They mostly welcome visitors, answer questions and collect camping fees. But they also ensure these fragile islands are not abused. Harassment of marine animals and sea birds is illegal. Those camping in undesignated areas are asked to move.

Parks has been considering for some time the introduction of a use quota and reservation system in the Broken Group Islands. It continues to be studied. As visitor numbers increase and negative impacts are observed, the pressures that come to bear could lead to its implementa-

Barkley Sound provides the
perservering paddler with just
reward. (*Ken Meadows*)

tion. Check the status of this issue with the Park Information Centre
well in advance of paddling in this area. Address this and other enquiries to the Park Information Centre (open from Easter to mid-October),
at (250) 726-4212, or by writing to Pacific Rim National Park, Box 280,
Ucluelet, BC, V0R 3A0.

Fires

Driftwood is scarce within the Broken Group and virtually non-existent near designated camp areas. It is also illegal to chop tree limbs or
downed logs for firewood. Smaller pieces of driftwood found in exposed locations and loaded into an empty kayak hatch can be brought
back to camp where fires are permitted below the high tide line. Rather
than create another unsightly scar, build fires in already-existing circles. Assume that most meals will not be prepared over a fire, and bring
a small stove.

Water

Drinking water is not available in this area. Coliform counts at all the
islands' water supplies indicate they are unsatisfactory for drinking
unless the water is boiled for at least ten minutes. During the summer
months, water is also hard to find as most sources are reduced to a
mere trickle. Bring your own supply, about 3 l (approx. 3 qt) per person
per day for drinking and cooking. This amount should be enough to

tide you over in case you have to stay longer because of bad weather. Dishes can be washed in salt water and sparingly rinsed with fresh.

Shellfish Harvesting and Fishing

Those tempted by the abundance of shellfish need to be aware that shellfish harvesting is banned in this entire area. If you are unfamiliar with paralytic shellfish poisoning (PSP) and the subsequent harvesting closures, refer to "Shellfish Harvesting and Fishing" in the "Introduction to the Gulf Islands."

Sports fishing in Barkley Sound is both safe and legal (as long as you have purchased a federal licence). Fishermen with power boats that can quickly access the offshore waters are the most successful, but paddlers with minimal gear will also find fishing in calmer waters productive. Bruce Obee, author of *The Pacific Rim Explorer*, recommends that small boaters troll for salmon with a bucktail fly or lightly weighted Kripple K spoon. He suggests that only about 15 m (50 ft) of line is needed to snare a chinook, while coho can be taken from the surface, 5 or 10 m (16-32 ft) behind the boat. If the salmon aren't biting, or if you are not equipped for trolling, try jigging for bottomfish.

Trip Planning

Daily Distances

The same daily distance planning applies to Barkley Sound as for the Gulf Islands. Refer to "Daily Distances" in the "Introduction to the Gulf Islands."

Route Options and Selecting a Trip

Route options are as numerous as the islands within Barkley Sound. This guide suggests several circuits in an attempt to cover major highlights, yet the author recognizes that the weather is always the final factor in any route-selection process.

Listen to marine weather broadcasts prior to heading out in the morning, and choose a route appropriate to the conditions predicted for that day. By taking a weather radio, you can listen to updated forecasts. They may force a change of plans. In this case, the more exposed the route, the fewer your options. Options are much more plentiful in sheltered waterways.

Inexperienced paddlers can determine if a trip is suited to their ability by reviewing the "Considerations" sections of this guide. For a detailed description of how to use "Considerations" during a trip-selection process, refer to "Trip Selection" in the "Introduction to the Gulf Islands."

Search and Rescue and Pacific Rim National Park

Parks Canada is implementing a cost-recovery program to cover costs

Route decision making in the Deer Group. On the West Coast, weather can be the most significant consideration during this decision process. (*Ken Meadows*)

incurred during search and rescue operations taking place within park boundaries. This program came into effect in 1996 for tour companies and for the general public in 1997. If your planning includes risk-taking ventures, Parks Canada suggests considering insurance coverage. For more information, contact Pacific Rim National Park Information Centre.

Nautical Charts

Two charts published by the Canadian Hydrographic Service, No. 3670 and No. 3671, cover the Barkley Sound area.

Chart No. 3670 (1:20,000) covers the area from Toquart Bay through the Broken Group, and of the two charts, it provides the most exacting detail. Designated campsites, water sources and detailed representation of shallows and shorelines are provided on this smaller-scale chart. (Older versions of this same chart did not have information pertaining to campsites and water supplies.) The only disadvantage for paddlers using No. 3670 is that it requires frequent removing from the chart case and constant refolding — not an easy feat in the middle of a downpour. In spite of this inconvenience, for the information provided (the entire backside is covered with valuable information put out by Pacific Rim National Park), this is the better choice for a paddling trip to the Broken Group Islands.

Chart No. 3671 covers the entire Barkley Sound area, including both the Deer Group and Broken Group Islands. On a larger scale (1:40,000), it is not as detailed as No. 3670 but provides the information required by most paddlers. This is the only chart that covers the Deer Group.

Getting to the Deer Group

The easiest access to the Deer Group is from Port Desire at the head of Grappler Inlet and adjacent to the tiny community of Bamfield. Although paddlers must cross the open waters in Trevor Channel, the crossing is just over 1 mi, and on most days, rough seas are avoided by crossing in the morning. A detailed description of the launch is provided later.

Getting to the Broken Group Islands

There are several ways to access these islands, with some routes easier and safer than others. Even experienced paddlers should not attempt to access the area by crossing the open waters of Imperial Eagle Channel. It is at least 1 mi across Trevor Channel to the Deer Group, then an additional 4 mi across Imperial Eagle to the Broken Islands. Both channels are open to westerlies and swell.

The crossing to the Broken Islands from Ucluelet through Newcombe and Loudoun Channels is 7 mi and is also extremely risky. It is possible to land on Chrow Island, 3 mi out of Ucluelet, but as I discovered myself, the beach on Chrow varies in size with the tide. At high tide it is completely covered with water, and there is nowhere to land! With its exposure to strong westerlies, this is not a recommended route.

The safest way to access the Broken Group is from Toquart Bay on the north corner of Barkley Sound. The paddle from Toquart Bay to Hand Island is sheltered compared to the previously described routes, and although there are open stretches of water, this is by far the most protected access. (A description on how to access the launch site is provided later.)

The easiest access is undoubtedly via the *MV Lady Rose* and *MV Frances Barkley*. Throughout the year these passenger/cargo vessels, operated by Alberni Marine Transportation Incorporated, travel between Port Alberni and Bamfield delivering goods to tiny West Coast communities. From late spring to early fall, an extended service runs across Barkley Sound to Ucluelet, including a stop at Sechart Whaling Station. Located at the north end of Barkley Sound this waypoint provides paddlers quick and sheltered access to the Broken Group Islands.

At Port Alberni Harbour Quay, passengers, kayaks, canoes and all the gear are loaded. Once aboard kayakers simply sit back in relaxed comfort and travel the 40 km (25 mi) down Alberni Inlet or they can head below deck where a food service provides delicious home-cooked meals. Upon arrival at Sechart the crew helps passengers unload boats and gear. The 1-mi wide crossing of Sechart Channel brings kayakers to the Broken Group and within an hour's paddle to designated campsites on Gibraltar and Hand Islands.

Sea cave in the Deer Group. Caves are common nesting sites for the pelagic cormorant. As tempting as it is to enter, keep in mind the success of a breeding season could depend on your choice to keep a reasonable distance from vulnerable nest areas. (*Bruce Holland*)

Scheduled sailings from June through September depart from Port Alberni in the morning, arriving at Sechart by noon. Canoe and kayak rentals are an integral part of this friendly operation. Assure a boat by reserving rentals well in advance. Reserving "boat space" when bringing your own kayak is also recommended.

For sailing schedules and rental rates, contact Alberni Marine Transportation Inc., PO Box 188, Port Alberni, BC V9Y 7M7, phone (250) 723-8313 or fax (250) 723-8314. Toll free reservations can be made April to September by calling 1-800-663-7192.

Paddling Etiquette

Cormorants, Caves and Paddlers

Many first-time visitors to the area do not know of the sensitive nature of nesting cormorants. Pelagic cormorant nesting sites are frequently located inside a feature that is also very attractive to paddlers – sea caves. Too often, paddlers enter caves completely unaware of the potential effect their intrusion has on nesting birds. Adult cormorants are not only alarmed by the intrusion but also by the paddlers becoming an obstacle within their natural escape route. They subsequently leave the nest and, in the scramble to do so, inadvertently kick out the young and the eggs. Eggs and hatchlings are also left open to their most-feared predator, the northwestern crow.

As tempting as it is to enter a sea cave, please refrain from doing so from June through August. The success of a breeding season could depend on your choice to keep well away from these vulnerable nest areas. Within the national park, the wardens do not take kindly to paddlers who get too close to sea caves.

Native History in Barkley Sound

Paddlers and Archaeological Sites

Paddlers visiting Barkley Sound are bound to be impressed by the remains of a native culture that once flourished in this entire area. Stonewall fish traps, shell middens, terraced villages, fortification sites and canoe runs are among the aboriginal features left by the several thousand Nuu-chah-nulth peoples who once lived along these shores. The overwhelming presence of these features demands in the very least that a brief account of native history be included in this introduction.

More importantly, these features also demand our respect. They have been here in some instances for many hundreds of years, and an assurance that they remain depends on how we treat them today. Do not tamper with them in any way, and do not remove anything from these historically significant areas. By moving as much as a single boulder within a stone trap alignment or native canoe run, we add to their further disintegration. Picking away at a shell midden only compounds the erosion that already whittles away at these shell deposits.

The importance of preserving the past by leaving all archaeological sites as they were found cannot be overemphasized. Take a look at these features, but please do not disturb them.

The Nuu-chah-nulth Peoples

For at least four thousand years, most of the Pacific side of Vancouver Island was occupied by the Nuu-chah-nulth (Nootka) peoples.

In the nineteenth century, at least five Nuu-chah-nulth groups shared the relatively small area within Barkley Sound: the Sheshaht, Toquaht, Ucluelet, Ohiats and Uchucklesahts. Although the groups shared a common way of life, they were politically separate, with each claiming a traditional territory.

Little is known of the extent of prehistoric territories. During the late 1700s and early 1800s, a series of wars and the devastating effect of "white man's" diseases resulted in the extinction of some groups and the coalescing of others. However, it is known that in the early part of this century, a typical territory likely consisted of locations on both the "inside" (Alberni Inlet and inner islands within Barkley Sound) and the "outside" (outer islands within Barkley Sound). Inside areas were protected and provided sheltered winter village sites. Outside areas, occupied from spring through autumn, provided access to seasonal food supplies such as whales, sea lions, salmon and halibut (McMillan and St. Claire).

A semi-nomadic lifestyle was exemplified in the seasonal movements of the Sheshahts, who began their annual move to Barkley Sound from the head of Alberni Inlet in January. Having stopped at various sites along the inlet, they made their way to Nettle and Keith Islands — the first sites occupied each year due to their protected location. The major village of Hiikwis near the west end of Sechart Channel was also occupied in the spring. In May, further movement led to the outer islands where the Sheshahts stayed until August. Seals, halibut, cod and salmon were among the resources obtained at Huumuuwa (the large summer village on the east coast of Effingham Island, pronounced "Omoah") right up until the 1930s. Much smaller sites were also occupied on the bay on the west side of Effingham, on Wouwer Island (a good sea lion hunting area), and on Dicebox, Clarke and Benson Islands. Upon leaving Barkley Sound in August and slowly winding their way back to protected winter villages, the Sheshahts completed an annual cycle following seasonal resources.

Shell middens, the accumulation of debris after countless years of occupation, remain where villages once stood. Larger middens represent major village settlements, while the much smaller ones represent seasonal camps. Eighteen major village sites have been identified in the Broken Group, although not all of them were occupied within the last two hundred years.

The Arrival of Europeans

Captain James Cook arrived in Nootka Sound on the west coast of Vancouver Island in 1778 — an event that was to have a major impact on all Nuu-chah-nulth peoples. The epic voyage brought to world attention the enormous profits to be made in selling the magnificent sea otter pelts. Between 1785 and 1825, almost five hundred trading voyages brought native groups in frequent contact with European traders (Inglis and Haggarty). During this same period, Captain Charles Barkley discovered and explored Barkley Sound aboard the trading vessel *Imperial Eagle*.

The natives supplied the traders with the highly prized sea otter pelts, yet the resource was limited. Hunting pressure intensified, and warring amongst Nuu-chah-nulth groups increased. Warfare coupled with the introduction of communicable diseases brought about a major decline in native populations.

After four decades of sea otter trade, native groups were relatively free of contact with the Europeans. However, by the mid 1800s, foreigners became a permanent presence. This time they sought to trade for dogfish oil, a commodity that was required in large quantities for lubrication by a developing forest industry (McMillan and St. Claire). Trading centres were set up, and natives gravitated toward them. For instance, when a store was established in the Deer Group at Dodger Cove around

1868, there was only one Ohiat house. By the end of the century, Dodger Cove was a major village.

The migratory habits of the natives were further influenced when BC joined Confederation and Indian affairs became a federal concern. Reserves were established, and a semi-nomadic people were no longer quite so free to roam.

Missionaries quickly followed, consciously attempting to change the native ways. A Reverend Willemar described it in the following way:

> ... *the wandering habits of the Indians are a very great obstacle to mission work: the Barkley Sound Indians are always dispersed during the year ... by teaching the natives to obtain their livelihood from agricultural pursuits, we might cure them of their migratory habits; and once settled at Alberni, we could possibly obtain a permanent hold on them.*

Traditions broke down further with the arrival of sealing schooners. From the 1870s to the early 1900s, these vessels called in at native settlements, looking for crews of hunters. At first, sealing grounds were just off Vancouver Island, but as seals decreased, the hunters had to sail further away. Subsequently, villages were abandoned for longer periods of time. By the end of the nineteenth century, populations had plunged due to a further introduction of communicable disease. Coastal peoples paddling from village to village by canoe were extremely vulnerable to the spread of smallpox, tuberculosis and measles.

It is hard to know exactly, but it is estimated that prior to European contact, Barkley Sound's Nuu-chah-nulth people numbered about 9,000. In 1874, 949 were left (Inglis and Haggarty).

Today, a proud Nuu-chah-nulth people live in communities adjacent to Bamfield, Port Alberni and Ucluelet.

AREA IX — THE DEER GROUP

Chart:	– No. 3671, Barkley Sound (1:40,000)
Tides:	– Reference Port: Tofino
	– Secondary Port: Bamfield
Duration:	– 3 to 4 days
Camp Locations:	– Diana Island, northeast corner
	– Sandford Island, east side
	– Holford Bay
	– Ross Islets
	– Stud Islets

Launches

The launch is located near Bamfield on the southwest side of Barkley Sound.

To get to Bamfield, paddlers from the mainland take a ferry to either Nanaimo or Swartz Bay on Vancouver Island. Once on the island, follow Highway 1 to the Cowichan Lake turnoff, just a few kilometres north of the town of Duncan. (Paddlers from Vancouver Island drive to the same turnoff.) Follow signs along Highway 18 to Youbou. A short distance beyond this logging community, the pavement ends, and the remaining distance to Bamfield is travelled over a gravel road that is owned and operated by MacMillan Bloedel Limited. Expect to encounter the company's logging trucks at any time, and always travel with your lights on. Otherwise, expect a safe journey on a well-maintained road. Confusing to first-time visitors is a profusion of secondary roads that shoot off in many different directions from the main route. Stay on the main road, follow the signs and within two hours you will reach the town of Bamfield. Allow four hours to drive to Bamfield from either Victoria or Nanaimo.

For those wanting to camp, there is a campsite just before Bamfield at Pachena Bay. The campground is operated by the Ohiat Indian Band and is accessed by driving past the sign-posted entrance to the West

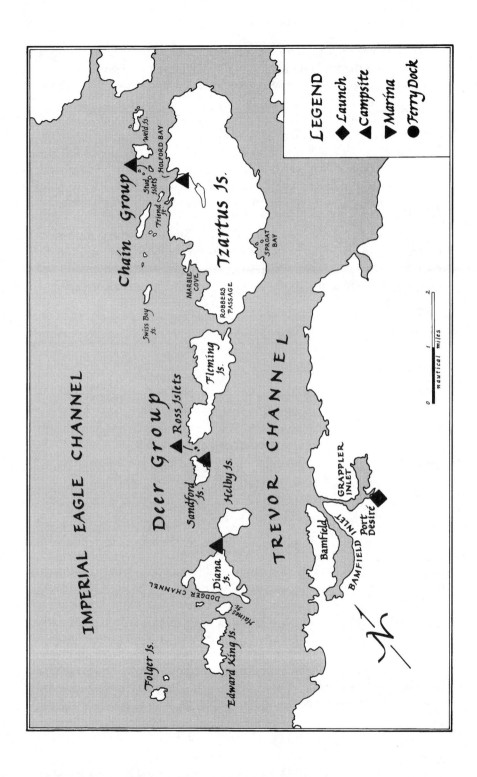

IMPERIAL EAGLE CHANNEL

Chain Group

Folger Is.

Edward King Is.

Haines Is.

DODGER CHANNEL

Diana Is.

Deer Group

Helby Is.

Sandford Is.

Ross Islets

Fleming Is.

Swiss Bay Is.

ROBBERS PASSAGE

MARBLE COVE

Tzartus Is.

SPROAT BAY

Friend Islets

Studd Islets

'weld Is.

HOLFORD BAY

TREVOR CHANNEL

GRAPPLER INLET

Port Desiré

BAMFIELD INLET

Bamfield

N

LEGEND

◆ Launch
▲ Campsite
▼ Marina
● Ferry Dock

0   1   2
nautical miles

Coast Trail, then taking the next left turn, passing through the reserve and following the Pachena River down to Pachena Bay. The sites are set in the forest above the kilometre-long Pachena Bay beach. The natives charge a minimal fee to use this facility.

Head to Bamfield, a delightful West Coast village located about 5 km (3 mi) from Pachena Bay. Make a right turn on Grappler Road, the first major intersection in the town. On the corner is the Tides and Trails Cafe, one of two eating places in town (the other is across the inlet). Next to the cafe is the Kamshee Store where you can stock up on last minute provisions. The tiny establishment also serves as a liquor outlet.

Continue along Grappler Road to Port Desire and the government wharf. Park to the right of the boat ramp to unload gear, and for the duration of the trip leave vehicles parked on the side of the road, well above the government wharf. (Be sure that vehicles are left locked.)

Trip 24 — Diana Island

Distances: – Port Desire to Diana Island campsite (3 mi)
  – Circumnavigation of Diana Island (3.5 mi)

Highlights

Diana Island is exceptional. Quiet, sand-fringed coves backed by towering cedar and hemlock, surf-lashed shores and fantastic sea caves are but a few of her highlights. Pass by an intriguing bit of history represented by the abandoned villages on Dodger Cove.

Considerations

Trevor Channel is open to both swell and wind coming in off the open Pacific; therefore it is important to know sea conditions prior to crossing to the Deer Group. Wind-generated waves and swell will hit paddlers broadside in Trevor Channel, a far-from-desirable condition, especially if winds are strong and waves are steep. As westerlies are most likely to come up in the afternoon, consider making the crossing in the morning.

The shores along Diana Island are only semi-protected from adverse conditions, with a couple of stretches that are fully exposed (Kirby and Voss Points). Listen to marine weather forecasts prior to paddling around the island.

Fog, low cloud and rain could affect visibility, so always travel with a compass.

The Deer Group Islands are not recommended for inexperienced paddlers. Sheltered areas in these islands are few and far between, and most shorelines are exposed to prevailing winds and swell.

Launch at the public ramp on Grappler Inlet.

The Route

Launch from Port Desire, the seaside village on Grappler Inlet. The few houses here — some new, some leaning out over the water, most looking weatherworn — all add to the unique ambience of this coastal community.

Paddle .5 mi to the entrance of Grappler Inlet, favouring the left-hand shore to avoid the boat traffic entering and exiting the inlet. For over fifty years, the large complex that is visible as you round the point housed the Bamfield Cable Station. After the cable office shut down (1959), the station was bought by five Canadian universities (1969) and now serves as a marine research centre.

A side trip to Bamfield West is a "must do." Cross the narrow entrance to Bamfield Inlet, and head to the government dock. The freight/passenger ship *Lady Rose* docks here, so it may be necessary to paddle over to the dock immediately in front of the general store. The general store (also a liquor outlet) and the adjacent post office function as the local gathering place. Take a wander along the boardwalk past cosy cottages, or head over to the Coast Guard Station (its red and white paint job is distinctive) where one of two West Coast lifeboats is stationed.

Paddlers may choose to head directly to one of two campsites located on Sandford Island and the Ross Islets. The crossing from Bamfield to either of these camp locations is about 2 mi. For a description of these sites, see "Trip 26 — Sandford and Fleming Islands and the Chain Group." Others may begin with the following exploration of Helby and Diana Islands.

The distance from Bamfield across Trevor Channel to Helby Island is just over 1 mi. Helby is one of the few islands in the Deer Group that is privately owned. From a distance, the island's road is clearly visible, but the homes are set back and are not visible from seaward. The owners, many of them staff at the Marine Research Station, have made a conscious choice to develop the island in this manner (Watmough).

If a landing is required, pull up on the sheltered beach just inside Self Point; if not, paddle across Mackenzie Anchorage to the northwest corner of Diana Island where a sand beach breaks an otherwise rocky shoreline. In the forest above is enough level ground for several tents, complete with rudimentary camp facilities made of driftwood. As the site is on the lee side of the island, it is sheltered from prevailing winds. Views out to Ohiat Island and the distant Mackenzie Range are magnificent.

Commence the 3.5-mi circumnavigation of Diana Island by paddling toward Kirby Point. Just inside the point is one of the most attractive beaches in all of the Deer Group. A beautiful meadow and open forest behind this sandy expanse inevitably beckon passersby. The entire point is Indian reserve and may not be used for overnight camping. However, having obtained a pass from the Ohiats, daytime exploration of beaches is permitted. (See "Native Reserves in Barkley Sound" for information regarding permission to visit.)

Hike across Kirby Point to a windswept bay on the opposite side of the peninsula. A single grave enclosed with wire fencing is all that is left of an old cemetery, last used in the 1940s by natives from nearby Dodger Cove. Look for Columbian black-tail deer, as they often browse on luxuriant grasses growing here. Or wander through the magnificent stands of cedar and hemlock, selecting any number of routes that lead to narrow surge channels and lofty bluffs overlooking the open sea. A view of the sun setting over Mount Ozard from Kirby Point is hard to forget, especially with the sounds of surf breaking on rocks below.

Expect large numbers of fishing skiffs off Kirby Point. This is a very popular fishing spot, and for good reason — the fishermen here are successful. Give their trolling lines plenty of leeway, and watch them for a short time — you are almost guaranteed to witness their landing a sizeable salmon.

Once around Kirby Point, shelter from westerlies is non-existent. This short section of Diana's coast is exposed. Waves slop up against rock bluffs, then drop back, confronting incoming waves and generating erratic seas. Swing well out from the point to avoid the turbulence.

Seppings and Edward King Islands break the waves from the open Pacific; therefore expect calmer conditions once within Dodger Channel. Dodger Channel was named by a historic schooner captain, who considered it "a fine place in which to dodge the weather." Today's yachtspeople obviously agree as two or three sailing vessels are often moored here.

Cross over to the south side of Seppings Island where a gaping cave entrance demands closer inspection. Continue south to Haines Island where once again the most inviting of beaches is on reserve land and not available for overnight use. Daytime stops are permitted only with the purchase of a yearly pass from the Ohiats. A small community comprised of several frame houses once stood on the grass berm above the beach. Occasional bits of porcelain and broken glass are all that remain of past inhabitation. Walk the beach at low tide, and explore extensive rocky islets off the south end of the island. Upon leaving Haines Island, look into the eel grass shallows for moonsnail casings.

The entire south end of Diana Island is also reserve land. This Dodger Cove community once flourished, as evidenced by an assortment of

Tilikum at Dodger Cove

In 1901 John Voss and his mate Norman Luxton spent several weeks at Dodger Cove before resuming a historic voyage that had started only days before. They departed from Victoria aboard a 9-m (32 ft) dugout canoe, the *Tilikum*, embarking on a voyage that they hoped would take them around the world. The cedar dugout was refurbished so that it contained forward and aft bulkheads, a cabin, galvanized water tanks and three masts.

Within days of their send-off, the two-man crew was forced ashore because of bad weather. They landed at Dodger Cove. Using her father's journal, Eleanor Luxton provides a glimpse of turn-of-the-century life in this native community.

It was the later part of May that the Tilikum blew in under and past Beale Light, and it was not until the 6th of July, 1901, that she eventually got under way to the Pacific for keeps. Weather conditions for the most of June were the worst that the coast had experienced for years. It seemed I and Voss had a lot of time on our hands. I spent most of my time exploring the surrounding country either by foot or canoe. Besides McKenzie's trading store, the village supported a school for Indian children and two villages of some forty or fifty houses, wonderfully furnished according to the success the owner might have had in seal hunting the year previous. It was a common thing to see several sewing machines in one house or half a dozen phonographs, and beds and tables by the dozen but never used. The floors of the houses or the beach were used for most domestic purposes. Invariably, dripping from huge slabs of blubber fat from whales or black fish, the grease fell on this display of wealth, amid smells reeking to the heavens.

Almost six weeks passed before *Tilikum*'s anchor was raised. The Pacific crossing that followed was full of mishap. Luxton abandoned ship in Fiji. Voss completed the voyage on the Thames River, September 2, 1904.

The *Tilikum* survives today, appearing much as she did throughout her voyage, in the Maritime Museum in Victoria, BC.

both collapsed and standing buildings. History describes a thriving village site inhabited by both natives and whites. A trading post established in the 1850s brought in various white traders. Missionaries attempting to keep up with natives on their seasonal migrations set up a mission and built a church here in the late 1800s; and at the turn of the century, sealing schooners repeatedly visited Dodger Cove to recruit natives for seal-hunting expeditions to the Bering Sea. One industrious captain transformed the derelict church into a dwelling and storehouse for furs. Little of this history can be gathered from the

During the latter part of the eighteenth century, two native villages stood on either side of Dodger Channel. A recently killed humpback whale lies on the shore fronting the Haines Island village in a photo taken around 1800. (*Royal British Columbia Museum*)

rubble that remains. Most of the village has long since surrendered to the elements.

Pass the cave entrance between the village and Voss Point. Although sea water covers the cave floor, there isn't enough clearance to enter the confined space by kayak or canoe.

Voss Point honours Captain John Voss and his around-the-world voyage in a dugout canoe. Waiting for an improvement in the weather, he stopped at Dodger Cove.

Explore the shallows in the bay north of Voss Point near Cia Rock, before returning to the Diana Island campsite.

Trip 25 — The Outer Islands: Edward King and Folger Islands

Distance: –   6 mi, round trip

Highlights

Nowhere in all the Deer Group is the drama of open coast more impressive than on these outer islands. Jagged shores hurl the incoming surf back to the sea in an ever-present display of foam and spray. The bare rocks on Folger serve as a haul-out site for California and Steller sea lions. The sheltered shorelines here are festooned with the blueberry beasts, and the air is filled with their interminable barks and growls. Beneath these waters is a historic ship, claimed a century ago by submerged reefs within Barkley Sound.

Considerations

Most of the distance between Diana and Folger Islands is across the open waters in Hammond and Imperial Eagle Channels. The area is fully exposed to prevailing winds and is subject to fogs that significantly reduce visibility. There are few landings along the predominantly rocky coastlines. Expect boat confinement for up to two or three hours.

The route should not be attempted unless weather forecasts indicate safe conditions. Nor should it be attempted by paddlers inexperienced with navigation by compass.

Even in calm conditions, this route is not for inexperienced paddlers.

The Route

The open-water crossing from Kirby Point to Folger and Leach Islands is just under 2 mi.

The sounds of the resident sea lions greet the adventurous paddler a fair distance from Leach and Folger Islands. Immediately upon entering the narrow passage between the two islets, you will see the dozens of animals that line the jagged shoreline from early fall until the spring. Sea lions are not usually aggressive but are a threatening presence once they enter the water, simply because they are so large. If paddlers get in too close, these mammals will swim to and fro in an attempt to discourage uninvited guests. Observe them from a respectable distance.

Be wary of swell passing over the shallows between Folger and Leach. Breakers are common in a channel that is riddled with kelp. Beneath the foam is the remains of the *Ericsson*, a historically renowned vessel that met her disastrous end in this windswept channel in the winter of 1892.

Those attempting a visit to Folger to view the sea lions will not be disappointed if they have not yet returned. The island boasts many other dramatic features often associated with such exposed land masses. Hundreds of sea birds, including pigeon guillemots, oystercatchers, cormorants and eagles, inhabit these shores. Harbour seals curiously eye paddlers from rocky lookouts. On exposed outer shores, the power of the open Pacific manifests itself when even the gentlest swell creates a thundering break. A sea cave is found on the northwest corner of the island.

Paddle on to Edward King Island, a place named after an ambitious young man, Captain Edward King, the founder of both the *New Westminster Times* and the *Victoria Gazette*. In 1861 King was accidentally shot on a deer-hunting expedition while removing a loaded gun from a canoe. He was twenty-nine years of age. Almost the entire island, except

The *Ericsson*

In 1985 divers of the Underwater Archaeological Society of BC located the remains of the *Ericsson*. Untouched since she sank in 1892, this wreck would soon become known as the most historically significant shipwreck in BC waters.

The *Ericsson* was the result of a single man's vision to build a ship that would mark the end of the age of steam. John Ericsson believed in a theory that heat was a material fluid called caloric and that it could be collected, regenerated and the energy used to turn a ship's paddlewheels. In 1853 his lifelong dream ship embarked on her inaugural voyage. No finer a ship had ever been built in the US, and initial reviews on both appearance and performance were rave. (The vessel cost \$.5 million to build. The engines alone were worth \$130,000.) Newspapers reported, "The age of steam is closed, the age of caloric opens."

Success was to be short-lived. The revolutionary engine certainly required far less fuel than steam-powered craft, but steamers easily travelled at 14 knots and yet the *Ericsson* couldn't exceed 6 knots. Also, the caloric engines took up so much space, there was little room for passengers. Ericsson, convinced that his ship could surpass steamers, set out to make the necessary modifications, and so in 1854 a refurbished vessel embarked on a test run only to meet with high winds. She subsequently sank in New York Bay. Now Ericsson himself abandoned the project. The ship was raised, but the caloric engine was converted to steam.

As a steamer, the *Ericsson* was used as a freighter and passenger vessel. Eventually, she was converted to sail, and as testimony to her superior design, she broke many sailing records. In 1890 she started to carry lumber and coal from BC to ports around the world.

Her remarkable career ended in Barkley Sound in 1892 when a winter storm blew her onto the rocks. The crew abandoned ship, scrambled to safety and watched as all visible traces of the *Ericsson* disappeared.

Ninety-three years later, the wreck of the only caloric ship ever built was found near Folger Island. Recognizing her historical significance, the Underwater Archaeological Society of BC urged her protection, and so she is now protected under provincial heritage laws. Three artifacts raised at the time of discovery — the ship's bell, one porthole and the ship's head — are on display at the Maritime Museum in Vancouver. (Based on "Discovery of the Ericsson," *Diver Magazine*, August 1985, article by David W. Griffiths.)

for a couple of sheltered pockets, is exposed to the effects of westerlies and swell. Make the 1-mi long crossing from Folger toward the largest bay located midway along the west shoreline of Edward King Island.

Landings along the jagged shores of Edward King Island are few and far between. (*Tracy Cornish*)

There is some shelter from westerlies here as the tiny islets at the entrance to the bay break the swell. Land on the sand beach, and during low tides, walk along the northern shore to the sea cave. Don't miss paddling through a miniature archipelago off the most northerly point of Edward King Island. Eagles typically watch the water from weatherworn snags on these exposed reefs. Harbour seals swim in the kelp beds. Their heads are often mistaken for the floating bulbs of the giant bull kelp.

Head back to the Diana Island campsite, passing around either Voss or Kirby Points.

(As an alternative route, paddlers may choose to follow the eastern shore of Edward King. This east side is considerably more rugged than the west and is exposed to swell and prevailing winds. There are virtually no landings here, but by paddling this side, you have the opportunity to view the sea caves. Look for them about midway along this eastern shore.)

Trip 26 — Sandford and Fleming Islands and the Chain Group

Distances: – Diana to Sandford Island (1.5 mi)
– Sandford to Friend Island (5 mi)
– Friend Island to Studd Islets (.5 mi)

Highlights

Here are islands rich in contrast. Paddle along wind-battered, surf-swept shores, past towering bluffs and the gaping entrances to sea caves. Enter the quiet waters of sheltered bays where sand beaches are as long and as white as any that you'll find in the Deer Group. Miniature islets, alive with the colour of intertidal marine life, offer forest-sheltered campsites at the end of the day.

Considerations

Since most waters along this route are open to prevailing westerlies, listen to wind forecasts prior to paddling. Some sections, especially along the southwest end of Fleming, shouldn't be paddled if strong winds are predicted.

Watch for turbulent waters off major headlands (generated by the pounding swell), and be on the lookout for offshore breakers. Most of the swell-generated turbulence is avoided by paddling a short distance offshore.

This trip is not for novice paddlers.

The Route

Cross from Diana to Ohiat Islet, a steep-sided isle named after the natives living on this side of Barkley Sound. As inviting as it appears from a distance, there is virtually nowhere to land.

Satellite Passage is the widest channel in the Deer Group, providing the easiest power-craft access to Bamfield. Paddlers should navigate toward the inside of the westernmost point on Sandford, all the while watching for offshore breakers. This south shore of Sandford Island is extremely rugged. Massive boulders and steep bluffs stand guard all along this fore- boding coastline. The dark entrances of two caves inspire speculation as to what may be hidden beyond their black portals. They are not accessible.

Round the easternmost point, and look for a rather precipitous cliff. Just beyond, facing out to the Ross Islets, is a small sand-lined bay, and above the high tide line are rudimentary campsites developed by past users. Follow the trail that pushes through the salal and terminates a short distance away. Here, hidden by the undergrowth, is an enormous bulldozer. The treads on the mechanical dinosaur are almost as high as an average-sized person.

I'm now going to give away a once-secret camp location. I promised a friend I would not describe this spot in the original version of *Island Paddling*. I kept my promise. He has since given his blessing to describing it, as it "has been discovered" by locals and visitors alike. So, here goes.

The best of all the campsites in the Deer Group is located on the largest island in the Ross Islets. It is closest to Fleming Island. You will have to do a little exploration to find it. The site is accessed from the north and is very obvious once found. A gorgeous sandy shore, exposed at low tide, provides easy access. Several level areas, enough to accommodate several tents, are found in the forest on two adjacent

The Ross Islets provide sheltered shores, forest-bordered camp spots and sweeping views of coastal mountains. (*Maurice Robinson*)

islets. (At high tide they are separated by water.) Be prepared to share these sites with others, especially during the summer season. This spot is not only discovered but is also understandably popular. Once camp is set, walk out to the south-facing shore. Here, pelagic cormorants, wings extended, pose on exposed rocks. Swell, cresting on offshore shallows, crashes with a deafening roar on nearby islets. Watch the setting sun from this safe, astonishingly beautiful vantage.

The only time I have ever experienced the loss of a kayak was in the Ross Islets. A large group of us arrived in May. We set up camp and placed boats, so we thought, above high tide levels. Upon waking in the morning our party of ten had nine kayaks. We were fortunate to have a two-way radio and an understanding Coast Guard auxiliary who agreed to assist with a search. The kayak was found 6 mi away, nestled in a kelp bed off Effingham in the Broken Group Islands. We were lucky. Do check tide levels before bedding down and make sure your boat is secure.

The tremendously beautiful southwestern shore of Fleming is a definite highlight on this route. Deep bays cut into a desolate shore, and jagged cliffs mark the entrances to several caves. Surf relentlessly pounds these rock faces, washing the entire landscape with a plankton-rich soup. Barnacles in search of microscopic food brought to them by the tides and swell sweep the sea water with feathery plumes. Look for the acorn, thatched and gooseneck barnacles — all three species live in close proximity here. Anemones, sea stars and mussels also inhabit this rich marine environment.

Paddle to the bay, a conspicuous feature located about halfway along

Barnacles

Once a barnacle settles, it is stuck for life, secured by a strong glue that does such a good job of cementing that scientists are investigating its adhesive capacity. No cement has been found that works so well in a moist environment. Fossil barnacles that settled onto surfaces some one hundred and fifty million years ago are still attached (Starbird). If a similar material is ever synthesized, the adhesive could well mend broken bones and serve as a cement and filler in dentistry.

Once secured, the barnacle builds an encasement resembling a miniature volcano with two movable plates at the summit. At high tide, the plates open, and feathery feet (cirri) sweep the plankton-rich waters for food.

The two barnacle species most prevalent on the Pacific coast are gooseneck and acorn barnacles. The latter is the most common and is easily identified by its volcano-like shape. Four rigid plates and two flexible plates at the top effectively protect this animal from pounding surf. At high tide, this barnacle beats its legs furiously to gather food.

The gooseneck barnacle is a laid-back feeder, simply fanning the water and waiting for a meal to happen along. A fleshy stalk distinguishes this barnacle from the others. Overall, it bears a strange resemblance to a bird's beak at the end of a rubber neck. The name "gooseneck" is in fact derived from a sixteenth-century botanist who attributed the birth of geese to this animal! So strong was the bird-from-barnacle belief in medieval Ireland that Catholics regarded the goose as fish, not fowl, and allowed it to be eaten on fast days.

A third species common on the Pacific coast is the thatched barnacle, easily recognized by its steep-walled, thatched appearance.

How do you find a mate when you are glued to one spot? Well, barnacles are hermaphroditic. That is, they have both male and female sex organs and a reproductive potential that is awe-inspiring. "A mile of shore can have more than one-and-a-half-billion potential barnacles bringing forth fifteen billion potential young!" (Hewlett and Gilbey) It is no wonder that a ship is fouled with barnacles in as little as eight months, adding tons of additional weight. Toxic paints, copper sheathing and radioactive paints have been used to help eliminate this problem, but to this day researchers still search for a lasting solution (Hewlett and Gilbey).

Fleming's western shore. In this large bight, the harsh sounds of the open sea give way to the quiet hush of sheltered waters. Anyone needing a stopover, a place to stretch cramped muscles or to perhaps take a snooze, will appreciate the vast, sandy shore here. A tiny rivulet pushes through the sand in the south corner of the bay, but the water appears brackish — not a recommended water supply.

The most spectacular cave on Fleming Island is located just north of here. Swell pushes through a kelp-riddled channel that leads to the cave's opening. From the light of the entrance, peer into a 20-m (65 ft) high cavern with arched walls that are a magnificent, algae-covered red and green. Rock ledges inside this cave are used as nest sites for several pelagic cormorants. It is most important that these sensitive birds are not disturbed, so listen to the croaks of the cormorants from outside the entrance. (The success of a breeding season could depend on your decision to respect their nesting territory. Refer to the "Introduction to Barkley Sound" for further information.)

Cross from the northwest point on Fleming to an island archipelago referred to as the Chain Group. The 1-mi crossing is open to the west, so be sure that weather conditions permit safe passage. Navigate toward Swiss Boy, the most southerly islet in the group. There are no landings on the island as the steep rock cliffs rise abruptly to a forested crown. The cave located halfway along the western shore is used by breeding cormorants.

A white-shell beach on the south side of the largest of the Meade Islets looks appealing as a stopover, except at low tides when slippery kelp-covered rocks make access difficult. Those tempted to camp on the beach may waken as I did to the sound of water approaching the tent entrance. If you do camp here, place tents well above the high tide line.

Paddle through the rocky islets off the west and north ends of the Meade group for a close-up look at the colourful marine life occupying the intertidal zones. Bands of orange and purple stars, green-blue leather stars, green anemones and blue mussels continue on through to the Geer Islets where the multicoloured viewing is best at low tide.

A beautiful sand and shell beach is there for the landing at the north end of Diplock (except at high tide when the tiny shore is almost completely covered by water). Paddle the remaining short distance to the largest of the Studd Islets.

The Studd Islets tent site is located by heading to the white-shell beach clearly visible from the water. It faces southwest, taking full advantage of the last hours of sunlight and offering a panoramic view of Imperial Eagle Channel. The only disadvantage is that it is exposed to westerlies and is therefore a far-from-ideal location in windy weather. In calm conditions, pull up onto the beach. Space for three or four tents is found above the high tide line and below the forest perimeter. Walk the forest trail to a boulder beach on the north side of the islet. At extreme low tides, walk the water's edge where moonsnail casings and multi-armed sunstars are visible a short distance away.

Holford Creek on Tzartus Island will appeal to the adventurous few who want to access the headwaters on Holden Lake. In my own attempt to reach the lake, I was quickly discouraged, as what appears to be a trail terminates after about 100 m (325 ft). Two or three clearings in the

Swiss Boy

The year was 1858. An American brig, the *Swiss Boy*, sprung a leak and beached for repairs near an island that was to eventually bear her name. A local band of Ohiats saw the foreign ship and, having somewhat accepted the British influence on this part of the coast, regarded her as an intruder in the King's waters. They boarded the ship, took the crew as prisoners, sent the mainmast overboard and stripped her of valuables.

The American captives were set free days later aboard the schooner *Morning Star*. Upon their arrival in Victoria, they told the Governor of the incident, insisting that it must not go unpunished. Governor Douglas offered to repair the ship, but the captain declined, insisting that the *Swiss Boy* was ruined beyond repair. He and his crew returned to San Francisco at the Governor's expense.

Meanwhile, a gunboat was sent to investigate the state of the *Swiss Boy*. As it turns out, the damages in no way approached those described by the crew. The cargo was still intact, and the supposed widespread pilfering was limited to a few small articles. Even more ludicrous, test-bores showed that the *Swiss Boy* was rotten —she should never have set sail in the first place!

An Ohiat sub-chief, detained by officials in Victoria, was released, and the bizarre case was soon forgotten. The *Swiss Boy* was last reported "on a sandy beach, much overgrown with barnacles." All trace of her has long since disappeared.

---

forest near the creek entrance could accommodate several tents; however, thick coastal rain forest effectively blocks the evening sun and makes these camp locations dark. But quick access to a fresh-water bath is a definite plus for those considering an overnight stop here. (Before drinking this water, boil it.)

Consider a side trip to Weld Island. At the midpoint on the south shore is a cave, one of the few in the Deer Group that is accessible. Landing on kelp-covered boulders is tricky, but those willing to negotiate over such obstacles can access the cave entrance. The cave penetrates the island for about 30 m (100 ft). Take along a flashlight.

At this point, some paddlers may wish to continue around the north and east sides of Tzartus Island. I have chosen to describe an alternative return route as, in my opinion, the east side of Tzartus is not as interesting as the west. (For those who choose to follow this eastern shore, there is some camping above high tide on the beach fronting the native reserve land, although permission from the Ohiats is necessary before going ashore. Other camp locations are found in Sproat Bay. An oyster lease operates in the entire bay, but the Bamfield-based owner doesn't mind if paddlers wish to stay overnight as long as they do not interfere with the oyster operation.)

Trip 27 — West Side of Tzartus and East Side of Fleming

Distances: - Holford Bay to Robbers Passage (3 mi)
- Robbers Passage to Port Desire via Roquefeuil Bay (4.5 mi)
- Robbers Passage to Port Desire via Fleming and Sanford Islands (5.5 mi)

Highlights

Nowhere else in all of Barkley Sound is there such an incredible concentration of sea arches as there is along this stretch of coast. Narrow and towering high above the sea, or long and tunnel shaped, all are magnificent features. Paddle on to Robbers Passage where quiet waters lap sandy shores. Then head to Trevor Channel where once again the sea puts on a rousing show, spilling over the rocks on the east side of Fleming Island.

Considerations

In calm conditions most of the shoreline along this route is free of turbulent waters, but if westerlies should blow, both Imperial Eagle and Trevor Channels are open to their influence. The only section sheltered from these conditions is Robbers Passage. There is virtually nowhere to land along the rocky eastern shores on Fleming. Listen to wind predictions, especially prior to crossing from the Deer Group back to the launch at Port Desire.

If fog prevails over these inner islands, it tends to burn off by the afternoon (unless it is extremely thick).

Once again, this route is not recommended for novice paddlers.

The Route

Paddle southward from Holford Bay along the western shores of Tzartus Island where close-ranked evergreens crowd the shore and there are few places to land. Just north of Marble Cove, the first of several sea arches in this area penetrates a rock cliff. The gaping entrance faces north and is therefore visible to southbound paddlers. The long, tunnel-shaped arch drastically diminishes in diameter — so much so that it's impossible to paddle all the way through. However, if conditions permit access, explore inside this one. The lower walls within a cathedral-sized cavern are covered with sea anemones of the brightest green I've ever seen. In the same zone, purple and orange ochre stars, bat stars and brilliant orange algae all contribute their unique splash of colour. And up above, fronds of green maidenhair fern drape from the ceiling. In both colour and size, this arch is perhaps the most dramatic.

Nowhere in all of Barkley Sound are the sea arches so prevalent as they are in the area surrounding Marble Cove. Most impressive among them is this arch, situated at the cove's southern entrance.
(*Mary Ann Snowden*)

Paddle through the kelp, following the inner shore of Fry Island, to access the sheltered waters within Marble Cove. Look for a tiny arch immediately upon rounding the most easterly point, then continue along Fry's south shore for a close-up view of the most unusual of these rock-arch formations. A single band of rock, perhaps 6 m (20 ft) in diameter, curves up from the sea to join with an adjacent bluff. Pass underneath the 12-m (40 ft) span.

The final and perhaps most impressive arch penetrates about 30 m (100 ft) through the tiny islet off the southern entrance to Marble Cove. In paddling from one side of the tunnel to the other, exercise some caution as swell funnels through the channel, shooting kayak and paddler through the narrow gap. The free ride can be a thrill, but kayaks can also get pushed broadside and possibly end up wedged between the tunnel walls. Those unsure of either their skill level or swell conditions might consider observing this one from the outside.

Several float homes, reaping the benefit of the protection offered by Fry Island, moor within Marble Cove. Paddlers may choose to take advantage of the same sheltered waters and stop over on one of several pebble beaches found along these protected shores.

Robbers Passage takes its name from the former name of Fleming Island, Robber Island. Several geographical name changes were implemented by the Hydrographic Survey Service in 1933 because some names "were similar to those of other places elsewhere on the coast of British

Columbia and the similarity often caused doubt and confusion" (Scott). Tzartus Island was also renamed. Prior to 1933, it was called Copper Island because the island contains huge amounts of copper ore. The name Tzartus comes from a Nootka word meaning "the place of seasonal or intermittent waterfall."

The Port Alberni Yacht Club must have recognized the mirror-like calm often prevalent in Robbers Passage since it has built an outstation on Fleming Island, providing club members with a floating cabin and dock space. On Tzartus' shores, the Canadian King Lodge caters to sports fishermen. Clients arrive via float plane and spend several days trolling the hot spots in Barkley Sound. A couple of private homes are also situated on the Tzartus side of the channel. At first glance, it would appear that most of the shoreline in Robbers Passage that is suitable for landing is taken. But an exceptional beach is located midway through the passage on Fleming's shore, to the inside of the islets. Neither westerlies nor the presence of private property take away from the welcoming presence of this sandy beach.

Leave this sheltered pass to enter open waters in Trevor Channel. As the channel is exposed to both westerlies and swell, listen to weather forecasts, and do not attempt a crossing if combined wind and swell conditions are likely to create steep seas. Given safe conditions, choose one of two route options. Return directly to Bamfield by angling across Trevor Channel to Roquefeuil Bay, then continue along this shore to Port Desire. The total distance from Robbers Passage to the launch is about 4.5 mi. The alternative route hugs Fleming's eastern shoreline. Steep-sided banks, boulder-strewn beaches and barnacle-covered ledges along this side of Fleming ensure that most paddlers will cover the 2.5 mi between Robbers Passage and Sandford Island without a stopover. Stop and relax for a couple of hours, or spend an entire night camped on Sandford Island. The crossing from here to Port Desire is about 2.5 mi.

AREA X — THE BROKEN GROUP ISLANDS

Charts:	– No. 3670, Broken Group (1:20,000)
	– No. 3671, Barkley Sound (1:40,000)
Tides:	– Reference Port: Tofino
	– Secondary Ports: Stopper Islands and Ucluelet
Duration:	– 3 to 7 days
Camp Locations:	– Hand Island
	– Gibraltar Island
	– Dodd Island
	– Willis Island
	– Turret Island
	– Clarke Island
	– Benson Island
	– Gilbert Island

Launches

The *MV Lady Rose* and *MV Frances Barkley*

The easiest way to access the Broken Group is via one of two passenger/cargo ships operated by Alberni Marine Transportation Inc., the *MV Lady Rose* or the *MV Frances Barkley*. This option is especially recommended for paddlers who want to avoid paddling open stretches of water. (For further information about Alberni Marine Transportation, refer to "Getting to the Broken Group Islands" in the "Introduction to Barkley Sound.")

To get to Alberni Marine Transportation facilities, paddlers must first drive to Port Alberni on the west coast of Vancouver Island. Paddlers from the mainland who arrive at Swartz Bay, follow Highway 17, and then Highway 1 to Nanaimo. Travel Highway 19 approximately 20 km (12 mi) north of Nanaimo, then turn left to follow Highway 4 to Port Alberni. Paddlers from Victoria, drive the same route. The total distance from Victoria to Port Alberni is 196 km (122 mi). Allow three hours to drive the distance. Paddlers from the mainland arriving at Nanaimo's Departure Bay terminal, take Highway 19 north for approximately 20 km (12 mi) and turn left, follow- ing Highway 4 to Port Alberni. The total distance from Nanaimo to Port Alberni is 85 km (53 mi). Allow an hour and a half to drive the distance.

Just outside of the town of Port Alberni is a major intersection of Highway 4 and the Port Alberni Highway. (This forking of highways occurs in front of Port Alberni's tourist information centre.) Take the left fork, and follow the Port Alberni Highway until becomes Redford Street, a main artery feeding into the centre of Port Alberni. At the bottom of Redford, make a left turn onto 3rd Avenue, then a right on Argyle Street. Alberni's Harbour Quay, a 1.2-ha (3 ac) platform of reclaimed land where the *Lady Rose* and *Frances Barkley* dock, is located at the bottom of Argyle Street. There is no charge for vehicles left for the duration of the trip in a lot on nearby Kings Way. Alberni Marine staff will direct passengers toward the service.

Early morning departures demand that paddlers spend a night close to the quay. The Dry Creek Campsite is the closest camp facility. Follow the previously outlined route to 3rd Avenue, except make a left turn off 3rd onto Napier. The campground, at the end of Napier, has taken full advantage of a forest grove. The sites are most inviting, and the quay is only blocks away. Others may choose to spend a night in one of Port Alberni's hotel or motel facilities.

From Toquart Bay

Toquart Bay, on the northwest corner of Barkley Sound, is also accessed by first driving to Port Alberni. (For directions on how to get to Port Alberni, refer to the preceding section.)

Pass through Port Alberni by following Highway 4 (Pacific Rim Highway) and the signs for Tofino and Ucluelet. The 85-km (53 mi) stretch of highway (measured from the last set of lights in Port Alberni) from Port Alberni to the Toquart Bay turnoff winds its way along Sproat Lake and the Taylor and Kennedy Rivers, then drops down to Kennedy Lake, a massive body of water often mistaken for the ocean by first-time visitors. Once the lake comes into view, look for an obvious logging road running parallel to the highway. (If you find yourself driving along the highway parallel to the logging road, then you have gone too far.) Make a 180-degree turn onto the gravel road and drive the bumpy 16 km (10 mi) to Toquart Bay. Allow almost two hours to drive from Port Alberni to the Toquart Bay launch.

The BC Forest Service provides an unsupervised campground and boat launch at Toquart Bay. Upwards of two hundred recreation vehicles are often parked on these shores, and paddlers must do some manoeuvring to launch from the sandy beach. You leave vehicles here at your own risk, so be sure to leave them locked, and take your valuables with you.

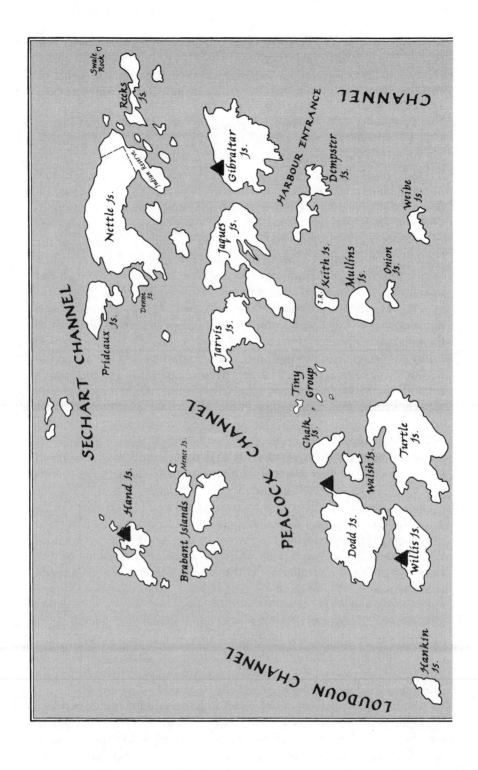

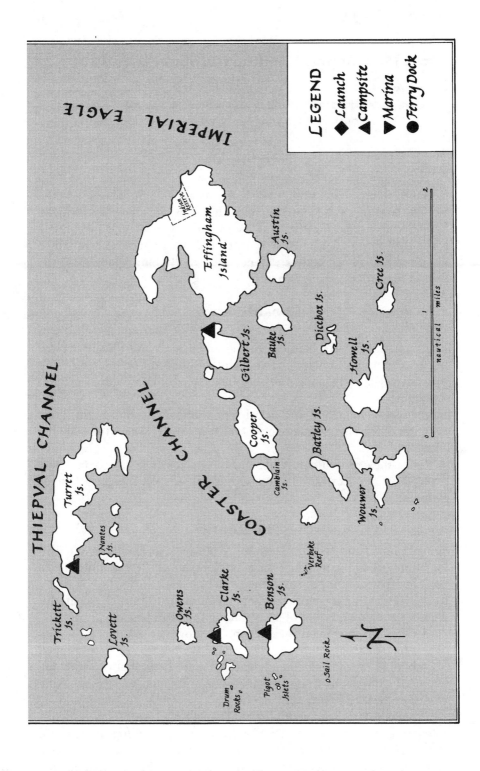

Trip 28 — Stopper, Hand and Brabant Islands

Distances:
  - Toquart Bay to Hand Island (4.5 to 5 mi)
  - Hand to Dodd Island, via the Brabants (2.5 mi)
  - Hand Island to Dodd Island, via Mence Island (2 mi)

Highlights

From Toquart Bay, paddle past virgin forest on the Stoppers, then head to Hand Island, a beautiful little isle that is a fitting introduction to the Broken Group. Its jagged coast is softened by shallow, sand-fringed bays. Set up camp amid the grasses on a nearby islet, and take in features that were left almost a century ago by natives. Paddle on to mirror-still shallows between Mence and the Brabant Islands and the first of the Broken Group sea arches.

Considerations

Westerlies occasionally affect the waters along this route, especially in Loudoun and David Channels. As these winds are most likely to blow in the afternoon, inexperienced paddlers should consider crossing open stretches early in the morning. Listen to wind predictions prior to launching.

Fog, low-lying cloud and drizzle could affect visibility in this area. As some of the crossings along this route are long, always travel with a compass.

Given the exposed nature of some of the crossings, novice paddlers may prefer to access the Broken Group Islands via the *Lady Rose* or *Frances Barkley*.

The Route

Toquart Bay is the primary launch site not only for paddlers, but also for hundreds of boaters accessing Barkley Sound. Recreation vehicles park bumper to bumper along the shoreline — up to two hundred at a time. Needless to say, most paddlers are anxious to leave these shores. Depart from any number of points along the sand beach.

An iron-ore crushing plant and concentrator once stood on the shores of this bay. Throughout the 1960s, crushed concentrates were shipped from here to Japan. Interestingly, the same ore body that provided the exported iron also contains the ore manganite, and as a result, compasses do not read accurately here.

From Toquart, head south toward the Stopper Islands. The rain forests on these islands are virgin, miraculously standing as they did centuries ago, but they must be admired from the water as suitable landings on the Stoppers are hard to find. Dense undergrowth quickly

Hiking gear across a shell beach to the Hand Island campsite, the closest of eight designated campsites in the Broken Group Islands to the Toquart launch. *(Ken Meadows)*

discourages any exploration beyond the forest fringe.

Pass between the two Stoppers, and round the easternmost point to land on a gravel beach on the most southerly of the two Stoppers. At low tide, the beach joins an unnamed islet to Stopper Island, but at high tide, the same beach is covered with water.

An alternative route follows the west side of the Stopper Islands and crosses to St. Ines Island. A beautiful sand beach on the north side of this island, sheltered from prevailing winds, provides easy landing.

The crossing from either the Stoppers or St. Ines Island to Hand Island requires paddling an exposed stretch of water. Listen to weather forecasts to be sure that westerlies will not endanger your Loudoun and David Channels crossing. Note the light on Lyall Point — it serves well as a point of reference.

Hand Island is the closest Broken Group island to the Toquart launch. Paddle the north shore of this island jewel, but shallow-draft boats should beware of offshore reefs that are barnacle covered. They will quickly lay claim to strips of gelcoat from a kayak's hull.

White-shell beaches such as those on the northwest corner of Hand are often associated with park campsites, but this campsite is unique from others in the Broken Group as it is in the open, set amid tall grasses on a tiny islet. Here, the final hours of evening light are not diminished by a dense evergreen canopy.

Stone Fish Traps

Within protected intertidal areas are crescent- and "V"-shaped rock walls constructed by native people who once lived in Barkley Sound. Located in small bays, channels and coves, the walls were used to trap inshore schooling fish. The exact species and specific methods of catching remain a mystery; however, evidence does suggest the fish were perhaps herded with canoes at high tide through openings in the walls and into the catchment pens. As the tide dropped, the stone wall trapped the fish inside. Smaller fishes such as herring and anchovy were likely caught behind the stone walls. (Inglis and Haggarty)

The circle of low-lying boulders found on the beach near the camp area is actually a fish trap. Native peoples enclosed a portion of the bay with boulders, creating a semi-circular trap. Look for it on the northwest shore where this unique alignment connects to bedrock found on the north end of the beach. The feature is easy to see at low tide. And please, do not alter the trap in any way.

Use the trail from the south end of the same beach. About 50 m (164 ft) from the head of the trail (on the left side) is a clearing in the forest. Two large hemlock trees stand at the entrance, and lying near the large cedar stump at the back of this forest opening is a weather-worn cedar. A flat section (however faded with age) shows where a plank has been removed. The natives split planks from trees by driving a series of yew wedges into the straight cedar grain and then prying the "boards" from the trunk. Shorter planks, such as this one, were likely used to manufacture boxes, while longer planks, split in the same manner, were used in the construction of the traditional longhouses. (Once again, do not alter this archaeological feature in any way.)

Continue southward along the trail to the shallow lagoon where an old steam donkey (evidence of the hand-logging that took place on this island) lays hidden in the bramble at the forest's edge. Walk around the salt marsh and the nearby islet for additional rusty evidence of former logging. The disturbed boulder alignments found on the beaches in this area once formed stone fish traps and a single canoe run.

Paddle from Hand to Dodd Island, either along the westernmost shores of the Brabants or along Mence Island. The west side of the Brabants are open to westerlies that periodically blow up Loudoun Channel, but in calm conditions, paddle around these outer shores to access Brabant's only sand beach. It is found in behind the tiny islet on the island's west side. At low tide, a rim of boulders block access to the beach. A tiny sea arch penetrates the nearby islet.

The Brabant Islands were originally called the Penders, but the name was changed to avoid confusion with the Gulf Islands' Penders. The present

Bald eagle preparing for takeoff. The name "bald" is derived from an Old English word, "balde," meaning white. (*Ken Meadows*)

The Bald Eagle

The Pacific coast has the largest population of bald eagles in Canada, and surveys from the early 1970s indicate that one of the greatest concentrations within the province occurs in Barkley Sound. In 1987 at least twenty-five nesting sites were recorded in the Broken Group Islands alone.

Eagles mate for life and return annually to the same nest location. Each year a new assemblage of sticks is added to the nest, eventually forming an aerie up to 4-m (13 ft) wide and 3-m (10 ft) deep. Within Barkley Sound, the tall Sitka spruce is understandably the tree of choice for nesting as many of the trees close to salt spray are spruce trees.

The eagle is a proficient predator, and the shorelines within Barkley Sound offer an inexhaustible food supply. Tide pools with shellfish and crabs and shallow bays teeming with unwary fish all provide the raptor with food. Sea birds are also preyed upon. No doubt paddlers have observed the respect paid a soaring eagle as hundreds of birds lift to the air and remain in flight until the eagle is out of sight.

Frequently, many eagles will flock around a rich food source such as carrion or a fish run. The most spectacular sighting in Barkley Sound was recorded in Imperial Eagle Channel in 1970 when sixty-three eagles were seen soaring and feeding around a shrimp boat during the summer. (Hatler, Campbell and Dorst) name honours Father Brabant, a nineteenth-century missionary who travelled by canoe in an attempt to keep up with his somewhat nomadic flock. He eventually set up a permanent mission at Hesquiat, north of Tofino.

A couple of stone fish traps are visible in the shallows between Mence and the easternmost islet. An enormous eagle nest located on the outer shore of the unnamed islet is a noteworthy landmark. The crossing from here to Dodd is about .75 mi.

Trip 29 — Dodd, Willis and Turtle Islands

Distances: – Dodd campsite to Willis campsite (1 mi)
                        – Willis to Dodd campsite via outside of Dodd (1.5 mi)
                        – Dodd campsite to Joe's Bay (.5 mi)

Highlights

Paddle sheltered waters in the lagoon defined by forested shores on Willis, Dodd and Turtle Islands. Onshore, explore an island kingdom scratched out of the West Coast by Salal Joe. Joe inhabited these shores for almost twenty years. Long ago, natives fished in this bay using stone traps — the rock enclosures still remain on the south end of Dodd Island. Under a magnificent canopy of evergreen on either Dodd or Willis Island, an inviting tent site waits for weary paddlers.

Considerations

This is one of the most protected paddling areas in the Broken Group. Waters are sheltered from prevailing summer winds, especially within the natural harbour defined by Willis, Dodd and Turtle Islands. Only on occasion do winds spill through the gaps on either side of Willis Island to the extent that they deter progress. The only semi-exposed stretch of coast along this route is on the west side of Dodd. Novices and those who are experienced but who are avoiding exposed coastlines because of bad weather will appreciate this predominantly sheltered route.

Fogs can affect this entire area.

Although the route is described starting from the campsite on Dodd Island, it is paddled just as easily from the campsite on Willis Island.

The Route

On a midden on the northeast corner of Dodd Island is a secluded, forest-sheltered campsite. Land on the south-facing beach to access several tent areas dispersed among close-ranked evergreens. Adjacent to

Calm seas. The sheltered waterways found between the inner Broken Group Islands are protected from prevailing winds and swell. (*Bruce Holland*)

the camp area is a garden cleared years ago by Salal Joe. Dilapidated fencing and untended fruit trees are all that remain of his remarkable effort to domesticate a West Coast plot.

At low tide, walk southward along the east side of Dodd to a shallow bay midway along this shore. A faint stream bed marks the locale of a native site where beach-boulder alignments form three canoe runs.

The Dodd campsite fronts onto a natural harbour bounded by Willis, Dodd and Turtle Islands. Known locally as Turtle Bay, it is protected from all winds and is a favourite anchorage for visiting yachts. Paddle the perimeter of the bay, following the southeast shore of Dodd Island.

Just prior to rounding the island's most southerly point, take time to look at two fish traps located in the adjacent bay. The semi-circular rock alignments at the very head of the bay stand out in bold contrast to the mud-grey bottom. Walk to them at low tide, or paddle over them at high tide.

The narrow channel between Dodd and Willis Islands is one of the stretches along this route where paddlers may encounter winds. Because of the funnelling effect, they may be strong enough to impede passage.

Whether staying overnight or making a short stopover, you will find that the Willis Island campsite offers an irresistible combination of rain forest and protected sandy shores. Tent sites extend along the entire length of two sand beaches, all nestled under an extraordinary canopy of cedar and hemlock. The water supply spills into a wooden catchment a short distance from the Canadian Parks Service sign. For magnificent views of the setting sun, choose a secluded site on the west-facing beach. At low tide, walk out to adjacent islets where mussels, anemones and sea stars all share crowded quarters on barnacle-covered boulders. Wander woodland trails where massive cedars tower

---

Salal Joe

Salal Joe lived in the Broken Group Islands for over two decades. His real name was Joe Wilkowski, an Iranian immigrant, who, after working his way across Canada, settled permanently in Turtle Bay (about 1960). He got his nickname as he made a living by collecting salal branches and shipping them to distant florists via the *Lady Rose*. When the park was established, the friendly hermit was not evicted. Instead, he was hired to do casual labour, and he continued to live at Turtle Bay.

Joe disappeared in the summer of 1980 and is believed to have drowned off the tiny islands nearby. His scow, *Hello Nature*, was found on the rocks on Chalk Island, the throttle wide open (Obee), Joe was never found. The well on Turtle Island and dilapidated fencing that surrounds the few fruit trees at his Dodd Island garden are all that remain of his island kingdom.

---

above the forest floor. The circumference of one forest giant obviously draws attention as a well-worn path leads directly to it.

Paddle the outside of Dodd Island (if westerlies are not too strong) where bald eagles search the shallows from elevated perches. A single white-shell beach, hidden behind an unnamed islet, provides one of the few landings along this exposed shore. Round the northeast corner of Dodd Island and reenter Turtle Bay by heading through the narrow channel between Chalk and Walsh Islands and then navigating toward Joe's Bay. (The bay is not officially called Joe's Bay but is known as such by many. It is the largest bay on the northeast corner of Turtle Island.) The leather star obviously prefers these quiet waters as many of these red-brown stars are visible here.

The bay was home to long-time resident Salal Joe. His floating cabin is long gone, and only a disintegrating stone trap stands near to where his float house was once moored. His water well remains. Look for it along the stream bed on the pocket-shaped cove just inside the entrance to the bay.

Trip 30 — The Tiny Group, Jaques and Jarvis Islands

Distances: – Dodd Island to Jaques Island (2 mi)
　　　　　　　 – Willis Island to Jaques Island (2.5 mi)
　　　　　　　 – Jaques Jarvis lagoon to Gibraltar campsite (1 mi)

Highlights

Miniature islets and secluded shell beaches are always enticing. Those found within the Tiny Group are no exception. The largest representation

---

Moonsnails

No other snail could possibly be confused with this one. It is huge! The shell itself is up to 10 cm (4 in) wide, and when extended, the immense foot is the size of a dinner plate.

The moonsnail is carnivorous, ploughing along under the surface of the sand in search of clams. Once it finds its food, the moonsnail drills a neat hole through the victim's shell and then sucks out the meaty flesh. Next time you walk a beach littered with clam shells, look closely for the neat hole bored by the moonsnail. Perhaps most unusual is the rubber-like collar constructed by the huge snail. First-time viewers are often puzzled by these unique formations as they bear a remarkable resemblance to discarded rubber plungers. In fact, they are an egg case, containing hundreds of thousands of eggs sandwiched between two layers of sand and held together by mucous secretions. In mid summer the egg case crumbles and half a million free-swimming larvae are committed to the sea. (Ricketts and Calvin)

---

of bat stars and moonsnails in all of the Broken Group is found in the calm shallows between the tiny islets on the west side of Jarvis, as are several native canoe runs. The lagoon defined by Jaques and Jarvis Islands simply must not be missed. Here is an ancient fish trap, so well preserved that the stone walls remain an impressive 1 m (3 ft) in height.

Considerations

The waters along this route are sheltered. Because winds are reduced by surrounding islands, waves seldom build to a significant height. (It occasionally gets choppy between the Tiny Group and Jarvis Island.) The swell that pounds in on the outer islands hardly affects these protected shores.

This is an area recommended for inexperienced paddlers and for those choosing to avoid exposed routes because of inclement weather.

Fog can cover these inner islands, but unless it is thick, it will often burn off by noon.

The Route

Paddle from either Dodd or Willis Island through Turtle Bay and out to the Tiny Group. This delightful archipelago is well worth exploring by shallow-draft boat. Pass by tiny islets to view harbour seals hauled out on exposed rock ledges, and watch pelagic cormorants in their clumsy attempts at aerial takeoff. These awkward flyers must flap the water for long distances before successfully lifting to the air. Listen for the yodel-like call of the arctic loon, a common migrant that visits these waters in the spring and fall. Stop on one of two beaches. A small pocket of shells exposed at low tide between the south islets is the first beach that you will come to. The second is on the largest islet within the Tiny Group, on the shore that faces Jarvis Island.

Enter the calm waters between the unnamed islets on the west side of Jarvis Island. The natives even recognized the predictable calmness of these waters as their word for the area translated to "where it is always calm" (Inglis and Haggarty). Huge numbers of bat stars are visible in the clear shallows. Moonsnail casings are also plentiful, but more impressive is the presence of the moonsnails. On a September visit, I counted more than ten of these rarely visible creatures creeping over the mud bottom on their huge, extended feet.

Land on the beach where it links the one islet to Jarvis Island and where three obvious boulder alignments are visible, especially at low tide. Rock formations such as these three, and a fourth one hidden behind a rock outcrop on the west end of the same beach, were used as canoe runs by native peoples landing on these shores. Further evidence of native habitation is the midden deposits found in adjacent banks.

Hike to a sedge-covered slough in the next bay, a unique marine environment that is often found where the gentle rise and fall of the tides are not complicated by pounding surf. Since wave action is so slight, silt and decayed vegetation build up, effectively generating this marshy environment.

The lagoon defined by the shores of Jaques and Jarvis is a "must do." At high tide, pass through the southwest entrance. At low tide, the narrow gap dries, but the north entrance is passable at all times. Either way, don't miss exploring this fantastic feature.

Within the lagoon, an overwhelming silence prevails. Raucous sea birds sit quietly idle on calm seas. Reflections of forested shores are mirrored by the placid waters. Most impressive is a stone fish trap found at the south end of the lagoon with its well-preserved outer rock wall — well over 1-m (3 ft) high. Internal stone walls further divide the enclosure into at least four separate trap areas.

From the lagoon, paddlers may either return to the campsite on Dodd or Willis or head to the campsite on Gibraltar Island.

Trip 31 — Gibraltar, Reeks, Nettle and Prideaux Islands

Distances: – Gibraltar to Reeks Island (1 mi)
   – Reeks to Prideaux Island (2 mi)
   – Prideaux to Gibraltar Island (1.5 mi)

Highlights

Here is a route rich in contrast. Paddle surf-swept shores, then quickly retreat to quiet coves, winding waterways and a multitude of tiny islands. Pass the entrance to a fantastic sea cave, explore the dilapidated remains of an old mine shaft, or take in evidence of long-ago logging, then return to a forest-sheltered campsite on Gibraltar Island.

Considerations

In circumnavigating Reeks and Nettle Islands, kayakers paddle through generally protected waters. Those sections closest to Imperial Eagle Channel (the southern and outer shores of Reeks) are exposed to westerly winds and swell. Novice paddlers could avoid these potentially rougher waters by choosing to paddle between Reeks and Nettle, keeping well away from Imperial Eagle Channel.

Very infrequently, a strong southeaster could come up and significantly affect most waters along this route. By listening to marine weather forecasts, paddlers can quickly determine whether or not this is a risk.

Fog occasionally affects these waters as well.

This route is suitable for inexperienced paddlers if exposed sections are avoided.

The Route

Gibraltar Island campsite can be busy as it is closest to Sechart where paddlers arriving via the *Lady Rose* or *Frances Barkley* disembark. At least three times weekly these motor vessels unload paddlers and all their gear. Although some passengers paddle to campsites further afield, many will set up base camp on Gibraltar Island. Several forest-sheltered campsites accommodate visitors here. The prime locations are on a knoll overlooking the beach area. A waterfall trickles over a rock face just inland from the west end of the beach, but use this water only after boiling it for at least ten minutes.

Take your time to paddle the 1-mi distance between Gibraltar and Reeks Island, meandering past tiny islets that speckle the crossing. It is well worth the effort to get past the kelp-choked passages to get in close to the south shore of Reeks Island, a shoreline serrated with narrow surge channels, sea caves and tiny sand-fringed bays.

Pass around the outer shores of Reeks Island, and peer from water level into the above-tide entrances to sea caves. (It is virtually impossible to land here as even on the calmest day the swell breaks onto jagged rocks all along this exposed stretch of coast.) Those set up with trolling gear might consider fishing here. Both Turner Islet and Swale Rock are renowned hotbeds for coho and chinook.

Immediately past the northeast corner of Reeks, the harsh open water gives way to calm sheltered bays. Land on either of the two beaches on the north side of the island. Watch for raccoons as they frequent both these sand-lined bays, especially at low tide.

Throughout the Broken Group, harsh open water gives way to calm sheltered bays. Paddlers come ashore, lured by exploration of low-tide habitats and the need to stretch kayak-cramped muscles. (*Bruce Holland*)

As inviting as the beach on the south end of Nettle Island may appear, the area above the shore is part of a reserve. Visitors must have written permission from the Sheshaht Band prior to exploring these private lands. (Refer to the "Introduction to Barkley Sound" for details.)

Paddle around to the north side of Nettle Island, passing Glen Islet. California mussels on this islet are among the largest I have ever seen. Unfortunately, the Broken Group Islands are closed to the harvesting of shellfish (mussels, oysters and clams) due to paralytic shellfish poisoning (PSP). (Those unfamiliar with the threat of PSP, refer to "Shellfish Harvesting and Fishing" in the "Introduction to the Gulf Islands.") Avoid the horrible risks involved in consuming potentially contaminated bivalves, and leave mussels such as these behind.

A beach stretches northward from a rock reef on the backside of Nettle Island. Land on the south end of it, and hike along hard-packed sand, or walk the forest edge to a nearby stand of alder, a deciduous species that is often found in areas once cleared by logging. Sure enough, a short distance from the alder stand are several large cedar stumps with markings that show the original trees were cut using springboards. Loggers used to chop rectangular notches into the butt of a tree into which a board was inserted. They could then stand on the springboard when operating a falling saw (Gold). The most visible of these notches is found on a stump located high on a bank to the left of the creek bed.

The Mussel

Mussels form a living blanket, covering every inch of available space on suitable, surf-swept rocks. They have devised an ingenious method of attachment called a "byssus." This flexible thread, secreted by a gland at the base of the foot, anchors the animal to the rocks and, in crowded areas, to other mussels. The slender threads can be voluntarily dissolved and new ones formed, allowing the mussel to move to vacant space, an ability that partly explains why the mussel is so dominant in many intertidal areas throughout the Pacific Northwest. (Werthiem)

Because the mussel's chief enemy is the ochre star, the hardy bivalve is confined to a specific zone around the mid-tide level, out of reach of hungry starfish predators.

Dining on the bivalve is not recommended during the summer (in fact, the Federal Department of Fisheries bans their collection) as the mussel accumulates a minute organism that causes paralytic poisoning in humans.

From Nettle Island, paddlers look directly across Sechart Channel to the remains of the only whaling station ever established within Barkley Sound. This turn-of-the-century operation was very successful – up to five hundred humpback and fin whales (no longer seen here) were taken in a season that stretched from April to August. But success also brought about the industry's demise. The station shut down when the whales became scarce. Sechart Whaling Station is now used as a port of call by Alberni Marine Transportation. Paddlers disembarking from the *Lady Rose* or *Frances Barkley* head to the Broken Group from this point.

Paddle on to the bay on the southeast corner of Prideaux Island. Out on the point is an old mine shaft. A cobble slag heap, concrete platforms, a cement staircase and the shaft entrance are all that remain of this copper mine. (Please, do follow the example of others and dump garbage down the shaft.)

Don't miss paddling the quiet waters between Nettle and Denne Islands. The only sound that breaks the silence here is the staccato call of a kingfisher.

You will pass several unnamed islets en route to the large bay on the south side of Nettle Island. The float cabin within the bay is used by the park wardens, but it is unlikely that you will find them here as they are often out on patrol in the park's zodiac. (A black triangle on chart No. 3670 pinpoints the exact location of the cabin.) In the event of an emergency, leave a message as the wardens are equipped to offer assistance and are in frequent radio contact with park headquarters.

The crossing from Nettle back to Gibraltar Island is .5 mi.

Grey Whales – The Gentle Giants

The whale that paddlers are most likely to see in Barkley Sound is the grey. These marine giants leave the warm calving lagoons off the coast of Baja, California, and swim slowly northward on the first leg of an incredible 20,000-km (12,4000 mi) round trip from Baja to the Bering Sea and back – the longest migration of any mammal. Most pass by the mouth of Barkley Sound in March and April, but summer paddlers who feel they have lost a chance to see the greys needn't despair. A small number spend the entire summer along the west coast of Vancouver Island. Sightings are not common, but they do occur, especially in Loudoun and Imperial Eagle Channels and offshore of the outer islands.

The grey whale is a bottom-feeder, diving to the ocean floor and twisting sideways to suck in mouthfuls of mud. The whale then rolls upright and swims toward the surface, pushing its immense tongue against the roof of its mouth. Water and mud are squeezed out through comb-like baleen. Anything too large to escape is trapped and swallowed.

Today, populations of grey whales on the Pacific coast are increasing, but this was not always so. In the year 1900, the once-abundant whale was almost declared extinct after American whalers discovered how easy it was to take the greys in calving lagoons. (The whaling station at Sechart did not take the greys. They were primarily interested in the humpbacks and fins. Over the several years that the station operated, only one grey was taken.)

Since 1947, international protection has been granted to the grey whale (although a couple of hundred are taken each year by Russian natives). Today, paddlers visiting Barkley Sound can scan the ocean surface, searching for a distinct double-spray of mist that indicates the presence of these gentle giants.

Trip 32 – Gibraltar, Dempster and Wiebe Islands

Distances:
 - Gibraltar campsite around outside of Gibraltar Island to Dempster Island (1.5 mi)
 - Dempster to Wiebe Island (1 mi)
 - Wiebe Island to Gibraltar campsite (1.5 mi)

Highlights

The open Pacific relentlessly assaults the outer shores of Gibraltar, Dempster and Wiebe Islands, shaping narrow surge channels, dramatic sea caves and sea arches. Nowhere in all the Broken Group are these magnificent features so prevalent as here.

Considerations

The same forces that make this stretch of coast so impressive could also generate dangerous paddling conditions (especially for kayakers who are tempted to get in close to view the dramatic results of wave erosion).

Swell alone creates hazardous waters when it breaks over offshore shallows and spills onshore. Watch for breaking surf while travelling this coastline and particularly before entering confined channels.

These shores are fully exposed to the prevailing westerlies and to the occasional southeasters that blow through Imperial Eagle Channel. It is absolutely necessary to listen to wind predictions prior to paddling this route.

If fog rolls in, avoid paddling until it burns off. Because it follows exposed shoreline and because offshore breakers are common, this route is recommended for experienced paddlers only.

The Route

Paddle the outer coast of Gibraltar Island – a rugged stretch of coast comprised of sheer cliffs and boulder beaches. The entrance to a large sea cave is found on the south end of the island. As is common to many of these isolated sea caves, rock ledges inside are used for nesting by pelagic cormorants. If the adult birds are alarmed, they momentarily vacate the nest, exposing the eggs or nestlings to predation by crows and gulls. Please respect the sensitive nature of nesting birds from June through September, and peer into the dark caverns a fair distance from the entrance.

Take a short reprieve from the outer coast and cross Harbour Entrance to a bay midway along Dempster's north shore. Rock reefs exposed at low tide form an entrance to this lagoon-like bay. Look into the shallows for the multi-armed sunstar and colourful bat stars, or pull up on the sand beach and cross the narrow strip of land to explore the south-facing shore.

Paddle on to the exposed outer shores of Dempster Island. A spectacular sea arch comes into view, but only if conditions permit access to the head of the island's most easterly surge channel. Entrance to the channel is determined by tide levels and swell since at low tide, offshore reefs cause breakers that make entering the channel almost impossible. High tides and calm conditions are required to approach this remarkable feature.

Most impressive is an exceptional cove on the southwest corner of Dempster. A snag supporting two eagle nests best marks the cove's locale. Within this single bay are the entrances to three sea caves, the largest of which is referred to as the "blowhole cave." With each surge, sea water funnels into the constricted channel, generating an almost deafening

Cormorants

As Tim Fitzharris points out, this unusual bird has some rather negative attributes: "The cormorant does not endear itself readily to humans. It has a sinister, hawk-like visage, dark, greasy plumage, and a sickly croaking call; it feeds its young on regurgitated fish, and its breeding territories are plastered with its own haphazard droppings." However, this initial impression does not take into account the cormorant's incredible adaptive abilities.

Four species of cormorants are found on the Pacific coast, three of which breed in BC. The pelagic cormorant is the smallest and shows white flank-patches in May and June. It breeds along the entire coastline, but the largest colonies are around Vancouver Island. Just over four thousand pairs nest on inaccessible cliff ledges, sometimes hundreds of feet above the water. A few nest in caves. The larger double-crested cormorant is distinguished by an orange-yellow throat patch and tufts of feathers on either side of its head, the characteristic for which it has received its descriptive name. These crests disappear later in the breeding season. The last species, the medium-sized Brandt's cormorant, breeds only off the central west coast of Vancouver Island (in the vicinity of Barkley Sound) and off Long Beach. Its bluish and buff-brown throat patch is characteristic. In winter this species is abundant in the Gulf Islands' Active Pass.

The reason paddlers so often see cormorants perched upright on drift logs and rock outcrops with their wings half-spread is that wing and tail feathers lack waterproofing. Wind and sun are used to dry the sodden plumage.

Cormorants prefer high nesting sites to facilitate aerial takeoff. Pelagic cormorants nest on narrow shelves located along steep cliffs. Double-crested cormorants nest on gentle, sloping sides of rocky islands, and in two areas (Ballingal Islets and Bare Point near Chemainus), this species nests in trees. Brandt's cormorants nest on the sides of rocky islets. In Barkley Sound, some pelagic cormorants build their nests on ledges in sea caves. Nesting usually begins in mid May, and some young are seen as early as late June. But there may be eggs present within the nests until the end of August as persistent parents will lay another set if an earlier clutch is lost. For this reason, paddlers are asked to not enter sea caves in Barkley Sound from late May through August. When alarmed by your intrusion, adult birds inadvertently kick out young and eggs as they scramble to leave the nest. As well, eggs and hatchlings are left open to their most feared predator, the northwestern crow.

The final word on cormorants comes from a fellow kayaker. He describes them as the "bureaucratic bird" because they all look alike, all do everything at the same time, all fly away at the slightest provocation and all have trouble gaining altitude.

Paddling the outer shores of Gibraltar Island can be an exhilarating experience. All along the exposed shores, surf meets rock in a dynamic display of crashing waves and perpetual mist. Paddlers swing out from shore to avoid the erratic seas. *(Michael King-Brown)*

blow. Mist continuously surrounds the entrance. The middle cave is smaller, but it also generates a dramatic sound as water fills the ever-tightening channel. Although it has the largest portal, the third cave is perhaps the least impressive as it penetrates the rock cliff for the shortest distance. Do not approach the "blowhole cave" entrance because pelagic cormorants nest inside. You can still hear the dramatic effect of water entering this cave from the entrance to the cove.

Several features on Wiebe Island make the .75-mi crossing from Dempster Island worthwhile. Although exposed to prevailing winds and swell, the narrow channels between the rocky islets and Wiebe Island form a paddler's haven during calm conditions. Seals haul out on drying reefs and swim in the kelp beds. Oystercatchers probe the rocky shores with long red beaks, while cormorants perch with extended wings on low-tide rocks. On one occasion I watched as a gull attempted to swallow a blood star. The spiny creature posed a unique set of problems for the gull, but the midday meal was eventually consumed.

A sand beach is found on the east side of the rocky isthmus on the south end of Wiebe Island, but access is limited to high tides since low-tide rocks separate the beach from the sea. Midway along the south shore is an impressive sea arch, and a short distance away is the entrance to a sea cave.

Paddlers may choose a return route to Gibraltar Island campsite, passing the tiny Elbow Islets.

Others may wish to cross Coaster Channel to get to campsites on Turret and Gilbert Islands. Prior to selecting this option, check the sea conditions. Coaster Channel is entirely open not only to the prevailing westerlies, but also to southeasters. Although these are not the prevailing summer winds, they do blow occasionally, generating steep seas within the channel. It may be necessary to return to Gibraltar Island rather than paddle this wind-vulnerable stretch of water.

Trip 33 — Turret, Trickett and Lovett Islands

Distances: – Willis campsite to Turret campsite (2 mi)
         (add another mile if paddling the islets on the south side of
         Turret Island)

Highlights

Turret, Trickett and Lovett Islands and the dozens of offshore islets form a magnificent archipelago that is bound to impress. The prettiest shell beaches in all the Broken Group Islands, located on the north side of Trickett Island, are mere steppingstones to the jagged, wave-battered shores of Lovett Island. Paddle mirror-still waters between the tiny islets on Turret's south side, then camp beneath towering spruce. If you are shore bound because of bad weather, you needn't despair — there are kilometres of exciting shoreline to be explored by foot from Turret's campsite.

Considerations

Westerlies do affect the outer shores on Willis, Trickett and Lovett (especially when both wind and swell roll into the seaward side of the islands). These same winds also affect the waters in Coaster Channel. Listen to wind and swell predictions prior to paddling in this area since it is only semi-protected by the outer islands.

If you wake up in the fog, wait until it burns off before setting out.

In calm conditions, this route is suitable for inexperienced paddlers. In the event of a sudden change in the weather, there are several landings that permit a quick retreat. Avoid the likelihood of this action by listening to weather predictions prior to heading out.

The Route

Depart from Willis Island, embarking upon a .5-mi crossing of Thiepval Channel. The name "Thiepval" honours a shipwreck that lies on the bottom of the narrow pass to this day.

Navigate toward the gravel bar that joins Trickett and Turret Islands. Only during extreme winter tides is the gravel link covered by water; whereas in the summer, paddlers can land anywhere along the isthmus and explore driftwood-strewn beaches that run southward on Turret and northward on Trickett Island.

Thiepval

The *Thiepval* went aground in February of 1930, on an uncharted rock in the channel that now bears her name. Tall tales that surround her sinking describe the hot pursuit of a rumrunner, but the true circumstances were far less dramatic.

The *Thiepval* was one of four sister ships that patrolled the coast, enforcing fisheries regulations. While on a routine run between Bamfield and Ucluelet, she struck the uncharted rock in fair weather and daylight. The tide was falling, and soon her propeller was above water. Attempts to secure her were unsuccessful, and a day later the *Thiepval* took her final plunge, bow first. No attempt to raise her was ever made. She lay untouched for about thirty years until 1962 when a local group of divers raised the bow cannon. Restored and mounted, it now sits next to the village office in Ucluelet.

Her rusting hull remains largely intact, alive with marine invertebrates. The wreck is a popular dive site.

Paddle the north side of Trickett Island. Narrow surge channels penetrate this entire low-lying island. But most inviting are the glistening white beaches found on the island's west end. At low tides, access to them is sometimes difficult as boulders block the beach, but at high tide, access is easy.

The waterways between Trickett and the unnamed islets to the west dry at low tide, but when water levels permit, paddle between the tiny isles. The intertidal life is both luxuriant and colourful. On the north side of the largest islet is another white-shell beach, easily accessed at most tide levels. Paddlers in shallow-draft boats can usually get through the narrow channel between the islet and Lovett Island. Access Lovett's shores by landing on the sand beach that faces out to the channel you have just paddled through. From the beach, hike along the exposed western coastline. It is a bit of a scramble climbing over the jagged rocks, but the effort is well rewarded.

Rather than head directly to the campsite on Turret, paddle through the archipelago of tiny islands scattered along the island's southern shore. Nantes Island and a host of unnamed islets are open to the winter storms that roar in off the Pacific with a strength that is evidenced by the windswept evergreens clinging to cliff edges. Lower down on the same cliffs, purple and orange ochre stars hang in the coolness of rock crevices. Inside the exposed islets are others that are sheltered from the stormy seas. The surrounding waters are particularly calm, and the shallows are abundant with moonsnails, bat stars and occasionally the multi-armed sunstar. In these quiet bays where long ago the Nuu-chah-nulth people caught fish in stone traps, the blue heron now searches for prey.

Stars of the Sea

The sea star has been called "blind, toothless and slow-moving" (Fitzharris). Yet this creature is an effective predator and tenaciously searches the intertidal zone for clams and mussels. Once its victim is subdued, the star pushes its stomach between the mollusc's shells, and the tender meat is digested before the star retreats. The preferred food is the mussel, and the sea star will eat about eighty of them per year. But being opportunistic feeders, they will also go for limpets, chitons and snails.

The most common star on the Pacific coast is the ochre star, ranging in colour from orange to brown to purple. A tough skeleton made up of calcium plates that are held together by a network of muscles protects this star from being shredded by extreme wave action.

Leather stars, distinguished by a blotchy red-brown colour, also possess these calcium plates, but the plates are not so massive as the ochre star's, hence their distinct slimy appearance. (Deep-water stars are generally softer since their need for protection from pounding surf decreases.) Pick up a leather star, and hold it close to your nose. It has a garlic aroma.

The bat star, with its wide disc, is easily identified in Barkley Sound. Unlike most of its relatives, this star is both carnivorous and herbivorous, feeding mainly on seaweed. Look for its orange, purple and green tones in areas where the sea floor is muddy.

The sunflower star is the "all star sprinter" of the intertidal zone, having been clocked at an exceptional one-metre-per-minute pace, all the while coordinating up to twenty-four arms and fifteen thousand tube feet. Like many other sea stars, the sunflower possesses an exceptional ability to regenerate a lost arm within a year.

The sea star has few natural enemies since it is spiny and not very palatable. Gulls take a few, especially the smaller blood star, but the sea star's greatest predator is man. Many of us are tempted to take a brightly-coloured star home. However, those who do so discover that they soften and quickly become smelly in the kayak's forward hatch. Leave these leggy creatures where you find them.

If turned upside-down, the sea star can right itself, but the process takes about an hour. Specimens that have been examined on the kayak's spraydeck should be returned to the sea in an upright position.

Land at the base of a clearly visible midden on the largest bay on this side of Turret Island. Have a midday meal on the secluded grass berm, then walk inland, following a nearby creek bed to a cedar stump that bears scarring from springboards.

On the northwest end of Turret is a campsite sheltered by an adjacent point of land and a small unnamed islet. Paddlers can land on the

Drift Logs

It's almost hard to imagine, but at one time drift logs did not line the beaches on our west coast. Most of the debris today is the result of logs being transported decades ago in Davis rafts.

These rafts were constructed of timbers, forming a log carrier almost 300-m (984 ft) long, 10-m (33 ft) deep and 13-m (43 ft) wide. They took weeks to build, and yet within minutes heavy seas could dismantle them, throwing hundreds of logs into the sea.

More-seaworthy barges have replaced these rafts, yet the logs that were washed ashore years ago still line most of our coast.

south-facing beach and climb a midden bank to the top of the hill where tent sites are found in spectacular rain forest settings. Most impressive — and towering metres above the tent clearings — are giant Sitka spruce. These spruce are extremely tolerant of salt spray and often dominate the coastal forest.

Paddlers who find themselves bound to shore by inclement weather will appreciate the exploring that can be done from here by foot. Follow the shoreline toward Trickett Island, initially clambering over a massive pile-up of drift logs. Head to the most westerly point on Turret Island where stone fish traps and a couple of canoe runs are visible, especially at low tide. Round the point, and continue to explore sand beaches that line Turret's northern shores, then cross the gravel bar that links Trickett and Turret Islands. At low tide, you can walk completely around Trickett. Make this a gumboot trek, and get in for a close-up view of the intertidal life found along these shores.

Trip 34 — Clarke and Benson Islands

Distances: – Turret campsite to Clarke campsite (1.5 mi)
   – Clarke campsite to Benson campsite (.5 mi)
   – Circumnavigation of Benson Island (1.5 mi)

Highlights

Clarke and Benson are absolutely stunning. Tiny islets and low-tide rocks line the access to sand-fringed shores. Onshore, there are open meadows, magnificent rain forests and primitive cross-island trails. The site of a turn-of-the-century hotel and a remarkable blowhole on the outer shore of the same island are just two of the rewards awaiting

Driftwood is scarce in the Broken Group, especially around the designated campsites. This paddler returned to Benson Island campsite with an empty hatch of driftwood found in an isolated cove. (*Mary Ann Snowden*)

those visiting Benson. Return to Clarke Island, or set up your tent under the shade of fruit trees in Benson's meadow. In the early morning, watch black-tail deer as they graze the nearby grasses.

Considerations

Coaster Channel is only semi-protected from prevailing summer winds, but most exposed are the outer shores of Clarke and Benson. Here, the force of westerlies is not diminished by other islands, so if strong winds are predicted, this route should be avoided.

Swell rolls unobstructed onto the outer shores of Clarke and Benson, and even to the experienced paddler, this can be unsettling. The greatest danger exists when swell breaks onshore. Swing well out from headlands to avoid the turbulence caused by these Pacific rollers.

Fog frequently covers these outer islands (especially in the late summer and early fall), and when thick, it drastically reduces visibility. Listen to fog predictions before heading out, and always travel with a compass.

Novices paddlers should across Coaster Channel from Turret to Clarke Island in calm conditions only. Paddling beyond these semi-protected waters, especially around the outer shores of Clarke and Benson, is not for the inexperienced, no matter how calm the seas.

The Route

The most direct route from the Turret campsite to Clarke Island includes a 1-mi crossing of Coaster Channel. Paddle the inside of Owen Island to access Clarke from the east.

While surf pounds the shores of the outer islets, waves quietly lap the

Japanese Drift

Walk the high tide line of any of the lesser-travelled outer beaches in Barkley Sound, and you are likely to find drift debris of Japanese origin. Plastic containers for products from motor oil to ketchup display familiar North American graphics, yet have Japanese characters. Glass balls that have broken away from Japanese fish nets are the prized find of beachcombers visiting the area early in the season. (Some of the "garbage" is not quite so exotic – it has been dropped overboard from freighters crewed by Japanese.)

The combined effect of the Kuroshio Current, the West Wind Drift and the North Pacific Equatorial Current carries objects along on a slow-moving circuit around the north Pacific ocean. Some items come across and land on our shores months after their release into the sea. Others are condemned to make several circuits, touching both sides of the north Pacific rim many times before landing. Strong onshore winds bring these high-sea voyagers onto our shores, ending their perpetual cycle.

Japanese Hydrographic Service vessels have dropped bottled messages off the coast of Japan in an attempt to determine how long these Pacific journeys last. The time between the date dropped overboard and the date recovered has varied from one to several years, although one bottle picked up near Kyuquot (at the north end of Vancouver Island) indicated a crossing time of only six months. (Nicholson)

white beach on the north side of Clarke Island. Land on the sandy shore, and access tent sites hidden in the forest fringe. Solitude seekers, head to the west-facing beach (the sundown side of Clarke) where the view of sunsets over offshore islets is unforgettable. (Past visitors will remember the cabin that stood on these shores. This shelter is no longer there.)

West Coast fog often settles in over the Broken Group, and although it may burn off over the inner islands by noon, it can persist over the outer islands for an entire day. In these conditions, many paddlers choose to stay onshore. On Clarke, spend some of these shore-bound hours exploring an extensive network of island trails. (These trails are not maintained by Parks personnel. They are here because of a summer residence that once existed in this area.)

The most visible trail leads to a delightful cove on the east side of the island. (Many visitors are tempted to pitch their tents here. Those who do so will be asked to move by the park warden as this is not a designated camp area.) Nearby is a concrete cistern that was likely the communal water supply for past summertime residents. Water collection is made easier by the cement structure, but be sure to boil the liquid before drinking it.

Hike a lesser-travelled route that departs from the main trail a couple of hundred metres from the campsite. (In wet weather, gumboots may be necessary on the muddy sections.) Follow this narrow path as it winds through the ever-present salal and exits onto a beautiful sand beach on the southwest side of Clarke Island. Early-season beachcombers should search the beach litter above the cove's high tide line. Much of the debris is of Japanese origin, and there is a chance of finding the comber's ultimate prize – the Japanese glass ball.

Return to the campsite, retracing the previously described route. Or if you prefer an orienteering challenge, head into the forest from the south end of the cove. From here I found a trail winding through the salal only to discover that it soon faded. A short distance away, another trail appeared, encouraging a search for what I was sure would soon be the obvious route. Eventually, the "on again, off again" trail led down to a sand beach – only 100 m (328 ft) from my campsite! See for yourselves how short a return route this is. While trekking through the forest, also be on the lookout for Columbian black-tails, a small deer that inhabits the island. A smaller version of the interior mule deer, the black-tail has adapted well to life on the coast and is often seen swimming across saltwater straits. Its distinct cloven-hoofed tracks are frequently visible along Clarke's sand beaches.

Paddle along the eastern or western shores of Clarke to Benson Island. The eastern shore is usually the more sheltered and offers views of Clarke's most impressive landmark – an enormous sea stack. This remarkable column of rock rises many metres from the sea, completely detached from adjacent cliffs.

Whereas the western shore of Clarke is the more exposed, it is also perhaps the more interesting. Prior to the 1800s, these waters were home to the sea otter, a mammal that no longer lives in Barkley Sound. Paddle through the luxuriant kelp beds between the islets, and listen for the shrill call of the oystercatcher. Look closely at the varied intertidal life ranging from barnacles and anemones to mussels and stars.

Although Pacific swell ravages exposed shores a short distance away, the narrow passage between Clarke and Benson is usually calm. Only if strong westerlies or southeasters are blowing do waves spill into this quiet channel. Land on the sand beach on the north side of Benson, just inside of a navigational beacon. Benson Island is a personal favourite with its unique history, open meadow and an enticing network of cross-island trails.

Set up tents in the meadow immediately above the beach or in forest-sheltered locations above the high tide line. Common throughout these damp woodland locations, and deplored by most newcomers, is the banana slug. Given a choice, these voracious eaters prefer wild mushrooms, but they will check out anything that smells good. Avoid slugs crawling along the inside of your favourite pot by covering all cooking utensils.

The Sea Otter

Let's start by clearing up a case of mistaken identity. The otter most often seen on the Pacific coast is not a sea otter, but rather the river otter, a species that has adapted well to a marine environment.

Prior to the 1800s, sea otters inhabited the entire coast of BC, yet by the 1900s this delightful little animal was approaching extinction. The reason for this was a dense coat of fur that was highly prized by Asian aristocracy. A single sea otter pelt fetched such a high price that it led to rampant exploitation, first by Russian, then American and European traders. There was no thought of conservation among those determined to gain immediate profit, and so after 150 years of unabated hunting, the animal was all but completely eliminated. Fortunately, remnant populations remained off the coast of Alaska and California.

Recently, 89 otters were transferred from Alaska to the Bunsby Islands, south of Vancouver Island's Brooks Peninsula. They have established themselves well in the area, and their numbers had increased to almost 350 in 1984 (Baird), but the sea otter remains a rare sight in BC waters. Otter sightings in Barkley Sound are almost guaranteed to be river otters.

John Benson is responsible for the island's name and the meadow that is such a popular camp location today. This sealing captain arrived on Benson in 1893, whereupon he constructed a small hotel. In order to provide for his guests, he cleared part of the island and planted a garden and orchard. Apple and cherry trees still grow in the meadow almost a century later. The hotel operated by him and his wife for almost thirty years finally closed its doors in 1922.

Start out on an exploration of this island by taking the trail through the meadow, then dropping down through the forest to an isolated cove on Benson Island's east side. A tree-crowned sea stack marks the seaward entrance to this delightful sand cove. Many paddlers choose to take advantage of sweeping views across Coaster Channel by setting up camp in one of the forest-sheltered sites. John Benson must have recognized the beauty of this location as he built his hotel here. A towering chestnut tree stands in recognition of his incredible effort to domesticate this isolated isle.

Return to the main trail, and follow signs that lead to the water supply. Prior to reaching the creek catchment, take a right turn onto a little-used path where a dense growth of salal causes many first-time visitors to turn back. Be persistent. Cross over logs, and continue along this overgrown path, and eventually the 400-m (1300 ft), tunnel-like route opens onto the outside of Benson Island. Drop down to the exposed beach, and head southward to a prominent surge channel. Water funnels into this constricted channel, producing a near-deafening thunder. At high tide, the enormous volumes of water create a dramatic blowhole. Natives gave this shore a name that means "sound of surf in the rock" (Inglis and Haggarty).

Walk from the blowhole to the outermost bluffs where alternating bands of black and white rock have formed extraordinary patterning in the steep cliffs. Continue exploring the boulder beaches and the surge channels that are so typical of such exposed shorelines. Watch the swell crash over Sail Rock, then return to Benson's campsite, following the previously described trail.

Few paddlers land on Benson without a desire to paddle around her outer coastline, and understandably so — this stretch of exposed coast is magnificent. But conditions can make paddling here dangerous. Offshore breakers are prevalent throughout the Pigot Islets and in shallows off Benson's south shore. Surf washes up over cliff edges, then sloshes back to meet incoming swell, creating erratic seas. Add wind-generated waves to these already tumultuous waters, and you have conditions that are unsafe for paddlers of all levels. Check the weather, and if calm conditions prevail, then paddle these shores, swinging well out to avoid close-to-shore turbulence and watching constantly for offshore breakers.

From Benson Island's campsite, paddle toward the Pigot Islets where pelagic cormorants are often found. Paddle on toward Sail Rock, a barren rock named by past schooner captains that bears a remarkable resemblance to a sail from some angles. From a comfortable distance, watch powerful cresting swells as they break over the shallows off the south end of Benson and nearby Verbeke Reef. Return to quieter waters on the east side of Benson, passing by the island's prominent sea stack.

Trip 35 — Batley, Wouwer, Howell, Cree and Dicebox Islands

Distances:
- Benson to Batley Island (1.5 mi)
- Batley to Dicebox Island via the outside of Wouwer and Howell Islands (2.5 mi)
- Batley to Dicebox Island via the inside of Wouwer and Howell Islands (1 mi)
- Dicebox to Cree Island and back (1.5 mi)

Highlights

Nowhere in all of the Broken Group is the ruggedness of the open coast more obvious than on Wouwer Island. Here, swell meets rock in a dramatic display of crashing waves and a welter of spray. Seemingly oblivi-ous to the furious seas are the sea lions that have dominion over the tiny islets off Wouwer. For the experienced only, this stretch of coast offers some exhilarating paddling.

Those who prefer to leave the harshness of the open sea for others to explore might follow an alternative route where calm seas lap the sandy shores of secluded coves. Cross a semi-sheltered bay to access a huge tide pool that is packed with intertidal life. And be sure to land on a remarkable little isle, Dicebox, where a fortification site, including no less than twenty traditional longhouses, once stood.

Considerations

The Coaster Channel crossing and the outer shores of Wouwer are un-protected from adverse conditions. If strong westerlies blow, they blow totally unleashed. Check weather conditions prior to paddling, and if strong winds are predicted, save paddling this route for a calmer day.

Even in calm conditions, both onshore and offshore breakers in the shallows around Verbeke Reef and off the south coast of Wouwer and Howell Islands would intimidate the novice. Coupled with the fact that there are no suitable landings on these exposed stretches of coast, pad-dling in these areas is not for the inexperienced.

If visibility is good and seas are calm (and weather forecasts indi-cate they will likely stay that way), inexperienced paddlers could consider paddling sheltered sections along the inside of Wouwer and Howell Islands, but keeping in mind the exposed waters in Coaster Channel that must be crossed to get there. Exercise extreme caution before choosing to paddle in this area.

Fog is always a possibility here. If you wake up to it, or if it is pre-dicted, avoid this route.

The Route

Access to Batley Island requires crossing the exposed, 1-mi wide en-trance to Coaster Channel, during which paddlers should keep well away from cresting waves around Verbeke Reef.

Batley's wind-battered shores are fantastic, especially when viewed from a paddler's vantage. Two sea caves on the northeast corner of the island are particularly noteworthy. The larger of the two is the more impressive since dramatic cliffs surround its entrance. Listen from a distance for a thunderous noise as surging waters fill the confined space. Do not enter the surge channel that fronts this particular cave for two reasons. First, the swell that is forced into this constricted pass creates hazardous conditions for paddlers. Second, cormorants nest on ledges inside the cave.

Few intertidal animals inhabit these surf-swept shores, and those

Both California and Steller sea lions pull up onto jagged rocks around Batley and Wouwer Islands. They are not generally aggressive, but do watch them from a respectable distance. (*Bruce Holland*)

that do must be specially adapted to tolerate the rigorous pounding of heavy seas. Sea stars, with their numerous tube feet, and mussels, anchored to the rock by thread-like hairs, are among those that can hold on in the face of crashing waves.

One other creature that is seemingly oblivious to pounding surf is the sea lion. Both California and Steller sea lions pull up onto the jagged islets between Batley and Wouwer Islands, arriving here from distant breeding grounds in the late summer. They are generally not aggressive, but do watch them from a respectable distance. Paddle in too close, and they plunge into the water, intimidating most paddlers simply because of their size.

Paddle sheltered waters to a sand-fringed bay fronting the narrowest neck of land on Wouwer Island. A trail starts from this cove. Within a short distance it leads onto the island's exposed southeastern shore where a tangled mass of drift logs covers the upper beach. Adventurous hikers can scramble southward along the jagged rocks to a grass berm where, centuries ago, a native village once stood.

Return to the sheltered cove on the north side of the island to continue on with one of two route options. The first route follows Wouwer's exposed outer shores, and the second follows a sheltered inside route. Weather conditions and paddling ability (this section is not for the inexperienced) will determine which is the better of the two choices.

Follow the outer route to view two islets off Wouwer's western shore. Here is the most renowned sea lion haul-out within Barkley Sound. In their attempts to capture these magnificent animals on film, photographers will

California and Steller Sea Lions

Both the California and Steller sea lions return annually to winter haul-outs at the south end of Vancouver Island. Although the two species are often found together, they are easily distinguished as the Californias are smaller and have a darker pelage. They bark, whereas the Stellers have a deep growl.

Only the males return, appearing in late summer and early fall on rocky islets adjacent to Wouwer Island in the Broken Group and the Deer Group's Folger Island. Early arrivals to Race Rocks near Victoria appear in September. Many individuals remain at these three haul-outs throughout the non-breeding season, although some disperse to haul-outs scattered throughout the Gulf Islands. Most of them return to distant rookeries in the spring, and of the few who remain, most are adolescents. The California sea lions return to islands off the coast of California and Mexico, while the Stellers return to one of three rookeries off the coast of BC: Cape St. James on the south end of the Charlottes, Danger Rocks in Hecate Strait or the Scott Islands off the north end of Vancouver Island.

When the rigorous battle for territory begins (on distant rookeries only), the bulls are in splendid physical condition (weighing up to 1,000 kg, or 2,200 lb). During the next two months, they do not leave their chosen ground for food or drink and must rely upon stored fat reserves. Most will lose up to 200 kg (450 lb) (Bigg and Olesiuk). Soon the females arrive and within days give birth to offspring of the previous year's mating. Meanwhile, impatient bulls are anxious to accept them into their territory, so within two weeks of the birth of pups, the fervent activity of mating begins.

Newborns quickly learn to avoid wrestling bulls, but pup mortality at this stage is high. They receive only minimal care from indifferent and otherwise-occupied mothers. During sporadic nursings, the pups do receive a fat-rich milk that guarantees a rapid accumulation of necessary body blubber.

By the end of July, excessive physical activity and a lack of food reduce the once-arrogant males to exhaustion. They must now return to the sea to replenish body stores. The Stellers travel within a few miles of shore to southerly winter haul-outs, while the Californias begin their northward migration. Although the females also move out, they remain closer to the breeding rookery, tending the newborn pups.

All species of sea lions and seals have been protected from commercial hunting with predator control programs since 1970. As a result, the numbers of California sea lions in particular have increased considerably. However, controversy surrounds these increased populations. Fishermen claim sea lions drastically deplete fish stock, especially salmon, and that these huge mammals destroy nets. Thus far, biological studies indicate that they feed mainly on herring and hake. (Bigg and Olesiuk) appreciate the dramatic backdrop provided by barren, surf-swept islets. Note: the best shots will be taken with a telephoto lens since swell and the behaviour of the sea lions (they will dive into the water if you get too close) prohibit getting near the islets.

If swells are high, watch for offshore breakers all along this side of Wouwer. Charts indicate where there are shallows, and in particular, note those offshore and inside of the sea lion haul-out. (This island was at one time appropriately named Storm Island.)

In adverse conditions, paddle the inside route along Wouwer's northern shore where beaches are protected from most westerlies by tiny offshore islets. Spend some time exploring the shallows between the islets, or head for shore to stretch out in the sun.

Whether you have paddled the inner or outer route, be sure to visit Wouwer's southeast bay where at low tide an extensive reef encloses a large area, trapping receding waters and forming a huge intertidal aquarium. (You can access this impressive feature from the bay to the west where potential landings along a rocky shore vary with the tide. Most are far from ideal, yet in spite of landing obstacles, this stopover is well worth the effort. Just be sure to tie boats securely as a flooding tide will quickly fill this shallow bay.) Walk the perimeter of the giant tide pool to view resident anemones, purple ochre stars, red coralline algae and California mussels.

Head to the middle of the bay (above the tide pool) to see three aboriginal fish traps. They are easily spotted as the boulder alignments stand out in bold contrast to the muddy bottom. Return to the boats, and if conditions permit, head toward the outside of Howell Island.

The outer shores of Howell and Wouwer are similar, yet the cliffs on Howell are steeper, higher and generally more impressive, especially when viewed from a paddler's vantage. But this island's outer shoreline is totally exposed to wind and swell. This section is not recommended at all for the inexperienced, and if weather conditions are at all doubtful, even the experienced should paddle the sheltered waters on the inside of this island.

Dicebox Island is a favourite stopover. Paddlers who return to the Broken Group year after year simply do not tire of this island gem. Even the natives honoured this spot with a name that translates as "a place where you don't feel like leaving" (Inglis and Haggerty). Land on one of two pebble beaches found on the north and south sides of the island. The north beach is the more sheltered.

Dicebox is comprised of two elevated bluffs joined in the middle by a lower berm. A trail traverses the berm, linking one beach to the other. The canoe run, visible at low tide on the south beach, was used long ago by the native peoples who landed here. A major village once stood on the berm, but of greater significance is the huge defensive site that formerly stood on the east bluff. Scramble up the steep slope from the eastern end of the south beach. Shell midden is visible all along the upward climb. Archaeologists have identified more than twenty house platforms extending along the top of this hill, across the lower saddle and over the slightly higher hilltop. All evidence of these historic dwellings is hidden by dense undergrowth, but anyone attempting the climb can't help but feel awed by the location of this remarkable site. The group who once lived here abandoned the area in the early 1800s, but not before they successfully defeated an Ahousat war party by rolling logs down the steep slopes onto the attackers (McMillan and St. Claire).

Explore the remaining Dicebox shores by boat. A sea cave is visible from the water on the island's southeast end and can be entered by foot at low tide. The tunnel penetrates the island to an opening on an adjacent shore.

Cree Island, a little more than .5 mi from Dicebox, might appeal as a sidetrip, but weather conditions demand consideration since this area is fully exposed. Watch for cresting waves where swell pushes over the shallows between Dicebox and this outermost Broken Group isle.

Cree's precipitous cliff was once used as a lookout by natives watching for invading tribes and seeking pelagic wanderers such as the grey whale. Today, few land here. The entire shoreline is lined with jagged rocks and steep cliffs. Only pigeon guillemots build nesting sites on the remote island where their eggs are effectively isolated from predators (Campbell). Offshore, sports fishermen seek the chinook salmon that are so plentiful here.

From Dicebox, paddlers can return to Clarke and Benson campsites or head north to the campsite on Gilbert. The return to Benson and Clarke Islands is about 2.5 mi. The distance to Gilbert Island is just under 1 mi.

Trip 36 — Gilbert, Austin and Effingham Islands

Distances:
- Gilbert to Austin Island (.75 mi)
- Austin Island to Effingham Bay (2.5 mi)
- Effingham Bay to Gilbert Island (.5 mi)

Highlights

No islands could more fittingly outline the eastern edge of the Broken Group than Effingham and Austin Islands. They possess all the features attractive to exposed shorelines: the remains of shipwrecks, impressive bluffs, a native village site, caves and sea arches, tiny offshore islets and pelagic birds in abundance.

Cedar Bark Harvesting

The inner bark of the red cedar was harvested by virtually all native groups along the coast of BC. In split, twisted or shredded forms, it provided clothing, mats, blankets, brushes, torches, towelling, rope, bandages and even diapers. (Elldridge and Stryd)

Suitable trees for stripping had to be small in diameter as a young cedar's bark is more pliable. The trees had to have straight trunks, be without large branches and be easily accessible from the water – an exacting set of criteria that is met by the cedars on Gilbert.

Bark gathering was a task carried out almost entirely by women. After selecting a tree, they would make a cut near the base of the trunk. Then, grabbing hold of the freed bark, they would back away from the tree, pulling the long ribbons with a twisting motion. Strips anywhere from 3 to 5-m (10-16 ft) long were removed in this manner during the summer and spring when the sap was running. The inner and outer bark were then separated, and the inner bark was bundled and packed into waiting canoes. (Stewart, 1984)

On the inside of Effingham is a huge bay where, two centuries ago, Captain Barkley embarked upon an exploration of an area that would eventually bear his name. On Gilbert, historically significant cedar trees, long ago stripped of their bark, stand amidst secluded tent sites.

Considerations

Swell rolls up Imperial Eagle Channel, breaking over cliffs on the outside of Effingham and Austin Islands and creating erratic wave activity. The turbulence is avoided (in calm conditions) by travelling a short distance from shore.

Of greater risk is the openness of these shores to prevailing westerlies. (When winds blow, they form waves, and when these waves combine with the existing swell, they create hazardous paddling conditions.) Listen to wind predictions prior to selecting this route.

All these hazards are compounded if fog rolls in. Avoid paddling here if fog is present or if it is predicted. Even when visibility is good, take your compass with you.

Since most of its shoreline is cliff-edged and exposed with few places to land, this route is recommended for experienced paddlers only.

The Route

A delightful pocket-shaped beach welcomes paddlers to Gilbert Island, and although the campsite appears dark from the water, visitors will discover the forest is surprisingly open. Several large areas for setting up camp are available here.

Wreck of the *Vanlene*

The *Vanlene* sailed from Nagoya, Japan, on February 24, 1972, with a crew of thirty-eight and a cargo of three hundred Dodge Colts. On March 4, she grounded on a reef off Austin Island in heavy fog. At that time, an S.O.S. gave her location as somewhere off the Washington coast – almost 100 km (60 mi) away from where she actually was!

How the *Vanlene* could have been stranded so far off her estimated position was a mystery until further investigation revealed the ship's echo sounder, radar and radio direction-finder were not operational when she approached the West Coast. Apparently, the radar had failed while the ship was in Japan, but the set was not attended to because of the vessel's short twelve-hour stay in Nagoya. The *Vanlene* had crossed the Pacific using compasses!

Almost half of the cars were airlifted by helicopter, while scavengers attempted to remove what was left. The maimed *Vanlene* was visible for several years, but by the late 1970s, she had slid beneath the waves. The Pacific had claimed yet another vessel, and a decaying hulk became home to innumerable marine creatures.

Nearby cedar trees show a unique scarring left behind by natives who once stripped their bark. Because both the inner and outer bark were removed, bare wood shows on the small-circumference cedars between the outhouse and the shoreline.

(Please, do not deface these significant trees in any way.)

Explore the forest beyond the campsite, and scramble through the salal to access a secluded south-facing cove. Take in the impressive panorama that includes Bauke and Dicebox Islands.

Gilbert's campsite provides the shortest route to Effingham Island. Paddlers can embark on a circumnavigation of this largest of the Broken Group Islands by heading through the narrow gap between Effingham and Gilbert Islands. Forested shores and steep cliffs deter landing along the initial stretch of this route, so be prepared for an hour or two of boat confinement.

Paddle between Austin and Bauke Islands, navigating toward the outer shores of Austin where incessant waves have carved a sea cave. Look for its gaping portal halfway along Austin's eastern shore, but do not get in close as once again cormorants nest in this cave. This rugged stretch of coast has claimed several ships over the years, the most recent being the *Vanlene*, an 8,000-ton freighter that smashed into a reef off Austin in March 1972.

From Austin, cross to Effingham Island where sheer rock bluffs rise over 50 m (165 ft) above sea level. Chasm-shaped surge channels and

Charles and Frances Barkley

Two hundred years ago, tiny vessels and bold sailors travelled the seven oceans in search of exotic places. In 1786 a young and beautiful Frances Trevor met and fell in love with the intrepid mariner Captain Charles Barkley. As a bride of seventeen, she left her English home and embarked upon a voyage during which she not only circumnavigated the world, but also became the first white woman to land on the coast of British Columbia.

Within five weeks of marriage, the couple left on a fur-trading expedition in a refurbished vessel, the *Loudoun*, which was later renamed the *Imperial Eagle*. They sailed around the Horn, landed in Hawaii, then sailed on to Vancouver Island's Nootka Sound. Once trade with the natives for the highly prized sea otter pelt was completed, they sailed southward and entered what henceforth was called "Barkley Sound."

Frances was an observant woman, recording her travels in a diary —from which in later life she wrote *Reminiscences*. Her diary has vanished, but *Reminiscences* exists today and is held by the BC Archives in Victoria. From it, the following account elaborates on the historic discovery of Barkley Sound: "We came to another very large sound, to which Captain Barkley gave his own name, calling it Barkley Sound. Several coves and bays and also islands in this sound we named. There was Frances Island, after myself; Hornby Peak, also after myself; Cape Beale, after our purser; Williams Point and a variety of other names, all of which are familiar to us. We anchored in a snug harbour in the island, of which my husband made a plan as far as his knowledge of it would permit. The anchorage was near a large village, and therefore we named the island Village Island. From here my husband sent the boats out to trade."

Three major channels, although not named by Barkley, eventually honoured the expedition. Imperial Eagle and Loudoun Channels recognize the sailing vessel, and Trevor Channel uses Frances's maiden name.

The Barkleys and crew eventually sailed to China, sold the sea otter pelts and returned to England, having circled the world. But the Barkleys' achievements received little attention — in part due to Charles Barkley's publishing no account of them, and in part due to a Captain John Meares's acquiring the Barkleys' log. Meares, a rather unsavoury character by most accounts, subsequently returned to the Pacific coast, and it is his published reports that take credit for the discoveries made a year before.

steep cliffs line this entire southern shoreline. Many paddlers lured by the hopes of attaining fresh water head into the bay where the outflow from the lake on Effingham enters the sea. The surf that pounds the rest of Effingham's shores also enters the bay, and if this constant wave action doesn't deter landing, then barnacle-covered boulders that line the entire shore will. I have spoken to several zodiac owners who have landed here and successfully reached the lake. However, as they described it, their endeavour was not worth the trouble. Thick undergrowth surrounds the lake, making it almost impossible to get to the water.

Effingham's easternmost point is Meares Bluff, a magnificent 100-m (328 ft) rock face commemorating Captain John Meares. He explored these islands in 1788, one year after the Barkleys made the initial discovery.

Just north of the bluff is one of the most impressive sea arches in all of the Broken Group — a massive rock bluff carved out by the sea. Pass through the wide tunnel if swell and tide levels permit safe passage.

Almost immediately upon exiting the arch, you will see the entrance to another wave-carved feature, a sea cave; however, access to it is dependent upon tides. The cave floor is sandy and at high tide is easily accessed, but at low tide, a rim of boulders stands between paddlers and the entrance. Evergreen boughs sweep across the cave mouth, effectively obscuring the opening. Inside, maidenhair fern drapes from the roof and walls of a massive cavern.

The bay fronting the Indian reserve is choked with tiny islets and low-tide rocks, creating a yachtperson's nightmare but a paddler's paradise. Paddle through the shallows to observe countless shore birds perched on exposed ledges, including pelagic cormorants, black oystercatchers, glaucous-winged gulls and bald eagles. Belted kingfishers sweep overhead, and harbour seals swim in the kelp-riddled waters.

A major village once stood on these shores, inspiring Captain Barkley's naming of Village Island. (Although the name was changed to Effingham one year later by Captain Meares, it was not recognized as such until the Hydrographic Service officially called it "Effingham" in 1933.) As the entire area above shoreline is reserve land, paddlers must have obtained written permission from the Sheshahts to explore ashore here. From the water you can see the grass-covered terraces where longhouses once stood. Besides a shell midden, there is little left of an exceptional village that was finally abandoned in the early 1900s.

A short distance beyond the reserve boundary is another sea arch. The narrow band of rock curves upward to join with yet another distinct feature, a sea stack. The base of this sea arch is well above high tide.

Paddle around the north tip of Effingham to an adjacent west-facing bay. There are a couple of native canoe runs here. Both of the white-sand tracks are visible, even when high tides cover them. Land on the pebble beach at the head of this bay to explore the forest fringe and the faint outline of a historic cabin. There is archival reference to this cove in the form of a letter from Anderson and Company, a London-based firm that built BC's first export sawmill in the Alberni Valley. Another of its ventures included a fishing station, and the letter of application written in the 1860s asking permission to set up the enterprise distinctly refers to this sheltered bay.

Jubilant paddler in Coaster Channel. (*Mary Ann Snowden*)

The best all-weather anchorage in the outer islands of the Broken Group is in Effingham Bay — a bay where the swells do not reach and the winds have little effect. Captain John Barkley chose to anchor here in 1787. He describes the port as "sufficiently capacious to contain a hundred sails of ships, and so fortunately to secure them from any storm."

Only paddlers who have permission to explore reserve areas may travel along a trail that leads from the cove at the head of Effingham Bay and heads to the village site on the south side of the island.

Past versions of chart No. 3670 indicate the water source on Effingham Island to be in the cove farthest along the south shore of Effingham Bay. Corrected charts show the water in its proper position, in the cove closest to the head of the bay. Paddle toward it while searching the eel grass shallows for moonsnail casings. Land on the sand beach, hike across the shell midden and wander through the open stands of cedar and hemlock. The nearby creek provides water.

Return to the designated camp area on Gilbert Island.

Trip 37 — Cooper and Camblain Islands

Distance: – Gilbert to Cooper Island (2.5 mi round trip)

Highlights

The Broken Group Islands are not often associated with sunbathing, but if weather permits, there are a couple of sand and shell beaches on this route that beckon would-be bathers. One shell beach is particularly alluring as it is very secluded. Another beach boasts one of the most reliable water sources in all the Broken Group. There is some paddling to be done among the tiny islets between Cooper and Camblain.

Considerations

Although the shores along the north side of Cooper and Gilbert Islands are predominantly sheltered from the prevailing winds, the waters on the south side of Cooper and in the pass between Cooper and Camblain Islands are not. The area is also exposed to the southeasters that infrequently blow. Check weather conditions prior to paddling this route.

In calm conditions, this route is relatively free of hazards and therefore can be enjoyed by novice paddlers. However, access to the area demands a long crossing through the exposed waters in Coaster Channel. Inexperienced paddlers should listen to weather predictions to be assured that seas will remain calm long enough for the return paddle to protected waters.

The Route

This is the final and the shortest of all the routes within the Broken Group area. A narrow passageway bounded by the unnamed islet off the northwest corner of Gilbert Island and Gilbert Island itself shouldn't be missed. The pass dries at the lowest tides; otherwise, paddle through to a tiny beach on the southeast side of the islet. The glistening white shells appear almost luminescent below the dark forest. Spend a couple of lazy hours in this secluded cove, far away from designated campsites and hidden from view to most passersby.

Continue toward Cooper Island. Midway along the southern shore is a tiny islet connected to Cooper at low tide. Land on the nearby beach. A tiny sea cave, only 1-m (3 ft) high, marks the eastern edge of this sandy shore. Walk westward along the forest perimeter to a creek that spills onto the sand. This is the most reliable (although uncharted) water source I've found in the Broken Group. Freshwater flows continue right through until September, but as with all water, boil the liquid for at least ten minutes before drinking.

Round the western tip of Cooper, and enter the shallow waters between it and Camblain Island. Here is an archipelago of tiny islets that is bound to please. Seals often haul out onto the sun-warmed rocks. Loons frequent these waters, especially in the spring and fall when migrant arctic loons pass through the area. In the shallows are countless clam shells, moonsnail casings and sea stars of every colour and size. Nearby is a sand and pebble beach on Cooper's shore, remarkable in that it is one of the few west-facing beaches in the area that is almost completely devoid of drift logs and debris. Look across to the steep-sided bluffs that line the entire perimeter of Camblain Island.

Return to Gilbert Island, following the northern shore of Cooper. Any one of several sand beaches found along this stretch of coast serves as an enticing stopover place.

APPENDICES

Kayak Speciality Shops and Rentals

Alberni Marine Transportation
PO Box 188
Port Alberni, BC   V9Y 7M7
phone: (250) 723-8313; fax: (250) 723-8314
Toll free reservations: 1-800-663-7192
Rentals and transportation to Broken Group Islands

Ecomarine Ocean Kayak Centre
1688 Duranleau Street
Vancouver, BC   V6H 3S4
phone: (604) 689-7575
Retail and rentals

Gabriola Cycle and Kayak Ltd.
RR 1, Site 1, C-23
Gabriola Island, BC   V0R 1X0
phone: (250) 247-8277; fax: (250) 247-9788
Retail and rentals

Gulf Island Sea Kayaking
RR No. 1
Galiano, BC   V0N 1P0
phone: (250) 539-2442
Retail and rentals

Island Spoke Folk/Saltspring Kayaking
104 McPhillips Avenue
Saltspring Island, BC   V8K 2T5
phone: (250) 537-4664 or (250) 653-4222
Retail and rentals

Jeune Brothers and Peetz
570 Johnson Street
Victoria, BC V8W 1M3
phone: (250) 656-9888; fax: (250) 380-1533
Retail and rentals

Mayne Island Kayak and Canoe Rentals
PO Box 40
Mayne Island, BC V0N 2J0
phone/fax: (250) 539-2667
Retail, rentals and camping

Mouat Point Kayaks
1615 Storm Crescent, RR #2
Pender Island, BC V0N 2M2
phone: (250) 629-6767
Rentals

North Island Water Sports/Discovery Kayaking
2755 Departure Bay Road
Nanaimo, BC V9S 3L7
phone: (250) 758-2488
Retail and rentals

Ocean River Sports
1437 Store Street
Victoria, BC V8W 3J6
phone: (250) 381-4233; fax: (250) 361-3536
Retail and rentals

Sea Trek Sports
9813 3rd Street
Sidney, BC V8L 3A6
phone/fax: (250) 656-9888
Retail and rentals

Tofino Expeditions
PO Box 620
Tofino, BC V0R 2Z0
phone: (250) 725-4222
Retail and rentals, B&B

Kayak Tour Companies

There are several kayak tour companies operating in the Gulf Islands
and Barkley Sound. Some have operated for many years, others are
relatively new, and others have folded. In order to obtain the most
current information, contact Tourism BC at 1-800-663-6000.

Equipment Checklist

Kayak Equipment

paddle(s)
spare paddle
spray skirt
life jacket
pump or bailer
sponge

Safety Equipment

flares and smoke device
marine weather radio or VHF
rescue equipment: paddle float, rescue loop
whistle
tow line
fibreglass repair kit (where applicable)
rudder repair kit
duct tape
wet suit (if desired)

Navigation Equipment

Tide and Current Tables
compass
navigation charts
chart case

Wet Weather Gear

foul-weather jacket and pants
sou'wester
pogies or paddling gloves
waterproof footgear (rubber boots or wet suit booties)

Personal Gear

quick-drying pants, synthetic pile jacket
polypropylene underwear
wool socks
wool hat
sun hat
shoes for walking
sunglasses with cord
sunscreen
toiletries
toilet paper
towel
first aid kit
flashlight and spare batteries
knife

waterproof storage bags and containers
water bottle
money

Camping Equipment

tent
sleeping bag
sleeping pad
stove and fuel
cooking pots
cooking utensils
eating implements
cup
tin foil
waterproof food storage bags
waterproof matches or lighter
dish soap and scrubber
water storage containers
tarp and nylon cord

Extras

camera gear
binoculars
guide book(s)
book(s)
fishing gear and licence
sail or kite

BIBLIOGRAPHY

Abbott, D.N. "A Study of Factors Relevant to the Interpretation of Archaeological Remains on Southeastern Vancouver Island."
Master's thesis, Washington State University, Department of Anthropology, 1971.

Arima, E.Y. *The West Coast People*. British Columbia Provincial Museum, Victoria, 1983.

Baird, Robin. "Sea Otters Around Victoria." *The Victoria Naturalist*, 44 no. 5, 1988.

Baird, Robin, and Pam Stacey. "Foraging and Feeding Behavior of Transient Killer Whales." *Whalewatcher: Journal of the American Cetacean Society*, Spring 1988.

Bentley, Ted, and Mary. *Gabriola: Petroglyph Island*. Sono Nis Press, Victoria, 1981.

Beram, Luisa. "Petroglyphs: Messages in Stone." In *Archaeology Programs in Capital Regional District Parks – 1987* (unpublished).

Berton, Pierre. "The Strange Case of The Brother, XII." In *My Country*. McClelland and Stewart, Toronto, 1976.

Bigg, M., I. MacAskie, and G. Ellis. "Photo Identification of Individual Killer Whales." *Whalewatcher Magazine*, Spring 1983.

Bigg, M., and P. Olesiuk. *Seals and Sea Lions on the British Columbia Coast*. Fisheries and Oceans, Pacific Biological Station, Nanaimo, BC

Burch, David. *Fundamentals of Kayak Navigation*. Pacific Search Press, Seattle, 1987.

Canadian Hydrographic Service. *Current Atlas: Juan de Fuca Strait to Strait of Georgia*. Ottawa, 1983.

Ceska, Adolf. "Trial Islands: Wild Flower Paradise." *BC Naturalist,* Summer 1983.

Chettleburg, Peter. *An Explorers Guide to the Marine Parks of British Columbia.* Special Interest Publications, Vancouver, 1985.

Connors, Elizabeth. "Dead Silence." *Monday Magazine,* October 13-20, 1988, p.10.

Cummings, Al, and Jo Bailey-Cummings. *Gunkholing in the Gulf Islands.* Nor'westing Inc., Edmonds Inc, Edmonds, WA, 1986.

Daniel, Linda. *Kayak Cookery.* Pacific Search Press, Seattle, 1986.

Dowd, John. *Sea Kayaking.* 3rd ed. Douglas and McIntyre, Vancouver, 1988.

Elldridge, M., and A. Stryd. "Meares Island Tree Utilization Study," unpub. report submitted to MacMillan Bloedel, Vancouver, 1984.

Fitzharris, Tim. *Birds of Canada.* Oxford University Press, Toronto, 1989.

Fitzharris, Tim. *British Columbia Wild.* Terrapin Press, Vancouver, 1986.

Fitzharris, Tim. Text by John Livingston. *Canada: A Natural History.* Penguin Books, Canada, 1988.

Forester, Anne, and Joseph. *Fishing: BC Commercial Fishing History.* Hancock House Publishers, Saanichton, BC, 1975.

Freeman, Beatrice, and J. Spalding, comp. *A Gulf Islands Patchwork.* Gulf Islands Branch, BC Historical Assoc., Sidney, 1969.

Gold, Wilmer. *Logging as it Was.* Morriss Publishing, Victoria, BC, 1985.

Gould, G. *Genoa Bay Reckonings.* Lambrecht Publications, Duncan, BC, 1981.

Griffiths, David. "Discovery of the Ericsson." *Diver Magazine,* August 1985.

Griffiths, David. "The Thiepval," *Diver Magazine,* June 1982.

Gustafson, Lillian, comp., and Gordon Elliot, ed. *Memories of the Chemainus Valley.* Chemainus Valley Historical Society, Chemainus, BC, 1978.

Hatler, D., W. Campbell, and A. Dorst. *Birds of Pacific Rim National Park.* British Columbia Provincial Museum, Victoria, 1978.

Hewlett, S., and K. Gilbey. *Sea Life of the Pacific Northwest.* McGraw-Hill Ryerson Ltd., Toronto, 1976.

Hill, Beth. *The Remarkable World of Frances Barkley: 1769-1845.* Gray's Publishing, Sidney, BC, 1978.

Hill, Beth, and Ray. *Indian Petroglyphs of the Pacific Northwest.* Hancock House, Saanichton, BC, 1974.

Ince, John, and Heidi Kottner. *Sea Kayaking Canada's West Coast.* Raxas Books, Vancouver, 1982.

Inglis, Richard, and James Haggarty. *Pacific Rim National Park, Ethnographic History.* Environment Canada Parks, microfiche series #257, 1986.

Kozloff, Eugene. *Seashore Life of the Northern Pacific Coast.* J.J. Douglas, Vancouver, 1973.

Leighton, Tony. "Stalking the Blues." *Equinox Magazine,* May/June 1983.

Lillard, Charles. *Seven Shillings a Year.* Horsdal and Schubert Pub. Ltd., Ganges, BC, 1986.

Lilly, Kenneth. *Marine Weather of Western Washington State.* Starpath School of Navigation, Seattle, 1983.

Luxton, Eleanor, ed. *Tilikum – Luxton's Pacific Crossing.* Gray's Publishing Ltd., Sidney, BC, 1971.

McMillan, Allan D., and Denis St. Claire. *Alberni Prehistory.* Alberni Valley Museum, Port Alberni, BC, 1982.

Muller, J.E., and J.A. Jeletsky. *Geology of the Upper Cretaceous Nanaimo Group, Vancouver Island and the Gulf Islands.* Geol. Sur. Can.,1970.

National Geographic Society. *Water, Prey and Game Birds of North America.* Nat. Geo. Soc., Washington, DC, 1965.

Nicholson, George. *Vancouver Island's West Coast 1762-1962.* George Nicholson, Victoria, BC, 1965.

Obee, Bruce. *The Gulf Islands Explorer.* Gray's Publishing, Sidney, BC, 1981.

Obee, Bruce. *The Pacific Rim Explorer.* Whitecap Books, Vancouver, 1986.

Parks Canada. *Grey Whales in Pacific Rim National Park* (brochure). Ministry of the Environment, Canada, 1983.

Rankin, Laird. *The Nonsuch.* Clarke, Irwin and Company, Vancouver/Toronto, 1974.

Ricketts, E., and J. Calvin. *Between Pacific Tides.* 4th ed., revised by Joel Ricketts. Stanford University Press, Stanford, 1968.

Rogers, Fred. *Shipwrecks of British Columbia.* J.J. Douglas Ltd., Vancouver, 1973.

Rozen, David. "Permanent Winter Villages and Resource Utilization of the Indian People in the Valdes, Galiano and Thetis Island Areas of the

Gulf Islands." Report submitted to Heritage Conservation Branch of BC, 1978.

Scott, Bruce. *Barkley Sound.* Sono Nis Press, Victoria, 1972.

Sloan, N.A. "Underwater World: Red Sea Urchin (brochure). Department of Fisheries and Oceans, Ottawa, 1986.

Starbird, Ethel. "Friendless Squatters of The Sea." *National Geographic Magazine*, November 1973.

Starkin, Ed. "A BC Leper Colony." In *Raincoast Chronicles: The First Five*, edited by Howard White. Harbour Publishing, Madiera Park, 1976.

Stewart, Hilary. *Cedar.* Douglas and McIntyre, Vancouver, 1984.

Stewart, Hilary. *Indian Fishery: Early Methods on the Northwest Coast.* J.J. Douglas Ltd., Vancouver, 1977.

Thomson, Richard. *Oceanography of the British Columbia Coast.* Department of Fisheries and Oceans, Ottawa, 1981.

Walbran, John T. *British Columbia Coast Names.* The Library Press, Vancouver, 1971.

Watmough, Don. *Cruising Guide to BC, Volume IV, West Coast of Vancouver Island.* Maclean Hunter Ltd., Vancouver, 1984.

Washburne, Randel. *The Coastal Kayaker.* Pacific Search Press, 1983.

Washburne, Randel. *Kayak Trips in Puget Sound and the San Juan Islands.* Pacific Search Press, 1986.

Werthiem, Anne. *The Intertidal Wilderness.* Sierra Club, San Francisco, 1984.

Weston, Jim, and David Stirling. *The Naturalist Guide to the Victoria Region.* Victoria Natural History Society, Victoria, BC, 1986.

White, Howard, and Margaret McCaffrey. "Tides." In *Raincoast Chronicles: The First Five*, edited by Howard White. Harbour Publishing, Madiera Park, 1976.

Wolferstan, Bill. *Cruising Guide to British Columbia, Volume I, Gulf Islands.* Whitecap Books, Vancouver, 1987.

Wyett, W. "Pacific Rim National Park — Interpretive Potential." A study for National Parks of Canada, 1970.

INDEX

For almost a decade *Island Paddling* has provided the sea ka
canoeist with a comprehensive introduction to some of the
paddling water in the world. Now, in an extensively updated and revised
edition, this best-selling guidebook again takes the paddler into the
spectacular Gulf Islands and Barkley Sound, showcasing these magnificent
marine areas. Including many new references and all the new parks,
Island Paddling once more takes it's place as *the* indispensable resource
for kayakers.

The Gulf Islands, a protected group of islands in the Strait of Georgia,
and Barkley Sound, located on the more remote and wild west coast of
Vancouver Island, offer all levels of paddlers a true wilderness experience
ranging from sheltered bays and crystal clear water to pounding waves
and exquisite scenery.

The updated edition of *Island Paddling* contains:

*   information on new parks including Dionisio Point Provincial Park,
    Wallace Island Provincial Marine Park and Prevost Island Park
*   hints on trip planning and preparation
*   detailed descriptions of many marine parks and camping spots
*   information on tides and currents, wind and weather
*   fishing and shellfish gathering tips
*   history and background of the area
*   paddling etiquette and safety

For the seasoned sea-kayaker or the curious beginner, this updated
version of *Island Paddling* is essential equipment for any trip.

ISBN 1-55143-065-

ORCA BOOK PUBLISHERS

$16.95 CAN
$14.95 USA

9 781551 430652